Greil Marcus is the author of the influential and widely acclaimed *Mystery Train*, as well as *The Dustbin of History* and *Lipstick Traces* (both published by Picador), *Dead Elvis* and *In the Fascist Bathroom*. He lives in Berkeley, California.

ALSO BY GREIL MARCUS

MYSTERY TRAIN:

Images of America in Rock 'n' Roll Music (1975)

LIPSTICK TRACES:

A Secret History of the 20th Century (1989)

DEAD ELVIS:

A Chronicle of a Cultural Obsession (1991)

RANTERS & CROWD PLEASERS:

Punk in Pop Music, 1977–1992 (1993)

THE DUSTBIN OF HISTORY

(1995)

STRANDED

[editor] (1979)

PSYCHOTIC REACTIONS & CARBURETOR DUNG

by Lester Bangs

[editor] (1987)

"In these recordings American culture found a voice that was equal to its history. With an astonishingly eclectic ease, Marcus brings together folklore, labour, politics, civil rights, and urban myths, suggesting how the texture of Dylan's music is haunted by the ghosts of its past. This book is hardly a study of Dylan at all, but rather a poetic encounter with the latent stories of America's manifest dreams. Non-fiction novel of the year"

Graham Caveney, *Arena*

"*Invisible Republic* [revolves] around Dylan's *Basement Tapes* making a case for those songs being the repository of the American folk tradition that seemed to have been lost in the pop boom of the Sixties. A fascinating book"

GQ

"Reading this book confirms that Greil Marcus is a rare specimen among the innumerable Dr Whos of cultural studies: a true Timelord, with his own key to the Tardis"

Ben Thompson, *New Statesman*

"Greil Marcus is a lateral thinker par excellence and his rapid and prodigious leaps across the vast breadths of his erudition don't make this an easy read. So much the better that you'll need to come back for seconds, thirds and fourths."

David Stubbs, *VOX*

"It's in exploring *Invisible Republic*'s central theme that the deepest thinker in music journalism (and much else besides) pulls off a remarkable achievement. Readers of his 1975 masterpiece *Mystery Train* know that in Greil Marcus the Great American Song has a Great American Critic, whose range of reference is as panoramic and richly layered as the Grand Canyon"

Mat Snow, *Mojo*

"A mystery train"

Jade Gordon, *Uncut*

INVISIBLE REPUBLIC

BOB DYLAN'S BASEMENT TAPES

GREIL MARCUS

PICADOR

First published 1997 by Henry Holt and Company, Inc., New York

First published in Great Britain 1997 by Picador

This edition published in Great Britain 1998 by Picador
an imprint of Pan Macmillan Ltd
Pan Macmillan, 20 New Wharf Road, London N1 9RR
Basingstoke and Oxford
www.panmacmillan.com

Associated companies throughout the world

ISBN 978-0-330-51151-3

1 3 5 7 9 8 6 4 2

A CIP catalogue record for this book is available from
the British Library.

Printed and bound in the UK by
CPI Mackays, Chatham ME5 8TD

For Pauline

CONTENTS

INTO A LABORATORY

Once a singer stood at a world crossroads. For a moment he held a stage no one has more than mounted since—a stage that may no longer exist. More than thirty years ago, when a world now most often spoken of as an error of history was taking shape and form—and when far older worlds were reappearing like ghosts that had yet to make up their minds, cruel and paradisiac worlds that in 1965 felt at once present and impossibly distant—Bob Dylan seemed less to occupy a turning point in cultural space and time than to be that turning point. As if culture would turn according to his wishes or even his whim; the fact was, for a long moment it did.

As a public matter, his story went back only a few years. He was born Robert Allen Zimmerman, in Duluth, Minnesota, in 1941, and grew up in Hibbing, a town in the northern part of the then northernmost state. He first made himself known to more than a few in the early 1960s, in New York City, as the self-proclaimed heir to Dust Bowl balladeer Woody Guthrie.

His first album, *Bob Dylan*, released in 1962, was a collection of folk performances about frolic and death; by 1963, after "A Hard Rain's A-Gonna Fall," "With God on Our Side," and "The Times They Are A-Changin'," he was no longer merely a singer, or a songwriter, or even a poet, let alone simply a folk musician. In a signal way, he was the Folk, and also a prophet. As he sang and wrote he was the slave on the auction block, the whore chained to her bed, a questioning youth, an old man looking back in sorrow and regret. As the familiar standards of the folk revival faded from his repertoire, he became the voice left after the bomb had fallen, the voice of the civil rights movement; then he became the voice of his times and the conscience of his generation. The sound of his hammered acoustic guitar and pealing harmonica became a kind of free-floating trademark, like the peace symbol, signifying determination and honesty in a world of corruption and lies.

All of this was suspended in the air—and, for thousands who had followed Bob Dylan's progress as a confirmation of their own, dashed to the ground—when in July 1965 the folk singer who once dressed only in fraying cotton appeared onstage at the Newport Folk Festival with an electric guitar in his hands and a high-style black leather jacket on his back ("a sellout jacket," someone whose name is absent from history called it). With a five-man band around him, a band he would quickly leave behind, he made the most raucous sound he could: an electric noise that to many signified corruption and lies. Though today there may be no person left on earth who would admit to having booed Bob Dylan at Newport, the result on July 25, 1965, was an uproar: a torrent of shouts, curses, refusal, damnation, and perhaps most of all confusion.

Beginning earlier in 1965, with *Bringing It All Back Home*, Dylan balanced a side of visionary acoustic ballads—"Mr. Tambourine Man," "Gates of Eden," "It's All Over Now, Baby Blue"—with one of comic tunes recorded with a band, and there was little controversy. After Newport, in the fall of 1965, he released the almost fully orchestrated *Highway 61 Revisited*, which took him to the top of the charts and, to many, onto the back of the Golden Calf. In May 1966 the Depression soul of the folk movement was erased by a dandy dropping the glamorous *Blonde on Blonde*. Taken together, as a single outburst, these records rank with the most intense outbreaks of twentieth-century modernism; they join the whole Gothic-romantic traverse of American self-regard. But the true result of this long year of creation and discovery was no aesthetic artifact to buy or sell, to hoard or discard, but rather a set of public performances: a tour that from the fall of 1965 through the spring of 1966 grew almost nightly in fervor, drama, and, near the end, conflict. Officially all but undocumented, these nights, these events, found their form in rumor, tall tale, and memory.

In a combination completed by various temporary drummers, most notably Mickey Jones of Trini Lopez fame, the musicians Dylan played with on his tour were bassist Rick Danko, organist Garth Hudson, pianist Richard Manuel, and guitarist Robbie Robertson. They were four-fifths of an obscure Toronto honky-tonk outfit called the Hawks, once the backing band for Arkansas-born rockabilly singer Ronnie Hawkins; in 1968, after they were reunited with their original drummer, Arkansan Levon Helm, who worked with Dylan before jumping ship after two months on the road, they became known as the Band. Starting in Austin, Texas, in September 1965, they crisscrossed the U.S.A. four times. With Jones they pushed on to Australia, Scandinavia, France, Ireland, and the United Kingdom, with no end in sight.

In June 1966, during a brief hiatus, Dylan suffered a motorcycle accident near his home in Woodstock, the old artists' colony in upstate New York, and went into seclusion. Eventually Danko, Hudson, Manuel, and Robertson, now calling themselves the Crackers, or the Honkies, or nothing, made their way to Woodstock to regroup and to work with Dylan on a film about their tour. Soon enough, in the early summer of 1967, they and Dylan began to meet on an almost daily basis, most often in the basement of a place in West Saugerties they named Big Pink, a house Danko, Hudson, and Manuel were renting; there and elsewhere they made casual music and, after a bit, casual recordings, taping more than a hundred performances of commonplace or original songs. Fourteen of the new tunes they came up with were pressed as an acetate disc, titled "The Basement Tape," and sent to other musicians. Some of the songs—"Too Much of Nothing," "Quinn the Eskimo," "You Ain't Goin' Nowhere"—soon turned up as hits by Peter, Paul & Mary, Manfred Mann, and the Byrds, and tapes of the acetate itself leaked out to the general public in 1968. *Rolling Stone* called for its release, to no avail; by 1970 the music was being pressed onto vinyl and bootlegged everywhere.

The basement tapes—the name shifted slightly in the journey to contraband—became a talisman, a public secret, and then a legend, a fable of retreat and fashioning. When a collection of sixteen basement recordings, plus eight Band demos, was officially released in 1975 and reached the top ten, Dylan expressed surprise: "I thought everybody already had them." From the first, the most immediately striking basement tape numbers—"I Shall Be Released," "This Wheel's on Fire," "Tears of Rage," "Down in the Flood," "Million Dollar Bash"—were recognized for a peculiar grace and spark; for a spirit, as I wrote in the liner notes to the 1975 release, pitched somewhere between the confessional and the bawdy house. The music carried an aura of familiarity, of unwritten traditions, and as deep a sense of self-recognition, the recognition of a self—the singer's? the listener's?—that was both historical and sui generis. The music was funny and comforting; at the same time, it was strange, and somehow incomplete. Out of some odd displacement of art and time, the music seemed both transparent and inexplicable.

As over the years more and more of the basement performances appeared—as sold or stolen and then traded tapes, further bootleg lps and then cds, here and there an officially released track on a Dylan anthology—one could begin to hear something more than a number of interesting songs, or a moment in a particular career. Heard as something like a whole—as a story, despite or even because of its jumble of missing pieces, half-finished recordings, garbled chronologies of composition or performance—the basement tapes can begin to sound like a map; but if they are a map, what country, what lost mine, is it that they center and fix? They can begin to sound like an instinctive experiment, or a laboratory: a laboratory where, for a few months, certain bedrock strains of American cultural language were retrieved and reinvented. That was the notion that occurred to me in 1993, driving from California to Montana and back again listening to nothing but weather reports and a five-cd set of basement tapes bootlegs. Twenty-six years after they were made, years during which Bob Dylan had, it seemed, long since lost all maps to any crossroads beyond those within the ever-diminishing confines of his own career, the basement tapes were creeping up and out of their laboratory as if for the first time. Without knowing quite what I meant by "a laboratory," I tried the notion out on Robbie Robertson, a friend since the early 1970s. "No," he said. "A conspiracy. It was like the Watergate tapes. A lot of stuff, Bob would say, 'We should *destroy* this.' "

"We went in with a sense of humor," he said. "It was all a goof. We were playing with absolute freedom; we weren't doing anything we thought anybody else would ever hear, as long as we lived. But what started in that basement, what came out of it—and the Band came out of it, anthems, people holding hands and rocking back and forth all over the world singing 'I Shall Be Released,' the distance that all of this went—came out of this little conspiracy, of us amusing ourselves. Killing time."

Music made to kill time ended up dissolving it. As one listens, no date adheres to the basement tapes, made as the war in Vietnam, mass deaths in black riots in Newark and Detroit, the Beatles' *Sgt. Pepper's Lonely Hearts Club Band*, and the Summer of Love all insisted, in their different ways, on the year 1967 as Millennium or Apocalypse, or both. The year "America fell apart," Newt Gingrich has said; "deserter's songs," a skeptic called the basement tapes in 1994, catching an echo of a few people holed up to wait out the end of the world. Yet the basement tapes could carry the date 1932 and it would be as convincing, as one listens, as 1967, if not more so—as would, say, the dates 1881, or 1954, 1992, 1993. In those last two years, Bob Dylan, then in his early fifties, suddenly recast what had come to seem an inexorably decaying public life with two albums of old blues and folk songs, *Good as I Been to You* and *World Gone Wrong*. Ranging from the sixteenth-century children's ditty "Froggie Went A-Courtin' " to the 1890s murder report "Stack A Lee," from the archaic Child ballad "Love Henry" to Blind Willie McTell's 1931 "Broke Down Engine," the songs were played on acoustic guitar and harmonica, with no other accompaniment; in Bob Dylan's repertoire they preceded the material on his first album, issued thirty years before. Unlike other songs he had sung in nearly a quarter century, they removed him from the prison of his own career and returned him—or his voice, as a sort of mythical fact—to the world at large.

"It is almost inconceivable that this is the man who once broke rock—as a form, as a mode of experience—in half," critic Howard Hampton had written of one of Dylan's albums of a few years before. "Now he's the dutiful repairman. 'Everything is broken,' he sings, but promises the pieces can be put back together in his art as assuredly as they cannot be in the world. This is an inversion of what his work once meant, but it is also a continuation of the political world of the last twenty years. Society has structured itself around the suppression of the kinds of demands Dylan's music once made, that it might make such speech unimaginable all over again." But it seemed as if it were precisely an unimaginable form of speech—a once-common, now-unknown tongue—that Dylan had found, or was now proffering, in ancient songs. "Strange things are happening like never before," went the first line of

World Gone Wrong, from the title song, the Depression-era words from the Mississippi Sheiks sung in a weary, unsurprised voice; the tune, Dylan wrote mysteriously in his liner notes, "goes against cultural policy." Just as the basement tapes escaped the monolithic pop immediacy of their year—a year of such gravity, it could feel at the time, that it was like a vacuum, sucking everything into itself, suffering nothing to exist outside its own, temporal frame of reference—these old-timey albums were bereft of any nostalgia. If they were a look back they were a look that circled back, all the way around to where the singer and whoever might be listening now stood.

More than anything Bob Dylan had done in the intervening years, these records were a continuation of the story the basement tapes told, or an unlocking of their laboratory. They "sound like they were made in a cardboard box," Elvis Costello said in 1994 of the basement tapes, with *Good as I Been to You* and *World Gone Wrong* playing in his head. "I think he was trying to write songs that sound like he'd just found them under a stone. As if they sound like real folk songs—because if you go back into the folk tradition you will find songs as dark and deep as these."

"He would pull these songs out of nowhere," Robbie Robertson said. "We didn't know if he wrote them or if he remembered them. When he sang them, you couldn't tell." That, in the basement tapes laboratory, is the alchemy, and in that alchemy is an undiscovered country, like the purloined letter hiding in plain sight.

INVISIBLE REPUBLIC

ONE

ANOTHER COUNTRY

In the dressing room in London, the guitarist was looking for a melody. He picked tiny notes off the strings until they fluttered, snapping in the air. The singer turned his head, caught the tune, the title flashing up: sure, "Strange Things Happening Every Day," Sister Rosetta Tharpe, when was it, 1945? Closing in on Tharpe's own guitar line, the guitarist felt for the syncopation in the rhythm, and the song came to life in the singer's mind.

> On that last great Judgment Day
> When they drive them all away
> There are strange things happening every day

She was shameless, the singer remembered: purer than pure when her mother was alive, backsliding after that. She came onto the Lord's stage in a mink; she had a way with a guitar few men could touch. She was the black church in the Grand Ole

Opry—she'd even recorded with Pat Boone's father-in-law, Red Foley, Mr. "Old Shep" himself. On the other hand, Red Foley had recorded "Peace in the Valley," hadn't he, the spiritual the Reverend Thomas A. Dorsey had written as the Second World War began? The sainted gospel composer, in earlier days known as Georgia Tom, who'd put his name on dirty blues? The singer shook his head: why was he remembering all this? His memory raced ahead of him. For some reason he remembered that "Strange Things Happening" had topped the black charts the same week Hitler killed himself. It was April 30, 1945; the singer was a month short of four, Sister Rosetta Tharpe was thirty. "There's something in the gospel blues," she would say years later, "that's so deep the world can't stand it." Now he heard the song as if the war had ended yesterday, as if it were the first time he'd heard it, wherever that had been—off some road he'd never remember anything else about, like waking from a dream you had to get up and live through.

> If you want to view the crime
> You must learn to quit your lyin'
> There are strange things happening every day

The guitarist was beginning to mumble the words, faking them, getting only the title phrase. The singer grinned as he made for the door. " 'Strange things happening every day,' " he said. "She got that right."

Bob Dylan walked out of his dressing room in the Royal Albert Hall. It was May 26, 1966; for two weeks he'd been up and down England, Scotland, Ireland, Wales. Two days before he'd crossed the English Channel to celebrate his birthday onstage in Paris, dropping a huge American flag as the curtains opened for the second set, the crowd going mad with rage as if he were throwing America's war in Vietnam in their faces—come on, hadn't they started it?—then taking in the headline in *Le Figaro* the next day: "LA CHUTE D'UNE IDOLE." It was kind of a quiet night, actually, compared to . . . he'd been in control. It wasn't usually like that, not this month, when the whole previous year felt like it was packed into a bomb that wouldn't stop exploding. Most nights abuse came raining down as if he could bring the weather with him, as if hate were the wind at his back, the storm waiting in every next town.

He walked out of his dressing room. He knew that when he sang his folk songs—most of them no more folk songs than a Maytag washing machine, except unlike a Maytag washing machine they didn't rely on electricity—a few older numbers, to please the crowd, or tease it, but mainly those long, odd songs that no longer made anyone laugh, "Visions of Johanna," "Mr. Tambourine Man," "Desolation Row," when he stood still, picked strings, and appeared as any singer might have appeared in the years or centuries before him, the people in the audience would show respect, even approval. He knew that when he finished that set, left, and came back with the Hawks—the piano player on one side of the stage, the organist on the other, the bass player and the guitarist at his sides, the drummer on a riser behind them—the trouble would start; the problem was, he never knew just when it would start. "How do you get your kicks these days?" an interviewer asked him a few months before. "I hire people to look into my eyes, and then I have them kick me," Dylan said. "That's how you get your kicks?" "No," Dylan said, "then I *forgive* them. That's where my kicks come in." It wasn't that easy, though; once the second set began, it was as if the two sides—the six on the stage, those in the crowd who had set themselves against them—were trying most of all to drown each other out.

"Dylan questions the comparisons drawn between charity rock events like Live Aid and USA for Africa and the student activism of yesteryear," a reporter wrote in 1985, then let Dylan speak: "The big difference between now and the sixties is that then it was much more dangerous to do that sort of thing. There were people trying to stop the show any way they could. . . . Then, you didn't know which end the trouble was coming from. And it could come at any time." He could have been talking about politics, in the narrow sense that the reporter was framing the issue; he could have been talking about the kind of politics that in 1966 occurred whenever he opened his mouth. And it was so stupid. Almost every night, the music lifted off the stage, so strong it was like a body, and there were moments when he couldn't believe he couldn't take his hand off his Fender Stratocaster and touch it. It was hard to hear, and hard to believe anything could ever be better. And then, at just that instant when the timing between a group of musicians was life itself, when the smallest mistake, the mistake you knew could never happen, would throw the world off its axis, when a physics no scientist would ever understand was all there was, the shouting would start, as if the audience that understood nothing understood one thing: ambush. A note, a chord, the start of a rhythm, and, then, "COCKSUCKER."

On May 26, 1966, at the Royal Albert Hall, they were just

about to move into "Leopard-skin Pill-box Hat"—a yet-to-be-released *Blonde on Blonde* tune that after a month or so on the road had turned into a big, noisy, vulgar Chicago blues carrying hilariously sneering lyrics ("I saw you making love with him / You forgot to close the garage door")—when it started. The tape that survives from this night doesn't register the crowd; you can't hear what Bob Dylan is hearing, but by now his senses are strung so tightly any discord is painful, and even as you might imagine him standing straight to face the crowd, three decades later you can hear him sag. "Oh, God," he says, like someone who has seen this too many times; the good lines that took him out of the dressing room, that great beat, are out of reach. The one shout he'd caught from the crowd is already growing, the once-timid now screaming: TRAITOR. SELL-OUT. MOTHERFUCKER. YOU'RE NOT BOB DYLAN. And then laughter. "Are you talking to me?" Dylan says, theatrically; you can feel him strike a pose. There are more shouts; you can't decipher them, but he can. "Come up here and say that," he says, and the great hall falls away. It is gone. We're in a bar in a town whose name you didn't catch when you drove in and won't remember to notice when you drive out, and in this bar "Ballad of a Thin Man" is all that is left.

In the fall of 1965, as the last song on the first side of the just-issued *Highway 61 Revisited*, the performance was almost laconic. Dylan's hipster piano, all reverb and menacing languor, led a high, ghostly organ sound, but mostly the music communicated distance, cool, disregard. There was more of the Midwest in Dylan's voice than in anything else on the disc—more dust. The singer has seen it all before. You can't surprise him. Bearing down just slightly for the chorus, repeated again and again without change—"You know something is happening, but you don't know what it is"—on record Dylan found an instant catchphrase for the moral, generational, and racial divisions that in this moment found Americans defining themselves not as who they were but as who they were not, and he also found a commercial hook. *"You know something's happening, but you"*—you could hear it everywhere over the next months, out of anyone's mouth. By definition, if you knew the song, you knew what was happening. If you wanted to know what was happening, or appear as if you did, you had to buy the album. Before the year was out, *Highway 61 Revisited* was only two places short of the top of the charts.

But on this tour, in May of 1966, up and down the British Isles, it is not this "Ballad of a Thin Man" that raises the bar it finds you in. Now it has become the most bitter, unstable song; with Dylan turning to the piano for this single number, it is also the song that is somehow most alive to the particular ambience of any given night, the weather, the frame of the hall, the mood of the crowd, sucking it up and using it like a karate fighter turning an opponent's strength against him. Some tunes in the set Dylan offers with the Hawks—"Tell Me Momma," "Baby Let Me Follow You Down," "One Too Many Mornings," "I Don't Believe You"—fly or they don't, but formally they are always the same. "Ballad of a Thin Man" is always different, always changed by the crowd, then moving as if to change it in turn.

The song begins and ends with the oldest, corniest beatnik cliché: the square. Some poor sap, well dressed, well heeled. As a listener, in the crowd, you're set up to imagine him as whoever you're not. The song puts him through the wringer.

Always at home in the streets of his town, he is now trapped in a demimonde, in an after-hours club where he is neither welcome nor permitted to leave. He's heard about the kind of people who inhabit these places: drug addicts, homosexuals, Negroes, intellectuals, homosexual Negro intellectuals like the funny-looking man with the beret and the popeyes. The square has seen the man's picture in the papers; he's even seen his like, men and women, black and white, in the streets. They used to live in the shadows; now they appear in public, as if the town is theirs.

The square watches as a man in high heels kneels at his feet and smiles up at him like a snake. He's taken into a room where everyone is shouting slogans, the kind of slogans the square has seen on the protest placards people carry on their marches, but here the slogans are in a different language, if it is a language at all: "NOW," they say blankly; "YOU'RE A COW." The square wants to run but he doesn't even know where he is—and by now whoever is listening is beginning to recognize his or her own dim shape in the song. Whoever is listening is beginning to flinch.

The walls of the Albert Hall rise up again, the noise from the crowd stays constant, but seated at the piano Dylan starts the music. The song is a blues, no more, on some nights the biggest blues anyone has ever heard, with Garth Hudson's organ finding a mode so mocking it is sadistic, a whirlpool opening and then laughing at your fear as it closes, with Robbie Robertson's first guitar notes enormous, Godzilla notes, so big they throw the audience back, daring anyone to say the first word—but not this night.

On this night, the last night but one of these weeks in the

United Kingdom, the last time but one this music would ever be played, no one is thrown back. Instead wounds are exposed, and the ugly sight quiets the crowd. "Are you sure?" Dylan asks Robbie Robertson, just three weeks past twenty-two; Bob Dylan is an old man, twenty-five years and two days. The crowd can't hear the singer whispering to the man at his side as if he's never been less sure of anything, but they can feel the way he's hovering, or tottering, and the sight is a kind of violence, a terror, a negative, a nothing.

Here it is: nothing. Here you are, all of you. It will take four thousand holes to fill the Albert Hall, and four thousand times nothing is nothing.

Even as recorded on *Bringing It All Back Home* and *Highway 61 Revisited*, the songs Bob Dylan began offering in 1965, most with rock 'n' roll accompaniment rattling and grand, took shape as treasure maps, and the treasure toward which they pointed was a still-undiscovered sound. By the spring of 1966 the songs had become the treasure. The tale of how this transformation came about is inseparable from the tale of how the music was received. In 1965 and 1966 Bob Dylan's music made a social drama, a drama that resisted all the charms of resolution.

It began at the Newport Folk Festival without any plan. On June 15, in New York City, Dylan had recorded "Like a Rolling Stone" with a band that included New Yorker Al Kooper on organ and Chicagoan Mike Bloomfield, of the Paul Butterfield Blues Band, on lead guitar; meeting up with the two in Rhode Island on July 24, the day "Like a Rolling Stone" went into the charts, the notion of a festival surprise seemed irresistible. Electric music had never been played at Newport, but the Butterfield band was itself set for a blues workshop; the equipment was there. Completing a pickup band with pianist Barry Goldberg, plus Butterfield's drummer Sam Lay and his bassist Jerome Arnold, Dylan rehearsed through the night and showed up the next day, on Newport's main stage, ready to experiment. Pete Seeger, the paragon of the folk revival, the man who represented all of its compassion and nobility, who as the son of the revered folk scholar Charles Seeger embodied a whole, people's enactment of an American folk century, had begun the evening by playing a recording of the cry of a newborn baby. He asked that everyone in the audience sing to the baby, that they tell it into what sort of world it had been born—and "he already knew," wrote Jim Rooney, a mainstay of the folk scene in Cambridge, Massachusetts, "what he wanted others to sing. They were going to sing that it was a world of pollution, bombs, hunger, and injustice, but that PEOPLE would OVERCOME." That was the call. Bob Dylan was the last act.

Watching the film of this night, one can see eager young men—Dylan and Mike Bloomfield in particular—taking their cues straight from *High Noon*, or the one-on-one shootouts that throughout their teenage years opened and closed almost every episode of *Gunsmoke*. Cheers greeted a simpering introduction by Peter Yarrow of the folk trio Peter, Paul & Mary, which two years before had made Dylan's "Blowin' in the Wind" a huge national hit and a touchstone of the era—"The person who's coming up now, is a person who has, in a sense, changed the face of folk music, to the *large American public*, because he has brought to it, the point of view of a *poet*"—but as the band took the stage and commenced tuning up the crowd was quiet.

Dylan's cry of "Let's go!" is like a leap out of a plane. He leans back on his bootheels, as if daring gravity, an erotic nimbus of certainty and pleasure around his face. Bloomfield crouches low, holding his guitar as a rifle with bayonet fixed, lunging for the sound with crackling noise every time Dylan takes a breath. Dylan is shouting out the caustic black humor of "Maggie's Farm" without range, without any need for it, as if he's just discovered that as a singer he can stomp his foot through the boards. Everything in the music is percussive, a beat building on itself. What began as blues careens into rock 'n' roll a few steps past anything else then abroad in the land.

Backstage Pete Seeger and the great ethnomusicologist Alan Lomax attempted to cut the band's power cables with an axe. Peter Yarrow and singer Theodore Bikel blocked them until a full guard could be rounded up, and the band moved into the slow, stately introduction to "Like a Rolling Stone"—which immediately regressed almost to its studio beginnings as a waltz. The song has a spine that's hard to find, and the band can't find it. As if to compensate Dylan puffs himself up with the declamatory intonations of Humphrey Bogart at the end of *The Maltese Falcon*, Mary Astor in his arms but spurning her pleas for deliverance: *"I won't because all of me wants to."* The rhythm is lost. Then "Phantom Engineer," an early version of what on *Highway 61 Revisited* would be called "It Takes a Lot to Laugh, It Takes a Train to Cry," and again the music is running. With Dylan singing a barbed Plains States drawl and his rhythm guitar pressing for speed, Bloomfield jumps the train and drives it: "I remember," said Sim Webb, Casey Jones's fireman when the Illinois Central 638 smashed into a freight train near Vaughn, Mississippi, on April 30, 1900, "that as I jumped from the cab Casey held down the whistle in a long, piercing scream." Bloomfield gets that sound. "Let's go, man, that's it!" Dylan calls; he left with the band. The sound was harsh at the beginning and it was harsh at the end, and not as harsh as the sound coming from the other side of the stage.

From the crowd there were rolls of boos, shouts of derision and contempt, some applause, and the vacuum of people sitting on their hands. Or so it seemed at the time—the so-called booing, many who were there would later claim, was merely a protest against a muddy sound system. Or it was the people in the back, in the cheap seats, who were booing—having misunderstood the well-meant complaints the elite of the folk movement were making in the front, the people in the back not wanting to appear unhip. Within a year, Dylan's performance would have changed all the rules of folk music—or, rather, what had been understood as folk music would as a cultural force have all but ceased to exist. The train was leaving the station, and who wanted to admit he hadn't had a ticket all along? From notes scribbled in the moment by critic Paul Nelson, a friend of Dylan's since 1959, when they were part of the folk scene in Dinkytown, the bohemian enclave near the University of Minnesota: "There followed the most dramatic thing I've seen: Dylan walking off the stage, the audience booing and yelling 'Get rid of the electric guitar,' Peter Yarrow trying to talk the audience into clapping and trying to talk Dylan into coming back"—"He's going to get an *acous*tic guitar," Yarrow said, unctuously pursing his lips around the middle vowels—"Dylan coming back with tears in his eyes singing 'It's All

Over Now, Baby Blue,' a song that I took to be his farewell to Newport, an incredible sadness over Dylan and the audience finally clapping now because the electric guitar was gone." "In penance—in penance!—Dylan put on his old Martin and played," Mike Bloomfield said years later. "To the folk community, rock and roll was greasers, heads, dancers, people who got drunk and boogied. Lightnin' Hopkins had made electric records for twelve years, but he didn't bring his electric band from Texas. No, sir, he came out at Newport like they had just taken him out of the fields, like the tar baby."

"Were you surprised at the first time the boos came?" Dylan was asked at a press conference four months later. "You can't tell where the booing's going to come up," he said, taking in the twenty-five shows he'd played since Newport, from Carnegie Hall to the Hollywood Bowl, from Dallas to Minneapolis, Atlanta to Seattle. "Can't tell at all. It comes up at the weirdest, strangest places, and when it comes it's quite a thing in itself." But "Newport," Dylan said with great amusement, as if looking back on a childhood prank that by some twist of fate got him on national TV and made him a hero to all his friends, "well, I did a very crazy thing. I didn't know what was going to happen, but they certainly booed, I'll tell you that. You could hear it all over the place. I don't know who they were, though," he said—as if, the next time he had the chance, he might see if he could find out.

With Newport behind him Dylan went back to New York City to finish recording *Highway 61 Revisited*. That done, he set about assembling his own band. For two weeks prior to a scheduled appearance at the fifteen-thousand-seat Forest Hills Stadium in Forest Hills, New York, he rehearsed new songs and old with Al Kooper, who had traded organ for electric piano, bassist Harvey Brooks, and guitarist Robbie Robertson and drummer Levon Helm of Toronto's Hawks—a foursome that would last through only one further performance before Dylan made common cause with all five of the Hawks—but if Newport was a spark, Forest Hills was a wildfire.

Fans of Dylan's recent Top 40 hits—"Subterranean Homesick Blues" from the spring of 1965, the new "Like a Rolling Stone"—were there, outnumbered by longtime followers. Appearing first alone, with acoustic guitar and harmonica, Dylan was introduced by hysterical Top 40 disc jockey Murray the K, "The Fifth Beatle" (some said the sixth): "It's not rock, it's not folk, it's a new thing called Dylan! There's a new, swingin' mood in this country, and I think perhaps Bob Dylan is the spearhead of this new mood! It's a new kind of expression, a new kind of telling it like it is, and Mr. Dylan is definitely"—he had to get in his signature phrase, though he sounded almost embarrassed by it—"what's happening, baby." Murray was roundly booed, but Top 40 disc jockeys introducing concerts expected nothing less. Dylan came on, sang songs mostly from *Bringing It All Back Home*, drifting songs of love and transcendence performed in a familiar way. As he almost always did, he included a song the audience had not heard before—in this case "Desolation Row," which would close the still-unreleased *Highway 61 Revisited*: a funny, tense, graceful eleven-minute parable of utopia as absolute exile and twentieth-century culture as the *Titanic*. The crowd cheered.

When buttoned-down Top 40 disc jockey Good Guy Gary Stevens appeared to introduce the second half of the show, he was booed off the stage almost before he could open his mouth, and with amplifiers and a drum set now waiting in plain sight, these were not the good-natured boos that had greeted Murray the K. This was mean, and just a warm-up. Dylan and his band launched themselves into "Tombstone Blues"—like five of the eight songs in the set, from *Highway 61 Revisited*—and suddenly, from the crowd, not the stage, the sound is that of someone being torn to pieces. People are screaming. Boos like cheers are now only occasional. Instead, in song after song, in instants that seem brought on by nothing in the music, it is as if some barely detectable gesture, somewhere in the audience, momentarily turns factions or merely clumps of bystanders into greater bodies. Again and again a violent shudder passes through the crowd. What one hears on tape thirty years later feels like a riot, or a panic, Forest Hills Stadium now the Odessa Steps, and part of the audience alive with the chance to drive everyone else down them.

The music couldn't keep up with such a frenzy, and in any case it was straight, one-dimensional, with only flashes of worry or lift, sometimes stiff, sometimes lumbering—sometimes shining, as if in spite of a distracted sound, with the light of its own lyricism. Dylan was not yet singing from inside a band, just fronting one; only on "Ballad of a Thin Man" or the rockers "Tombstone Blues" and "From a Buick 6" was he even able to reach for anything he hadn't already done in a studio. Al Kooper's piano caught a trashy streak in "From a Buick 6," showcasing the purest rock 'n' roll of the day, Dylan's fierce and exultant delivery of "I need a steam shovel, mama, to keep away the dead"—a line that brought laughter and applause through a hole in the sheets of demented noise that upended other songs, less drowning them out than, inside the crowd, shattering them.

This sound had been heard before, in the years leading up to this performance—but not in such a setting. The shouts and cries of individuals merging into a sound far more ugly and cruel than any one person could produce was the sound of white men and women, girls and boys, addressing nine black teenagers as they walked for the first time, and the second, and the third, into the halls of Central High School in Little Rock, Arkansas, in 1957; it was the sound of white students rioting, and killing, as Federal troops brought black student James Meredith to the campus of Ole Miss in Oxford, Mississippi, in 1962; it was the sound of white men in the Greyhound bus station in Montgomery, Alabama, in 1961, beating Freedom Riders—black and white Americans who had determined to travel together through the South as if the Constitution guaranteed their right to do so—to the edge of death, leaving unconscious bodies scattered like trash on the benches and the floor. And it was partly this sound that, just after the Forest Hills concert, led folk singer Phil Ochs to say what many other people were thinking—something Al Kooper was thinking as he bailed out of Dylan's band one show after Forest Hills, contemplating two scheduled dates in Texas: "Look what they did to J.F.K. down there."

It wasn't the first time Kooper had such a thought. Since they lived nearby, he and Harvey Brooks had driven to Forest Hills themselves and parked in the regular parking lot. With the show over and Kooper filled with thoughts of the moment when people rushed the stage and he was knocked off his piano stool, of the shouts of "fucking scumbag," of how for "Ballad of a Thin Man" Dylan, at his own piano, had tried to quiet the crowd by playing the opening notes again and again, for minutes, until finally he gave up and finished the song and the show—after all that, Kooper and Brooks realized that to get to their cars they were going to have to walk through the crowd.

It sounds funny; it wasn't at the time. "I was scared," Kooper, a tall man with presence and authority in the way he moves, said in 1995. Going back, he is all strategy: "We realized they would recognize us. It was best we walked straight ahead, close together. I didn't know if we were going to get out of there alive."

Phil Ochs had the nerve to say it out loud, in print, at the time:

> I wonder what's going to happen. I don't know if Dylan can get on the stage a year from now. I don't think so. I mean the phenomenon of Dylan will be so much that it will be dangerous. . . . Dylan has become part of so many people's psyches—and there're so many screwed up people in America, and death is such a part of the American scene now.

These were not idle words, and for reasons that go beyond the fact that Bob Dylan would not be on a stage a year from the time Ochs spoke, just as he would never again appear at the Newport Folk Festival. Ochs's scared, awkward language might have been that of anyone honestly attempting to acknowledge the awful current that had begun to run through public life in America. It was a current that had already left not only John F. Kennedy but Medgar Evers and Malcolm X assassinated; that in a few years would claim not only George Lincoln Rockwell,

Martin Luther King, Jr., and Robert Kennedy, but Andy Warhol; a current that as it diffused throughout the land as serial murder and the now commonplace one-day mass murder story of "MAN KILLS FAMILY/COWORKERS, SELF" would touch as well George Wallace in Laurel, Maryland; Marcus Foster in Oakland, California; Gerald Ford in Sacramento and San Francisco; Alberta Williams King—Mrs. Martin Luther King, Sr.—in Atlanta, and Larry Flynt in Lawrenceville, Georgia; Leo Ryan in Jonestown; George Moscone and Harvey Milk in San Francisco; Vernon Jordan in Fort Wayne, Indiana; Allard Lowenstein and John Lennon in New York City; Ronald Reagan in Washington, D.C.; Alan Berg in Denver; and Selena Quintanilla Perez in Corpus Christi, Texas. It is possible that for a time Bob Dylan took a place in that line, and even traced it—for a moment, by the intensity of his performance and the breach that performance opened up in his particular cultural milieu, extended it.

His milieu was that of the folk revival—an arena of native tradition and national metaphor, of self-discovery and self-invention. Here one sought and expected to take people as they appeared to be. It was a place of the spirit, where authenticity in song and manner, in being, was the highest value—the value against which all forms of discourse, all attributes inherited or assumed, were measured. One could make oneself up, as Bob Dylan did—creating a persona that caught Charlie Chaplin, James Dean, and Lenny Bruce in talk and gesture, Woody Guthrie and the French symbolists in writing, and perhaps most deeply such nearly forgotten 1920s stylists as mountain balladeer Dock Boggs and New Orleans blues singer Rabbit Brown in voice—but only if, whatever one's sources, the purest clay was always evident, real American red earth.

The folk revival, the historian Robert Cantwell wrote in 1993, looking back on a milieu that had disappeared, "made the romantic claim of folk culture—oral, immediate, traditional, idiomatic, communal, a culture of characters, of rights, obligations, and beliefs, against a centrist, specialist, impersonal, technocratic culture, a culture of types, functions, jobs, and goals." Folk chronicler Robert Shelton, writing in 1968, still believing he was part of a movement whose future remained to be made, set forth this argument not as argument but as wish, as faith:

> What the folk revivalists were saying, in effect, was: "There's another way out of the dilemma of modern urban society that will teach us all about who we are. There are beautiful, simple, relatively uncomplicated people living in the country close to the soil, who have their own identities, their own backgrounds. They know who they are, and they know what their culture is because they make it themselves." . . . Long before the Kennedy Administration posited the slogan, "The New Frontier," the folk revivalists were exploring their own new frontier, traveling to the country, in actuality or imagination, trying to find out if there was truly a more exciting life in America's continuing past.

Thus when Bob Dylan sang the antebellum song of runaway slaves, "No More Auction Block" (or "Many Thousands Gone"), or when he took its melody to fashion his own tale of repression and resistance, "Blowin' in the Wind," a tale for the present and the future, he symbolized an entire complex of values, a whole way of being in the world. But while he symbolized a scale of values that placed, say, the country over the city, labor over capital, sincerity over education, the unspoiled nobility of the common man and woman over the businessman and the politician, or the natural expressiveness of the folk over the self-interest of the artist, he also symbolized two things more deeply, and these were things that could not be made into slogans or summed up by programmatic exposition or romantic appreciation. As Bob Dylan sang—like Joan Baez, Pete Seeger, or any of hundreds of other folk singers, but more powerfully, and more nakedly—or as he was heard, he embodied a yearning for peace and home in the midst of noise and upheaval, and in the aesthetic reflection of that embodiment located both peace and home in the purity, the essential goodness, of each listener's heart. It was this purity, this glimpse of a democratic oasis unsullied by commerce or greed, that in the late 1950s and early 1960s so many young people began to hear in the blues and ballads first recorded in the 1920s and 1930s, by people mostly from small towns and tiny settlements in the South, a strange and foreign place to most who were now listening—music that seemed the product of no ego but of the inherent genius of a people—the people—people one could embrace and, perhaps, become. It was the sound of another country—a country that, once glimpsed from afar, could be felt within oneself. That was the folk revival.

As an art movement, the folk revival was rooted in the nineteenth-century and early twentieth-century song collecting—in England and Scotland, in Appalachia, in the Deep South—of Francis Child of Harvard, Cecil Sharp of London, John Lomax of Mississippi and Texas, Bascom Lamar Lunsford of North Carolina, and many more. As a social movement it emerged out of the aggressively defensive Americanism of the American Communist Party, the ideology of the Popular Front, and the vast and fecund art projects of the New Deal. As a fact, the folk revival was brought to life for the public at large in 1958 by the Kingston Trio's "Tom Dooley"—a hearty (perfect for singalongs), insistently mysterious performance of a traditional, quite local Appalachian murder ballad, with allusions to barely described characters and unspoken motives drifting into dark hollows and disappearing in the woods' surround. What *is* this? the radio almost asked every time the tune came on. It was, it turned out, a true-crime fable about the 1866 killing of one Laura Foster by her ex-lover Tom Dula and his new lover Annie Melton—an event that, depending on how you look at it, took ninety-two years, or just over the six months from the time of the disc's release, to travel from an unmapped corner of the national psyche to number one, from Wilkes County, North Carolina, to every town and hamlet in the Great Forty-eight.

For all this, though, there is a reason why, in the annals of American history, the folk revival is only a footnote, if it is that. More than its own art movement, its own social movement, or its own fact, the folk revival was part of something much bigger, more dangerous, and more important: the civil rights movement. That is where its moral energy came from—its sense of a world to rediscover, to bring back to life, and to win. The two movements were fraternal twins, for the civil rights movement was also a rediscovery, a revival: of the Constitution.

The folk revival reached its height in the summer of 1963, at the Newport Folk Festival and the March on Washington, the latter an event that itself entered into American folklore as the occasion of the speech by Martin Luther King, Jr., that ended with crescendos of "I HAVE A DREAM." At Newport on July 26, the festival closed with Bob Dylan, Joan Baez, Pete Seeger, Theodore Bikel, Peter, Paul & Mary, and the Freedom Singers—the stars white, the white-shirted Freedom ensemble black—singing Dylan's "Blowin' in the Wind," then linking arms and holding hands for the old Baptist hymn "We Shall Overcome," now the anthem of the civil rights movement. Symbolically, they spoke for the nation, or their nation; three weeks later, King spoke for and to the nation directly.

All who stood on the stage at Newport were present on August 28 when three hundred thousand people from all over the country gathered before the Lincoln Memorial. Some were black preachers and civil rights workers from Louisiana and Alabama who had left their fire-bombed churches and bullet-riddled communal homes to travel to the capital by bus or in old cars; some were affluent white college students who had flown in from California. They took their places in the Washington sun as the nation watched on television, as George Washington watched as pure abstraction from his monument in the distance, and then they called upon the sitting administration, the Congress, the courts, their own governors, their own legislators, their mayors, councilmen, school boards, sheriffs, police chiefs, and the people at large to honor themselves by honoring their national charter, to reaffirm the credo of equal justice under the law.

Bob Dylan like everyone else was there to hear King replace the Old Testament jeremiads of Lincoln's Second Inaugural Address with a New Testament sunburst that, so many years later, still sounds like a miracle unfolding, a waking of the dead. Speaking little more than a month before the surrender of the South, with John Wilkes Booth and his accomplices present in the crowd, Lincoln had taken the country back to the foreboding piety of its Puritan founders.

The Almighty has His own purposes. "Woe unto the world because of offenses! for it must needs be that offenses come; but woe to that man by whom the offense cometh!" If we shall suppose that American slavery is one of those offenses which, in the providence of God, must needs come, but which, having continued through His appointed time, He now wills to remove, and that He gives to both North and South, this terrible war, as the woe due to those by whom the offense came, shall we discern therein any departure from those divine attributes which the believers in a Living God ascribe to Him? Fondly do we hope—fervently do we pray—that this mighty scourge of war may speedily pass away. Yet, if God wills that it continue, until all the wealth piled by the bondman's two hundred and fifty years of unrequited toil shall be sunk, and until every drop of blood drawn with the lash, shall be paid by another drawn by the sword, as was said three thousand years ago, so still it must be said "the judgments of the Lord are true and righteous altogether."

With the rolling cadences of the trained orator, yet picking up the burrs and cracks of the Reverend J. M. Gates, the most famous black preacher of the 1920s, whose recordings of thrilling sermons sold in the hundreds of thousands, King invoked the Declaration of Independence, the Gettysburg Address, and "My Country 'Tis of Thee." He made them his own—and anyone's. Again and again he evoked the call and response of the black church, as the people nearest him turned themselves into an Amen Corner and answered his rhetoric with eager hosannas. And then, with all metaphors assembled, ranging across the continent from mountaintop to mountaintop, in one of only two American political speeches that can be compared to Lincoln's, he reached the peroration that shocked the nation with its eloquence. One could almost believe, listening then—or, worse, now—that the debt finally had been paid.

I have a dream that one day every valley shall be exalted, and every hill and mountain shall be made low, and the rough places will be made plain, and the crooked places will be made straight, and the glory of the Lord will be revealed and all flesh shall see it together.

That was the faith of the folk revival. This was its platform—the promise it made to the nation—and in the early 1960s the Newport Folk Festival was, for those who took part, a national convention, less a counter to the merely quadrennial conventions of Republicans and Democrats than a rebuke. Here were brought together the privileged and the forgotten, white students from the finest colleges and their academic elders along with rediscovered and reclaimed singers and musicians from the past, unheard for thirty, for forty years, black guitarists and white banjo players who now stood together on stage, gathered for photos, as they never had in the official America: Skip James of Mississippi, Buell Kazee of Kentucky, Mississippi John Hurt, Eck Robertson of Arkansas, Son House of Mississippi, Dock Boggs of Virginia, Clarence Ashley of North Carolina, legends all, now addressing an audience, a society in miniature, a country in fantasy, they could hardly have imagined existed. Their authenticity was in their hands and faces and it could not be questioned; as authentic beings they sealed the words and airs of those who now, Bob Dylan first among them, sought their many pieces that together made their one true voice.

Even as a folk singer, Bob Dylan moved too fast, learned too quickly, made the old new too easily; to many he was always suspect. From 1963 at Newport there is a photo that sums it up, a picture of graffiti scribbled on an ad, for sportswear, apparently: over bare legs and a pair of shorts someone has written "Bob Dylan doesn't know his ethnic musicology." *"That's the point!"* someone else has written; someone else has crossed out the last part of "doesn't" so that it reads "does"; and a fourth person, as if to seal this whole discussion (though for all one knows, in the archaeology of graffiti, this hand began it), has written "ASSASINS" in the biggest letters of all, though someone else has thoughtfully added the missing *S*. Still, as at the March on Washington Bob Dylan sang "The Ballad of Medgar Evers" (later released as "Only a Pawn in Their Game"), or shared a phone call with President Kennedy in "I Shall Be Free," or laughed at George Lincoln Rockwell in "Talkin' John Birch Paranoid Blues" (the "one man," he said of the head of the American Nazi Party, "who's really a true American"), his wit and passion—his ability to dramatize—overrode most doubts. Here he entered a kingdom where suffering and injustice, freedom and right, were the coin of the realm, and he spun injustice into right, straw into gold: this is where "With God on Our Side," "Blowin' in the Wind," "The Times They Are A-Changin'," and "A Hard Rain's A-Gonna

Fall"—the songs that took him past his contemporaries—came from.

These songs were embraced as great social dramas, but they were not really dramas at all. Whether one hears them ringing true or false, they were pageants of righteousness, and while within these pageants there were armies and generations, heroes and villains, nightmares and dreams, there were almost no individuals. There was no room for them in the kind of history these songs were prophesying—and certainly none for the selfish, confused, desirous individual who might suspect that his or her own story could fit no particular cause or even purpose. These songs distilled the values of the folk revival better than any others, and what they said was that, in the face of the objective good that was the Grail of the folk revival, there could be no such thing as subjectivity. Could anyone imagine Pete Seeger demanding a world organized, even for a moment, according to his foibles and perverse desires? Could anyone even imagine him having foibles or perverse desires? In the folk revival such a subjective demand on the world was all but indistinguishable from nihilism—the nihilism, in Manny Farber's words, "of doing go-for-broke art and not caring what comes of it"—and that was because of a fatal confusion in its fundamental notion of authenticity, at its heart the philosophy of the folk revival, its idea of the meaning of life.

Art was the speech of the folk revival—and yet, at bottom, the folk revival did not believe in art at all. Rather, life—a certain kind of life—equaled art, which ultimately meant that life replaced it.

The kind of life that equaled art was life defined by suffering, deprivation, poverty, and social exclusion. In folklore this was nothing new. "Thanks to folksong collectors' preconceptions and judicious selectivity, artwork and life were found to be identical," historian Georgina Boyes writes in *The imagined village*. "The ideological innocence which was the essence of the immemorial peasant was also a 'natural' characteristic of the Folk and their song." A complete dissolution of art into life is present in such a point of view: the poor are art because they sing their lives without mediation and without reflection, without the false consciousness of capitalism and the false desires of advertising. As they live in an organic community—buttressed, almost to this present day, from the corrupt outside world—any song belongs to all and none belongs to anyone in particular. Thus it is not the singer who sings the song but the song that sings the singer, and therefore in performance it is the singer, not the song, that is the aesthetic artifact, the work of art. In a perfect world, in the future, everyone will live this way.

That is a leftist translation of what began as a genteel, paternalistic philosophy; it is a version of socialist realism. In 1966 folklorist Ellen J. Stekert saw it alive in the folk revival, and traced it to Communist folk music circles in New York in the 1930s. Woody Guthrie and Aunt Molly Jackson, she wrote, celebrated as great artists by their sponsors, were not even good artists, judged either by the traditional standards they were seen to embody or by the urban standards of their primary, political audience, which embraced them for political reasons—because the singers brought authenticity to the politics. "It was a pitiful confusion," Stekert wrote. "It was monstrous for urbanites to confuse poverty with art." When art is confused with life, it is not merely art that is lost. When art equals life there is no art, but when life equals art there are no people. "The tobacco sheds of North Carolina are in it and all of the blistered and hurt and hardened hands cheated and left empty, hurt and left crying," Woody Guthrie himself wrote of Sonny Terry's harmonica playing. He didn't say if Sonny Terry was in it.

This, finally, is what Bob Dylan turned away from—in the most spectacular way. In September 1965, as the furor over his replacement of object with subject was growing, he tried, at a press conference in Austin, Texas, site of his first performance with the Hawks, to explain. He argued, it seems, that in a profound sense his music was still folk music, though that was a term he would refuse soon enough: "Call it historical-traditional music." Despite the phrase, it was as if he saw traditional music as being made less by history or circumstance than by particular people, for particular, unknowable reasons—reasons that find their analogue in haunts and spirits. One can hear him insisting that the songs he had been writing and performing over the previous year were those in which events and philosophies with which one could identify had been replaced by allegories that could dissolve received identities. Such songs as "Desolation Row," "Just Like Tom Thumb's Blues," "Bob Dylan's 115th Dream," "Highway 61 Revisited," "Tombstone Blues"—somber or uproarious songs populated by Beethoven and Ma Rainey, Ophelia and Cleopatra, Columbus and Captain Ahab, Poor Howard and Georgia Sam, Abraham and Isaac, Mexican cops on the take and the fifth daughter on the twelfth night—carried the tradition in which he had taken his place. "What folk music is," he said, it's not Depression songs . . . its foundations aren't *work*, its foundations aren't "slave away" and all this. Its foundations are—except for Negro songs which are based on that and just kind of overlapped—the main body of it is just based on myth and the Bible and plague and famine and all kinds of things like that which are nothing but mystery and you can see it in all the songs. Roses growing right up out of people's hearts and naked cats in bed with spears growing right out of their backs and seven years of this and eight years of that and it's all really something that nobody can really touch.

But this sort of talk was simply one more allegory. It quieted no one's anger and calmed nobody's despair. For when Dylan turned away from the equation of life and art, when he followed where his music led him, he turned away not just from a philosophical proposition but from an entire complex of beliefs and maxims that to so many defined what was good and what was bad. Thus when he appeared before them holding a garishly shaped and colored electric guitar and dressed in a bizarre tight suit that looked like a single piece of checkered cloth, like some medieval court fool's costume bought on Carnaby Street, he signified no mere apostasy, but the destruction of hope. As he stood on the stage he was seen to affirm the claims of the city over the country, and capital over labor—and also the claims of the white artist over the black Folk, selfishness over compassion, rapacity over need, the thrill of the moment over the trials of endurance, the hustler over the worker, the thief over the orphan. In the crowd, many would clench their fists and gather their breath in anger and disgust, feeling, if not quite picturing, whole dramas of despoliation: coal companies stripping eons of natural wonder and centuries of culture off the southern highlands where the treasured old ballads were still sung; police beating peaceful black teenagers bloody and even to death; the whole planet convulsed by hydrogen bombs.

Dylan's performance now seemed to mean that he had never truly been where he had appeared to be only a year before, reaching for that democratic oasis of the heart—and that if he had never been there, those who had felt themselves there with him had not been there. If his heart was not pure, one had to doubt one's own. It was as if it had all been a trick—a trick he had played on them and that they had played on themselves. That was the source of the betrayal felt when Bob Dylan turned to his band, and he along with Danko and Robertson turned to face the drummer, who raised his drumstick, the three guitarists now leaping into the air and twisting off their feet to face the crowd as the drummer brought his stick down for the first beat. That was the source of the rage.

When they landed on their feet before the crowd they realized it had become like a play, with the audience, having learned its part, now the performers, and the performers now the audience, there to react to the sound of the crowd.

The noise led Levon Helm to quit in doubt and despair by the end of November ("Everyone who wasn't telling Bob the combination was wrong for him," Robertson said years later, "was telling us it was wrong for us"), but by then the sound had caught up with the crowd. And the crowds were not all the same. In Berkeley, in early December of 1965, people fidgeted in their seats during the first, acoustic, solo half of the show.

Despite a "Desolation Row" that brought laughter and a still-unfinished version of "Visions of Johanna" that was like a bad dream the singer had the power to end at will, a power he refused to use, this was something to wait out before the promised shock and tumult. As Ralph J. Gleason so memorably put it in the *San Francisco Chronicle* a few days later, when the curtains opened for the second set "Dylan's band went over like the discovery of gold."*

It was as if the people there desperately wanted the performance to be as good as it was, as if they wanted it to be the best they'd ever seen. It was the best I ever saw. There was rattle and crash in an opening "Tombstone Blues," and a momentum, a charge over the next hill, that the earlier combos had not touched. Overwhelmingly loud, the sound had room in it. "It

*That is how I remember it, and a bootleg cd of the concert, *Long Distance Operator*, betrays not a curse or boo. ("Beautiful!" someone shouts as the show ends, a shout of equal parts joy and disbelief, disbelief that anything could be *this* beautiful.) But when, in Berkeley on December 3, 1994, I gave a talk referring back to the show that had taken place twenty-nine years earlier on the same weekend, three different people approached me later to tell me I had remembered nothing right. Groups of people had ritually risen from their seats and walked out of the hall when Dylan took the stage with the Hawks, one person insisted. "I was a welfare mother, I had nothing, and I saved for weeks to go," said a second. "And he didn't care, he only cared about the band, about Robbie Robertson—you could tell. He was stoned; he was somewhere else; he turned his back on the audience." She meant it literally; a third person recalled the same thing as metaphor. "That was the night he turned his back on us," he said, "and went for himself." All I could think was: what are the chances of walking into a medium-size meeting hall for a symposium on "The Current Political Situation" and finding four separate people who had been to the same Bob Dylan show almost thirty years before?

Ain't Me, Babe" was cut to a slow cadence, almost a march, on the verses; on the chorus Robbie Robertson threw out a flurry of notes like tiny firecrackers, and Dylan's singing shifted from certainty to wail. The arrangement was dark, gloomy, creating an ambience that made the listener feel trapped and implied the musicians held the key; there was happiness in the performance, and cruelty too. In a long break in the middle of the song, Robertson is contemplative, sure, mathematical; then it's as if, by accident, he chances upon a loose thread in the piece, so he pulls, the song unravels, it falls apart in your hands, but in his hands, on the stage, the song is suddenly whole again, and moving on. "I Don't Believe You," "Ballad of a Thin Man," and "Just Like Tom Thumb's Blues" don't have the careening, desperate cast they would take on a few months later in the United Kingdom—there was no need for it. Time after time Dylan turned to Robertson, their guitars just inches apart, his face cracked by a smile that didn't close: there was pleasure all over the music. The one song that did carry over into the last weeks in the British Isles was the one least burdened by the signs and portents fans heard in Dylan's music, or piled onto it: "Baby, Let Me Follow You Down." It was an old folk song, with a good guitar line; on Dylan's first album, where he carefully credited Eric von Schmidt, the man from whom he'd learned the tune, as folk singers were supposed to do ("I met him one day in the green pastures of, uh . . . Harvard University"), the music had a mournful tinge, the regret of a man coming on too strong. But now the music was an insistence that anything could be transformed and that there was no such thing as coming on too strong. As he would until that closing night in London, with this number Dylan drew the breath of the audience as one for the force he put into the sliding, then leaping harmonica notes that, with Rick Danko counting off the beat, spun the circling song into the air. Line by line, each verse grew in fervor and hilarity:

> I'll buy you a ball of twine
> Honey, just to see you climb
> I'll do anything in this godamighty world
> If you just won't again drive me out of my mind

In America, this music was, in a way, prophetic. At the very least the sound and its reception prefigured an America that, soon enough, for everyone, would be all too familiar: a country split in half over race and war, with battles in the streets, guns fired on college campuses, ghastly riots in cities across the nation, leaders falling to assassins as if on a schedule set by public fantasy, screamers driven from meeting halls with clubs, common citizens driven from their streets with gas and bullets. But in the United Kingdom, where after eight months on the road the ensemble had likely reached the limits of their capacities, and reveled at the fact, the hatred for Dylan's new music and for what he had become was somehow more abstract than in the United States, and more impersonal—uglier. It was as if he had betrayed not simply the Freedom Singers, or Woody Guthrie, or the fan who was now shouting, but the Folk immemorial, the mystic chords of memory, the very instinct that history contained identity and one could claim it. In any case the response now made the controversies of the past seasons fade into their own abstraction. In the music Dylan and the Hawks sent off stages in May of 1966, absurdity wars with terror, terror with exultation, exultation with loathing. It was all too much; it couldn't last, and it didn't.

Again and again, it is as if the whole of the drama is contained in a single incident. There is that famous moment in Manchester, at the end of the show. Dylan and the crowd have been fighting, sparring. Many in the audience clap slowly, in unison: *rap . . . rap . . . rap . . .* The sound defeats any other rhythm. Against a flurry of shouts Dylan begins to mumble what is apparently a story into the microphone, but as gibberish, until finally the crowd quiets out of simple curiosity: *What* is he saying? The music this night is overwhelming. "Tell Me, Momma," a song that emerged on the tour, opens every show, and there are never any boos for this one. It's too strong, it comes on too fast. Dylan rides the roar of movement the band throws up around him like a surfer in the pipeline, his only way home a wish to absorb every bit of energy in the physics of the instant and then add more. A snide, funny, baffled, empathetic set of lyrics seems no more than an excuse to prove this is the best band in the world. Garth Hudson seems to be playing a blast furnace, Rick Danko a monochord, Robbie Robertson a guitar yet to be invented. Listening to the way each musician seemingly plays off of every other's barely unfulfilled desire rather than whatever movement he has in fact made makes it impossible to believe that six people could ever know each other better. Yet all that comradeship will be burned off by the crowd as the night goes on; the chord Robbie Robertson gets to open "Ballad of a Thin Man" could not be more shocking, bloodier, and the crowd shuts down. And then, as if he had been waiting, well informed as to the precise order in which Dylan played his songs, a person rises and shouts what he has been silently rehearsing to himself all night. As over and over he has imagined himself doing, he stands up, and stops time. He stops the show:

"JUDAS!"

Dylan stiffens against the flinch of his own body. "I don't believe you," he says, and the contempt in his voice is absolute. As one listens it turns the echo of the shouter's curse sour, you begin to hear the falseness in it, that loving rehearsal—and yet that same echo has already driven Dylan back. "YOU'RE A *LIAR!*" he screams hysterically. A band member can feel the night beginning to crumble: "C'mon, man," he says helplessly. Dylan turns back to the band: "Play fucking loud." They dive into the last song, "Like a Rolling Stone"; there were no encores at these shows.

"Come on, Bob, SING!" roared a man out of a cold and growing hubbub in Sheffield; it's a wonderful sound, warm and coming from deep in the chest, but on the official and unofficial recordings of the tour it is unique. People rose from their seats and walked out en masse. People brought protest signs into the halls, including "STOP THE WAR"—not the war in Vietnam, but this one. The music grew in violence, in extremism. In Liverpool, in the midst of "Just Like Tom Thumb's Blues," a song about being in a place where you don't belong, the pressure increased with every verse. At Forest Hills, in Berkeley, across the United States, the performance of this song clung to its beginnings on *Highway 61 Revisited* as a lament, a twist of Marty Robbins's "El Paso" into the Coasters' "Smokey Joe's Cafe," a certain south-of-the-border who-cares dragging at the song's heels. But not anymore. Now every word is loaded, its delivery sounding alarms, the musicians ignoring them. Too much pressure—until you feel that if not the musicians, or the audience, then the characters in the song are about to burst from it—until finally the six on the stage are so caught up in the music they become mere figments of it. With only the thinnest gravity holding the performance together, a sound comes up from Hudson's organ, like the footsteps of a monster, a dragon bursting from its cave beneath the stage where it has slept for a thousand years, a roiling sound, the sound of a power beyond the ability of anyone on the stage or in the crowd to master, a genie out of its bottle for good. At just that instant when it seems the image can no longer hold, Dylan gives a long, high, wordless cry—a cry of delight. This is what it was for, that right to disappear, to be transfigured, to return an instant later as a being you yourself no longer recognize.

The same energies were sometimes at play in the first, acoustic half of the concerts, where, in false respect and false appreciation, the crowds conducted a kind of silent war, a phony peace. In Leicester Dylan began "Mr. Tambourine Man," and it would take him nine perfect minutes to find an ending in the song he could accept. As he sings his words are clipped, his diction almost effete, as if each word can and must be presented as if it means exactly what it says. But very quickly this odd speech becomes its own kind of rhythm, and paradoxically it releases the burden Dylan has seemingly placed on each word, and each word along with every other floats, and the song becomes a dream of peace of mind. You cease to hear the words. For nine minutes what you hear are two long harmonica solos, each pressing well past two minutes—solos that sway, back and forth, back and forth, a cradle rocking in their rhythm, until without warning the sound rises up like a water spout, hundreds of feet in the air, the cradle now rocking at its top, then down again, safe in the arms of the melody. "Who'll rock the cradle, who'll sing the song?" sang Dock Boggs of Norton, Virginia, in 1927, in "Sugar Baby," a record Bob Dylan loved, and Boggs answered himself, all menace, like a killer offering his victim the last words she will ever hear: "I'll rock the cradle, I'll sing the song / I'll rock the cradle when you gone." But there is nothing like that here, now; that comes in the second half of the show. "Nobody has any *respect,*" Dylan shuddered in the midst of "Ballad of a Thin Man" in Birmingham, the word shredding, as if it contained all the evil in the world and could not hold it, the crowd now flinching in its turn at what its rancor, what its hatred, what its bigotry had revealed.

On that night, then, in the Royal Albert Hall, "Ballad of a Thin Man" began slowly, as if all the motive in the song was suspended between each note of the first phrase, which itself seemed suspended, pressing against a freeze. The guitar began a theme but didn't shape it. The piano came in, as if it would rather have been anywhere else. The bass sealed the moment, for lack of anything better to do. The result was creepy—and simultaneously clandestine and public, inaccessible to anyone outside the group of six on the stage, yet as always beckoning, a secret language anyone could understand, that could break the code you used to hold yourself in place. The performance turned the wheel of its lassitude, and then without warning the wheel went off its track. "You *know* something is happening," Dylan screamed from the piano. "And it's happening without you!"

• • •

One night, in Cardiff, Wales, Dylan greeted Johnny Cash backstage. As caught by D. A. Pennebaker's camera, Cash is thin, his face scarred. At thirty-three he looks like cancer.

The two men sit down at a piano and begin searching for the melody in Cash's "I Still Miss Someone," a lovely, seemingly traditional ballad. Dylan bangs the keys with leaden fingers, and together he and Cash reach for the first line: "At my door—" They miss. "At my doooooor . . ." They stop. They're too tired, or too wasted, to find the song they're looking for. It's the simplest song in the world and they can't touch it. Cash punches Dylan in the chest. "Oh my God!" Dylan says, trying not to laugh. "You wouldn't do that to your best friend!" They turn back to the piano and stumble to the end of the chorus: "And I still miss someone." "You sing it," Dylan says, "I'll sing harmony." "At my *door*," Cash groans, then, "at my *doooooor*," lifting the last word. The piano begins to ring. Something begins to come into focus, then it's gone.

With everything coming out of their mouths a drunken slurring, the notes on the piano now begin to gong. Each note is separate, standing alone. You can hear one note fade completely into the air before the next note begins; the theme is all in pieces. Cash follows the broken line Dylan is drawing like a man trying to negotiate a DUI test on the side of a highway, but Dylan is on another road. His piano is stately now, full of silences and room for visions; the gonging has turned to chiming, and the chiming makes the ratty backstage into a church. As Cash begins to ride the melody, Dylan presses for a rhythm the country song won't give up. The notes come faster, hitting each other as they rise and fall, and the song itself begins to play. Its door opens, its leaves fall, its singer stands gazing out over his garden, or a prairie, or a river. He looks out across the landscape of his life, and all he sees are those blue eyes: "I see them everywhere." But the piano stops: ". . . the melody," Dylan says thickly, "I can't remember this." Cash mutters through a fog too deep to penetrate, as if from the far side of sixty. "That's the greatest song I ever heard," says Dylan, suddenly bright and eager, sounding at least seventeen.

They try again; Dylan picks up the pace slightly, takes the song, his voice raw and high, with Cash just a burr, the rhythm of his fatigue countering the rhythm of Dylan's reach for notes he can't hit, notes that seem to be straining as hard toward him as he is toward them. They go on; they fall short again.

"At my doooooor," Cash tries once more, then stops. "No, no," he says to Dylan, "let's do it your way." "Oh, my way," Dylan says, as if this is the best joke of the night, "my way *sucks*." "If I do it too," Cash says, unsteadily but warmly, like an older brother, "it'll make you look good." The best joke of the night is now a better one. "Well," Dylan says, "I'm not known for looking good—Don't you dare! I've—" (there are words that can't be made out), "I—" (or that never quite got made), "Why, I'll mystify this whole *room!*"

They banter for a moment more, Cash leans back, and then without a pause Dylan hits the keys hard. Coming directly off the last words of the conversation ("You didn't know I was a piano player, did you?" "Yeah, I did too"), a theme far more suggestive than any found in their earlier palavers comes up. Dylan opens his mouth, and wind and rain come out. The lights in the room seem to dim. Even if he is making it up out of the air, the song he's now singing feels older than the grandparents of anyone in the room and more familiar than anyone's own face. There are a few words, and a scattered blues melody—"I bought me a ticket, for a one-way train," Dylan sings, completely and happily lost, utterly alone even as Johnny Cash comes in for the next line, "I bought me a ticket, for a one-way track"—and as the film runs out in the camera Dylan disappears into the tunnel of the song. When he finally comes out on the other side he is in another country: the U.S.A., to be sure, though for the moment this is an America that exists only in the basement of a big pink house, a country that no one has exactly inhabited before. "Lo and behold!" he exclaims. "Lo and behold!"

T W O

TIME IS LONGER THAN ROPE

Inside Big Pink, "Lo and Behold!" opens on the rails, the first notes on the piano setting the wheels in motion, the singer with one foot on the platform and the other foot on the train as it pulls out within the basement walls. It's the summer of 1967, a couple of months into fooling with old tunes, moving across a common landscape, new songs now coming in a rush; three decades later, you can still hear Garth Hudson snap the switch.

He clicks on the tape recorder for the second take of the afternoon. They'd been pressing the first time through the number, the piano, bass, and acoustic guitar piling the rhythm up at the end of a phrase, the feel of a mind changing cramped by a tight vocal, the actor's mask not settling into the singer's skin, the singer improvising a last line out of frustration: "We're all gonna go to sleep!" Now Hudson turns back to his organ to catch up with the hard, hesitating count already locked in as a theme by the piano. Almost subliminally, he rolls the piano's one-step-forward, one-step-back into a better beat. The doubt and trepidation that mark the borders of the song aren't lessened, but the territory within is singing with energy, the uncertainty that a moment before said fear now saying who cares. Now the rhythm is a chase after pleasure that once it's caught its chase lets it loose for the pleasure of chasing it down again; with every chorus Bob Dylan and Richard Manuel lift their voices and then abandon them, stranding their words right at the edge of a cliff, suspending the sound in dead silence until the next verse begins. It's a stark, shuddering effect, the pleasure cut like a heater in a cheap hotel turning itself off; you stick in a coin, it starts up again.

The hesitation in the song is now dramatized, something to see, and also hiding inside the beat, a second song only the singer will recognize. Nevertheless the music has gained an irresistible momentum, a lift off the ground. This is a train you want to board, which may be a mixed blessing—like so many trains in American song, from Casey Jones's 638 to the sixteen-coach cannonball in the Carter Family's "Worried Man Blues," it's a train that could be easier to get on than to get off.

The train runs smoothly even as the rhythm pulls against itself: first stop San Antonio, Texas, next stop Pittsburgh, PA, a side trip to Tennessee, then back to Pittsburgh—you don't say. No wonder there's a kind of stammer in half the claims the singer makes. "I never felt so good," he tells us of the journey's start, relaxing into the memory. In the next instant the coachman asks him for his ticket, no problem, he's got a ticket, then for his name.

His name? He's not supposed to have to tell his name. Suddenly all his confidence is gone, as if the seat holding his back has fallen away like the chorus giving up its last word. Now he is faced with a demand that goes just past the endlessly rehearsed gestures of fellowship and distance, acknowledgment and evasion, presentation and disappearance, that in 1835, in *Democracy in America*, Alexis de Tocqueville caught as the very stuff of a democratic walk down the street of the American small town—"that same small town in each of us," as Don Henley could still imagine in 1989, in "The End of the Innocence." The video for the song was a montage re-creating photographs Robert Frank, from Switzerland, made in the mid-1950s, in Hoboken, New Jersey, Jay, New York, Iuka, Mississippi, Blackfoot, Idaho, Butte, Montana: insistently silent photographs, without movement within their borders, of individuals stranded in their own commonwealth. "I came home with good intentions / About five or six years ago," Elvis Presley sang in 1969 in an unreleased version of "Stranger in My Own Home Town." It was a blues song: "But my home town won't accept me / I just don't feel welcome here no more." He was recording in his hometown of Memphis for the first time in fourteen years—the town's most famous son, still scorned, still an embarrassment—but in the song he wasn't home yet. Singing slowly, as if he'd lived the story many times before, he rewrote the tune as he sang:

> I'm going back down to Memphis
> I'm gonna start driving that motherfucking truck again . . .
> All them cocksuckers stopped being friendly
> But you can't keep a hard prick down

The man on the train is here too—without this voice. All his rehearsed gestures—they were supposed to be those of surrendering a ticket and nothing more. This is an encounter in which the presumption of moral equality between one party and another guarantees that they can exchange moral goods—a ticket fairly purchased, fair value in return—without truly meeting: without asking who the other really is. It's a form of citizens' respect, a democratic deference, an American invention: that is why, in 1831, with Andrew Jackson in the White House trailing his campaign banner "LET THE PEOPLE RULE," Tocqueville responded to it. But the coachman has broken the rules. He has violated the presumption of equality and assumed a posture of authority; for no reason the man who felt so good can tell, the coachman has asked for too much. *Who are you?* Whatever the singer brought onto the train turns up worthless. His name? "I give it to him right away," Dylan sings, hurry and bafflement in his voice, then the hurry bleeding out, the bafflement joined with regret: "And I hung my head in shame."

From a country of thousand-mile vistas in the first line of the first verse, the man who as we met him there was filled with anticipation has by the end of the verse arrived in a country of hideouts and himself become a creature of guilt. With the verse over and the moving train now a trap, a mystery train, Manuel doubles Dylan from the other side of the room, his voice heavy, Dylan's straining; barely audible in Dylan's corner, Rick Danko adds a high echo.

> Lo and behold!
> Lo and behold!
> Looking for my
> Lo and behold
> Get me out of here, my dear man!

Hoisting himself onto the train, settling into his seat, the singer wasn't merely confident, he was cocksure. "And he asked me my name," the singer remembers; as he spins the incident back, he can feel how he'd pulled away, and underneath the worry that's how he sings it, a cold half smile on his face, his fish-eye all over the coachman's mug. "And he—" "—asked me my name." For as long as that little pause holds, with the pause weighting the last word, the singer is still telling this story, writing its script, acting it out; with an edge of amusement he retains his mask, holding his name like a poker player holding his cards to his vest. *My name? Perhaps you're lacking one yourself?* Yes, that's what he should have said! Too bad it's too late. "And he—"

Over the bright, playful pulse of the organ and piano, the former now swirling, sometimes leaping behind the latter, that pause suspends the story and the music with it, even as the music goes on. It's a perfect moment. The singer drags his breath across his tongue as if his fingers are caressing a gun. Now he's Clint Eastwood in *A Fistful of Dollars*. Serape on his shoulders, leather hat on his head, cheroot stuck in his face, the singer squints at the coachman, deadpan, until he sees that the coachman has turned into Billy the Kid, with Billy ramming his last words, "¿Quién es? ¿Quién es?" into the throat of the Man with No Name. By the time the singer gets to "my name" his knees are water. The coachman looks down at him, waiting. The singer says his name: *Nobody.*

One step forward, one step back: from within its rhythms of melody and speech, the first verse of "Lo and Behold!" makes a story as shapely and complete as one of Hawthorne's Twice-Told Tales of humiliation and withdrawal ("The Shaker Bridal," say, or "The Minister's Black Veil") and as casually doomstruck as one of Melville's fables of embarkment, most economically the first chapter of *The Confidence-Man: His Masquerade*, titled "A mute goes aboard a boat on the Mississippi" (a chapter where there is no dialogue, only hand-lettered signs proceeding from "Charity thinketh no evil" to "NO TRUST"). Still, the song hums along, from stop to stop, the train running from station to station, each succeeding verse promising a new adventure but never quite realizing it. The singer meets a woman on the next leg of his journey, but they fall into obscene banter ("What's the matter, Molly dear? What's the matter with your mound?"), and she hands him a dismissal as finished as the one he felt in the coachman's evil question ("What's it to ya, Moby Dick?"). Big deals turn into little dreams. A herd of moose the singer buys his girl becomes a truck he thinks he might pick up in Tennessee. "Gonna save my money and rip it up," he says hopefully, another trucker on his mind and maybe laughing at his conceit; the way the singer makes the words, ripping it up might as well be sweeping the floor. Every verse is full of fill-in-the-gaps, no tale holds and neither does the taleteller's voice—line to line, syllable to syllable, Dylan goes from eager to disgusted, smug to wary, prophetic to intrigued, bragging to couldn't-care-less. Soon it's as if all the openness in the song—the prospect of great novelties and thrills that at first seemed to be its subject—has been sucked up by the rhythm, pushing forward in a manner that all too quickly seems as blocked as it is swift: predetermined, inexorable, circular, a route that ultimately has nowhere to go but back to Pittsburgh.

The chorus goes in another direction. Self-mocking, it is

always yearning, even desperate, the sound of a man who wants to take off his mask and shout. But throughout every story told in "Lo and Behold!," in and out of every verse, there is really only one voice, and that voice is the mask itself: "a portable heirloom," Constance Rourke wrote in 1931 in *American Humor: A Study of the National Character*, "handed down by the pioneer." A hundred years after Tocqueville's arrival in the new United States, Rourke was looking into the face of the Yankee pedlar, the original traveling salesman, the confidence man, though the words that replaced this appellation, "con man," also took away its meaning: what the confidence man sells, proffering his calico and patent medicine, his aluminum siding and asbestos insulation, his Amway dealerships and breast implants, is confidence. He looks you right in the face; his betrays no doubt, no greed, no fear, shame least of all. Rourke wrote:

> In a primitive world crowded with pitfalls the unchanging, unaverted countenance had been a safeguard, preventing revelations of surprise, anger, or dismay. The mask had otherwise become habitual among the older Puritans as their more expressive or risible feelings were sunk beneath the surface. Governor Bradford encouraged its use on a considerable scale, urging certain gay spirits to enjoy themselves in secret, if they must be convivial. No doubt the mask would prove useful in a country where the Puritan was still a power and the risks of pioneering by no means over.

But it was not only risible feelings that were hidden, and the mask was not merely a disguise. Sometimes it was as if the mask could protect those who might gaze upon the real face of whoever wore it from awful sights—or even that the mask was a kind of defense against the mirror, protecting the wearer from his or her own face. "There is a gift held back," Perry Miller wrote in 1949 of the great Puritan preacher Jonathan Edwards, "an aboriginal and monolithic power" who in 1740 rang his words down the Connecticut Valley as the Great Awakening blew through him like a storm. "The way he delivered his sermons is enough to confirm the suspicion that there was an occult secret in them: no display, no inflection, no consideration of the audience." As "Edwards delivered his revival sermons—for example the goriest, the one at Enfield that goes by the title 'Sinners in the Hands of an Angry God' and is all that most people nowadays associate with his name," Miller wrote, "the people yelled and shrieked, they rolled in the aisles, they crowded up to the pulpit and begged him to stop, they cried for mercy," but "Mr. Edwards," one congregant remembered, "looked straight forward"; another said "he looked on the bell rope," hanging from the roof at the far end of the church, "until he looked it off." Setting down the words of those who heard Edwards, the scholar can look back two centuries and see clearly, but he wants most of all to reach back, to remove the minister's false face, to find out if it is false, if there is something or nothing behind it.

Edwards's mask too was handed down. It traveled from 1740 in New England to Memphis in 1968, where it was assumed one last time by Martin Luther King, Jr., as he preached in a church on the last night of his life. His voice rose and fell, the cadences of his speech making stairways for his words to climb, balconies from which they might plunge like spurned lovers. Like Moses, King said, he had gone "up to the mountain," and he had "seen the Promised Land," even if god would not permit him to cross over: "I may not get there with you, but I want you to know that we as a people will get to the Promised Land. So I'm happy tonight. I'm not worried about anything. I'm not fearing any man. Mine eyes have seen the glory of the coming of the Lord." "As he spoke," Lawrence Wright recalled in his memoir *In the New World*, "with that curiously impassive face of his, which was always like a mask of resignation, the congregation began to moan and cry out."

The mask passed from Edwards to King as if on a stream within a river, the gift of one divine to another, King's visions of justice with their source in Edwards's Awakening. Dissolving the earthly boundaries that separated the elect from the reprobate, Edwards forced his listeners to experience the thrill and terror of confronting god directly. Now, in fellowship, each congregant was Abraham and Moses, made to choose between god and Isaac, the right and the Golden Calf; each was obligated to begin the story again from the beginning, in his or her own heart. Speaking as one who came down from the mountain with the Ten Commandments in one arm, the Declaration of Independence and the Constitution in the other, King demanded that his listeners do the same; the mask was a bond between preachers who had reason to fear that the passions they sought to guide them toward righteousness might consume them.

"It was certainly a weird performance," Miller wrote of Edwards, and Wright was saying something similar about King. In 1968 people appeared in public not masked but convulsed with rage and fright. The mask was an occult secret no one had the time to decode, and the tumult was so great it seemed that all ancestors lived in another country, that the Puritans and their like had been altogether banished. It wasn't so in 1949, when Miller wrote. Again the Puritans seemed to rule, under new names but with no less power. As enemies of the people—those to whom such suspect words as "communist," "fellow traveler," or, so strangely, "premature antifascist" adhered—were taken from their homes and workplaces and exposed to all, many believed that the Puritans' witch trials were taking place before their very eyes, the centuries collapsed into each other. The frontier too persisted, a country within each citizen if it was anywhere; by this time the mask was all-American, and it had a new name: cool. James Dean wore it perfectly in *Rebel without a Cause*, where teenagers fought duels in the empty spaces surrounding the new suburban landscape; sitting in the audience, a twelve-year-old Randy Newman received the mask and tried to put it on. "The goal when I was a teenager was to be without affect, to have a masklike face," he said in 1995. "A lot of people I know never came out of it, and I barely did."

Discovered by Rourke as an eighteenth-century heirloom, the mask is what in the nineteenth century came to be called the deadpan, the poker face: precisely what the coachman wipes off the rider's face. The mask hides the voice no less than the face, and the voice it makes you might call Yankee Midwestern, though it is also Appalachian, mountain-still, a speech made as much of silences as of words, and the silence is the edge. *So what?* says the voice; it is dulled, unimpressed, as Rourke says, unsurprised. Those who use this voice claim they can't be surprised even by the weather—that is, by god—and that's their claim on life, why they expect you to listen to them, regardless of whether what they're saying makes sense. The voice is flat: so flat that with the slightest inflection it can say anything, imply anything, while seeming to do no more than pass the time.

This is the sound of bluesman Frank Hutchison, who Bob Dylan would return to in 1993 for the version of "Stack A Lee" he offered on *World Gone Wrong* ("a romance tale without the cupidity," Dylan wrote); it is the sound of drugstore speech in Hibbing, Minnesota, in 1949; it's the sound of William Burroughs waiting out a blizzard in a depot fifty miles north of Wichita. "Yes, that's ol' junkie Bill, over by the stove there, just whittlin' on his penis," says the stationmaster, while Bill mumbles to himself:

> . . . the buyer has a steady connection: the man within, you might say, or so he thinks. I'll just set in my room, he says: Fuck 'em all, squares on both sides; I am the only complete man in the industry. But a yen comes on him like a great black wind, through the bones. . . . The buyer had lost his human citizenship, and was in consequence a creature without species, and a menace to the narcotics industry, at all levels . . .

If you listen to Burroughs as he read these words into a tape recorder in Paris in 1965, what you hear is prairie-flat and Babbitt-plain, a world conspiracy lined out in the modest tones of a small businessman describing a small job. Just beneath the surface, or played back in memory, it's all music—"Fuck 'em all" expanding into a great curl, "Fuck 'em awww*lllll*," then the *q* in "squares" rounding, nearly flipping the word on its back—and simultaneously an anthropological document, no exile's art statement but a field recording, "American Vernacular, Kansas/Missouri (Science Fiction)." "The humorous story is American, the comic story is English, the witty story is French," Mark Twain wrote in "How to Tell a Story." "The humorous story depends for its effect upon the manner of telling; the comic story and the witty story upon the matter. . . . The humorous story is told gravely; the teller does his best to conceal that he even dimly suspects that there is anything funny about it." That is Bob Dylan all through the basement tapes, and most precisely, as if in summation of both manner and matter, in "Lo and Behold!"; that is Burroughs on *Call Me Burroughs*, his Ishmael's album of *Naked Lunch* readings that was a talisman of cool in Greenwich Village in the mid-1960s—and, cast as blues on a lap slide guitar, that was Frank Hutchison. On the old-timey lps and precious 78s of the folk revival, he was an even cooler talisman, to some.

It's Hutchison who Dylan takes for granted in "Lo and Behold!"—the speaker who Dylan, with intent or more likely without it, takes as a first principle. Hutchison's drifting, blasted, dead-drunk pieces are little exercises in sardonicism that by the end of a tune can lock a grin on the singer's face like tetanus; his songs lie behind the masked voice in "Lo and Behold!" as a tiny tradition of their own notes and phrases, winks and nods, not as something to best or transcend but as something to burrow into, to find what stories the tradition could have told but didn't.

Born in 1897, Frank Hutchison came from Logan County in southern West Virginia, near the Kentucky border. Logan had been anti-Union—for that matter, after West Virginia's pro-Union secession from Virginia in 1863, it was more or less anti–West Virginia, part of the rough, once-isolated inner frontier known as "the interior"; in the 1880s the territory was infamous throughout the nation as the home ground of the Hatfield side of the Hatfield-McCoy feud. There were few slaves in Logan before the Civil War and until the coal boom of 1910 not many black families after it; as a small boy Hutchison tagged behind a visiting black laborer—one Henry Vaughn, perhaps, residents told folklorists in the 1960s—drawn by the sound of the man's guitar. When Hutchison reached his late teens he went to work in the coal mines like everybody else, lucky to stay mainly on the surface, cooking and hammering nails—the farms and hunt forests of his parents' youth were just family stories. He married and settled in the small coal town of Ethel, in the shadow of Blair Mountain; before too long he made his living mostly as a musician, occasionally doubling as a blackface comedian. He recorded for the first time in 1926, for the last time in 1929, after which the Depression killed off such marginal enterprises as phonograph records for the blues and hillbilly trade; best remembered for "The Train that Carried the Girl from Town," Hutchison died in 1945, in Dayton, Ohio, disappointed and out of place. He had angel's fingers, and the voice of a man who's seen it all and loves more than anything to think back, facedown in a memory, in Rosanne Cash's phrase, as if some overlooked opportunity for revenge or solace might be found. More than anything there is in his music a detachment that goes beyond words, into a realm where only sound can follow, a loosening of ties that is so odd, and so strong, it leads one to ask not only what goes into a piece of music, but also a more intense version of the same question: what can you hear in it?

"Dylan manifests a profound awareness of the war and how it is affecting all of us," Jon Landau wrote in the spring of 1968, reviewing *John Wesley Harding*, the album Dylan recorded with Nashville musicians in the fall of 1967, when the basement afternoons were all but played out; the record was a quiet morality play, a sort of Puritan western. As Landau wrote, the country was about to split in half over the assassinations of Martin Luther King and Robert Kennedy, over race riots, political riots, police riots, a national election, the abbatoir of Vietnam; listening to an album that ended with a love song that rhymed "moon" with "spoon," Landau, like so many American GIs in the year to come, heard the war. "This doesn't mean that I think any of the particular songs are about the war or that any of the songs are protests over it," he said ("How do you know," Dylan would ask an interviewer in the summer of 1968, "that I'm not, as you say, for the war?"). "All I mean to say," Landau wrote, "is that Dylan has felt the war, that there is an awareness of it contained within the mood of the album as a whole"—and something similar may lurk within Frank Hutchison's music in the same way, as an occult social drama. Hutchison's music was made, after all, in the aftermath of a civil war in his own county: the West Virginia Mine War of 1920 and 1921. Hutchison lived dead center.

On January 30, 1920, John L. Lewis, the new president of the United Mine Workers of America, came to southern West Virginia to announce a drive to unionize the coal fields across the southern Appalachians. Miners there were tools, discarded when they broke or wore out. They were paid in scrip and kept in debt; with their families they lived in company housing. Injured miners were fired and evicted along with their wives and children, the widows and orphans of the hundreds of miners who each year died beneath West Virginia ground, and anyone who spoke the word "union." The hills were soon full of tent colonies housing striking miners and their families. In Matewan, in Mingo County, just over the line to the west of Logan, Mayor C. C. Testerman and Police Chief Sid Hatfield, an orphan raised by the once-mass-murdering Hatfield clan, aligned themselves with the strikers and guarded union meetings against company assassins; on May 19, 1920, they attempted to stop agents of the Baldwin-Felts Detective Agency from carrying out a new round of evictions. Hatfield was awaiting the arrival of warrants for the arrest of the detectives when Al Felts, a head of the agency, backed by twelve of his men, confronted Hatfield and Testerman with a warrant of his own—a phony warrant. When the facedown was over, Felts, his brother, five other detectives, the mayor, and two miners were dead in the streets, and the train carrying Hatfield's warrants arrived. Hatfield stood over Felts's body with a warrant in his hand. "Now, you son of a bitch," he said, "I'll serve it on you." In February of the next year Hatfield and twenty-two other Matewan men went on trial for Felts's murder; after almost six weeks, during which the presidency passed from Woodrow Wilson to Warren G. Harding, all of the defendants were acquitted. In July Hatfield was arrested on charges of harassing nonunion miners. It was a setup; when Hatfield arrived at the courthouse for arraignment, Baldwin-Felts detectives shot him down in broad daylight.

By this time Logan County was a state within a state: a police state. With Mingo terrorized, Logan sheriff Don Chafin barred union representatives even from entering his territory and deputized hundreds of company men to enforce a cordon sanitaire. Enraged by Hatfield's assassination, thousands of armed strikers, now pushed to the east, determined to seize Mingo. "No armed mob will cross Logan County," Chafin announced; defying their national union, the swiftly growing miners' army, led by such local union officers as Frank Keeney, Walter Allen, and Billy Blizzard, made to drive Chafin himself out of Logan. Chafin organized his own army of detectives, coal guards, American Legionnaires, and businessmen. By August 31 at least ten thousand men—and perhaps as many as twenty thousand—were firing across the ten-mile front line that snaked across the forbidding twin peaks of Blair Mountain. As Lon Savage noted in *Thunder in the Mountains*, "George Washington had fewer soldiers at the Battle of Trenton, the engagement which changed the course of the American Revolution."

The miners thought the Battle of Blair Mountain was as much a protest as a rebellion: a call to wake the nation to the fact that the Constitution was no law in Logan County. Instead President Harding sent Federal troops against the miners, and General Billy Mitchell of the Army Air Service, who had led air battles over France in the First World War, tried to bomb them. ("Gas," Mitchell said. "You understand we wouldn't try to kill these people at first.") Mitchell's squadron crashed, but the miners, many of them veterans of the same war that made Mitchell a national hero, would not fight their national government, and surrendered their arms. Expecting protection, they were arrested by the hundreds; Frank Keeney, Walter Allen, and Billy Blizzard were charged with treason. Keeney was never prosecuted; Allen was convicted, jumped bail, and disappeared; Billy Blizzard, tried in the same courthouse where

John Brown was convicted of treason in 1859, was acquitted—as was the man who led Sid Hatfield's assassins, tried in the same courthouse Hatfield was entering when he was killed. The border held; there was no union organizing in Logan until 1933, when Franklin D. Roosevelt became president.

In *Night Comes to the Cumberlands*, a study of the ruin of the Appalachians, Harry Claudill noted that as late as the early 1960s, the oldest residents of the coal fields still recalled "with pleasure W. J. Horsley, T. P. Trigg, E. B. Moon, John C. C. Mayo and a score of others, and nostalgically reminisce about their tours of the isolated backcountry." Full of wonderful stories of strange doings and faraway places, their faces cracked with open smiles seldom seen in a land where the pioneer's mask was rarely lifted, speaking a foreign tongue of flattery and praise, these were the men hired in the mid-1880s and 1890s by northern coal companies to buy up the mineral rights held by the hardscrabble hunter-farmers of the southern mountains. Constance Rourke sighted their Yankee ancestor "at the latter end of the eighteenth century . . . descending a steep red road into a fertile Carolina valley . . . In the end he invaded every house. Everyone bought. The Negroes came up from their cabins to watch his driving pantomime and hear his slow, high talk. Staying the night at a tavern, he traded the landlord out of bed and breakfast, and left with most of the money in the settlement." His seller's mask reversed for a buyer's, the confidence man reappeared a hundred years later; the result was the same. In Claudill's words:

With every convincing appearance of complete sincerity the coal buyer would spend hours admiring the mountaineer's horse and gazing over a worm-rail fence in rapt approbation of his razorback hogs while compliments were dropped on every phase of his host's accomplishments. He marveled at the ample contents of the mountaineer's smokehouse and savored the rich flavor of the good woman's apple butter and other preserved delicacies, while he assured her that no dainty to be found in the big city confectionaries was half so tasty. He ate the rough "grub" she prepared for him, and happily slept in the softest featherbed the cabin afforded. After such a visit he and "the man of the house" would get down to business.

It was mask against mask, and the smile won. Having secured the absolute right to extract whatever might lie beneath the farmer's ground, the buyers often left the putative owners of century-old land patents only the right to pay taxes. In most cases the buyers paid fifty cents for an acre of land that three decades later might produce twenty thousand tons of coal—and after that, nothing living, the buyer's signature and the farmer's mask having sealed an agreement by which the inner frontier of freeholders was opened to serfdom. "A new standard of morals is set up amidst the confusion," Emma Bell Miles wrote in 1905 in *The Spirit of the Mountains*:

This people who have no servant class are constantly made to feel themselves inferior to the newcomers, and so fall into servility. . . . Too late the mountaineer realizes that he has sold his birthright for a mess of potage. He has become a day laborer. . . . Need these razors be used to cut grindstones? Must this free folk who are in many ways the truest Americans of America be brought under the yoke of caste division, to the degradation of all their finer qualities, merely for the lack of the right work to do?

The buyers, Claudill reported with bitter wonder—gazing, as he wrote, upon a landscape reshaped by half a century of deep-mining and strip mining—could almost have been from another planet, they were so charming, making friends for life, even if the mountain people, or their children, one day awoke to find that their land and their history was no longer theirs, signed away, literally unwritten—and the buyers, who could have offered cards reading "Charity thinketh no evil" when they arrived and left others reading "NO TRUST" when they departed, never came back.

This is where the West Virginia Mine War began, before many who were part of it were even born—and one can perhaps hear a memory of these transactions, and a witnessing to war and surrender, in Frank Hutchison's unwavering detachment, in his distanced, worn-down, shaggy-dog blues, where the voice of the confidence man reappears so naturally, bereft as always of anxiety or surprise. In the shadow play of public happenstance and private regret, a great public disaster speaks the language of merely solitary unhappiness, not rage but guilt. That is the mask of shame unwritten history forces those who have lived it to assume. But here a single artist may come out of a time and place shared with many and offer a version of that time and place no one else could have made or even wished for. Others, perhaps enough to make the artist's living, may respond; much later, others may chance upon and follow the artist's clues. Thus the artist's work, commonplace and trivial on its face, may be charged with a power no intention could create and no particular geography or lifespan can enclose: the burning sensation produced when an individual attempts to resolve the circumstance of his or her life. Fashioning the sort of aesthetic artifact that dissolves into eccentricity or ethnography as soon as written history is pressed upon it, the artist may succeed in passing on the barest hint of a forgotten story and, blind to its source, the full weight of the impulse to tell it. That is how old stories turn into new stories; that is how stories get told.

"All right, boys, this is Frank Hutchison, settin' back in the Union Square Hotel, just gettin' right on good red liquor," he announced in "K.C. Blues"; it wasn't a typical sentiment. Hutchison liked to fade a note away from a theme, a word off of its phrase, to let his music go like smoke into the air. It's a typical blues technique, indicating the presence of something too dark or obvious to say out loud, though with Hutchison it doesn't feel like technique. It feels like musing, philosophy, his idea of revelation: the revelation that the meaning of any incident of love or money will always elude whoever wants it most, the fool who thought to ask. A high, thin bottleneck sound rises up in "Cannon Ball Blues," as if ready to escape the resignation the song describes so mordantly, then as if it isn't worth the effort. The back-and-forth tug-of-war the piano runs through "Lo and Behold!" is close to what Hutchison's music is about—a tired, so-what, whatever, never-mind refusal to wait around for the punch line to the joke everyone calls life combined with a willingness to wait around forever in the vague hope the joke might be on someone else. In the long, drawn-out "Worried Blues"—at times it almost seems to stop, so besotted with the pointlessness of it all—big notes slide up the strings, circling around and around, until sorrow fades into laughter, laughter into regret, regret into the oblivion of a six-day drunk, not a single word pressed harder than any other, everything as far from peaks and valleys as the patterns one makes tracing a finger in dust.

When I leave here
Just hang crêpe on your door
When I leave here
Just hang crêpe on your door
I won't be dead
Just won't be here no more

If you don't think that's funny, you're in the wrong country—or the wrong bar, not the bar Hutchison calls up in song after song with his trademark gather-round, bringing the boys together for one more drink before they head home to the joke that has no punch line. Small, prickling high notes are the pins and needles of Hutchison's worried blues, which

Make you b'lieve the world is upside down
They make you b'lieve, the world is upside down
I've traveled this world
Boys, it's all around

"All ay-round," he sings, treasuring the word, thinking it through, and it's this expiring tone—the tone of one who won't be dead, just gone—that allows Dylan in his turn to tell the most extravagant, half-cracked stories in "Lo and Behold!": to tell them as if there's no detail, no emotion, that can't be taken back, because with this tone whatever might sound uncertain, silly, or hysterical can as easily leave you wondering if you heard anything at all. "Now, I come in on a Ferris wheel,"

Dylan opens the last verse of the song, a hint of delight in his voice (why not, after coming up with an entrance worthy of Pecos Bill?), "and boys, I sure was slick. I come in like a ton of bricks, laid a few tricks on 'em"—and whatever delight there was dies with the drift of the language from the grand to the ordinary. You can imagine a man getting off a train with the flair and glamour of someone riding into town on a Ferris wheel; for that matter, the line is sung so matter-of-factly you can imagine someone riding into town on a Ferris wheel. Though you're framing the shot—the singer on his Ferris wheel like a cowboy on his horse—before Dylan is halfway through his next line, it's only the life in the image that pushes at the dulled voice, which is suspicious before it is interested, can't-fool-me before it's whatta-you-got; by the fourth line the mask is back in place, if it was ever off. "Goin' back to Pittsburgh," Dylan says to finish the verse, in the most elegantly, happily self-erasing lyric of his writing life, the joke finally complete, not that he won't embellish it. "Goin' back to Pittsburgh, count up to thirty," he says. "Round that horn and ride that herd. Gonna thread up." Got anything better you want to do? Well, then, might as well thread up. He'll go back to Pittsburgh if that's where the train is going.

All well and good, except that this journey—starting up eager with every verse, arriving nowhere soon enough—is only half of the song. Pressing against the masked face of its traveler is the plea of the chorus, the voice there breaking through the mask, for a moment disregarding its fatalism, its fear, its placid refusal to acknowledge the notion that there might be new things under the sun, its Appalachian aura of having seen everything twice: in the verses, the ethnomusicological message is if a man as still in his soul as Frank Hutchison doesn't know, what hope is there for you? "Gonna thread up," says the journey-man, perhaps disgusted, perhaps satisfied, perhaps satisfied nothing has broken his expectation of disgust. "Lo and behold!" says the tripled voice of his traveling companion, his Doppelgänger: "Looking for my lo and behold." With every chorus, the mask is stripped from the journeyman's face with a comic, frustrated, finally liberated demand for a new apprehension, a sighting of whatever has never been seen in those things that are seen every day, a demand for revelations in the face of a mask meant to deny them. Where is his lo and behold? Why won't the promised, perfect land reveal itself? Moment to moment he has glimpsed it; why won't it hold still so he can see it plain?

Retrieving the rhythm in the stopped moment after each chorus is done, the piano and organ gaily chug the piece on its way. Caught up in the pleasure of the motion, you need notice nothing more. The rhythm has such pull it is itself the listener's lo and behold—but the singer, caught up in his story, doesn't hear the music. He has joined that "long procession of dull-looking, unlikely oracles," as Rourke wrote of her masked ancestors, her avatars of the American mind and voice, preachers and yarn-spinners, schoolteachers and salesmen, the forgotten presidents who served through most of the nineteenth century but Lincoln too, perhaps yarn-spinner Lincoln most of all. It may not be the role the singer wanted, but he is an oracle in spite of himself, his mask a shield against his own desires, a clue to their enormity.

Just as the most delicate and intense of the basement tapes songs are like a play about the old American mask and the basement itself a theater for its ritual assumption, removal, and replacement, "Lo and Behold!"—pulling back and forth between adventures in nothingness and a cry to hear the truth or tell it—is a summation of the whole haphazard, instinctive basement project. All too aware of how silly its chorus sounds—"Get me out of here, my dear man!"—the song is a demand less for deliverance than for visions, an insistence that the singer and the musicians around him deserve nothing less, even if visions must be found in the most obvious, everyday facts, in a stumble through the most commonplace traditions, the faces everyone pulls, the songs everyone once sang, now cracked like nuts and shuffled like cards. "I found myself, a vacant seat, and I . . . put down my hat," the singer says on his way out of Pittsburgh, the first *I* free and unburdened, the second seemingly carrying all through the next line, a hesitation so deep it reverses all meaning and deflects all blame, then a pause before *put* as the hat goes down that's deeper still, weighted with a deliberateness that carries an acceptance of whatever the consequences of the act may be.

A new nation, reclaimed in this song as if the country were still new, still unsettled, is in this wariness, this holding back, these sly and careful shadings. But in the basement the country was still new and the Puritan and the pioneer anything but ancient history. Memories were still flesh. Puritans had filled the halls in 1965 and '66, demanding purity before anything else; their pioneer, they thought, had left his community behind because he heard the call of gold. "Time is longer than rope" runs an old saying. In the basement the Puritan and the pioneer were roped together, if only in the emerging fantasies of the music—the sort of music-led, almost abstract fantasies within which will or even bodies are nothing and unbidden signs the whole of life. As spectral actors, the Puritan and the pioneer found themselves in the towns and uncleared forests present on the basement floor. Though this is a landscape where few dare trust anyone else and each doubts his or her own self most of all, it is also on the traverse of this territory, out of fear or the wish for love that fear can bring, that the Puritan climbs down from the pioneer's back, here that the pioneer bucks the Puritan off, after which for an untimed moment at least as long as the rope that binds them they continue west or double back in step, every now and then with visions hanging in the sky before them, Judgment Day or just weather they can't tell.

THREE

BASEMENT NOISE

There's weather—the ordinary, the everyday, dirt kicked up by wind, a joke that leaves everyone gasping for breath, ten nights in a barroom and the boredom of waiting around for something to change—in the basement recordings most suffused with Judgment Day, and there is Judgment Day—a sense of visitation, the smell of fear, the appearance of the unwanted, ten nights in a barroom and the thrill of waiting around for the end of the world—in the most weather-bound. The most primitive stabs at a vague rhythm can suddenly bring forth a vehemence that the song forced to carry it can barely support; the most finished piece, all knowledge and experience, is never more than a step away from a place and time where hardly anyone can read or write. All across the basement tapes the people making them, and the characters moving through them—the happy fatalist of "See that My Grave Is Kept Clean," T-Bone Frank from "Tiny Montgomery," the schizophrenic preacher in "Sign on the Cross," the mail-order bridegroom of "You Ain't Goin' Nowhere," the doomed woman in "I'm Not There"—are learning and forgetting.

Time is longer than rope, and more supple. It unwinds lazily, snaps back in an instant, shocking you awake in a bed you cannot remember entering. Different memories, different wishes, are entered on different calendars and trace different histories. A national chronology marked by the dates memorized in the public schools of the 1940s and 1950s opens into neither the same past nor the same future as does a chronology remade according to the '40s and '50s as they happened. "Elvis as he walks the path between heaven and nature," Bob Dylan wrote in 1994 of Peter Guralnick's *Last Train to Memphis: The Rise of Elvis Presley*, "in an America that was wide open, when anything was possible." When did the last train leave the U.S.A.? In the mid-1950s, as a young Memphian took giant steps between heaven and nature, others would have placed the time when America was wide open—when one could expect to touch both heaven and nature with no more than a deep breath and an outstretched arm—scores or even hundreds of years in the past, and some would have said that such a time would always be. In 1994 Dylan was saying that time was now past to him; in 1967 the moment he would describe so vividly in 1994 was only eleven, twelve, at most thirteen years back. The year 1956, when Elvis walked the nation's airwaves like a laughing god; 1955, when the King of Western Bop barnstormed the South in a fleet of Cadillacs; 1954, when a nobody in pink and black first made Memphis turn its head—the moment was close enough to touch, and also gone. In 1967 the orderly assumptions and good-natured disruptions that in the 1950s bordered real life were melting down in riot and war; the civil rights movement, the great wave of belief in a republic fulfilling its own promises, disappeared into the Summer of Love, into the undertow of belief in a world where everyone was his or her own Christ. "When anything was possible," Dylan said. When was it, to his mind, in his voice, that America began to go into the past, changing shape from flesh to ghost?

It's not a personal question. The republic itself asks it; you simply answer. Just as every schooled American carries a sense of the country's beginning as event, so too does every such American harbor a sense of national ending, less as a historical event than as a fading away, a forgetting, a common loss of memory experienced all at once in a single heart: a great public event locked up in the silence of the solitary. For any American it is a defining moment; no promise is so precious as in the moment one knows it can never be kept, that now it belongs to the past. In 1967, in the basement of Big Pink, this event was in the air, the peculiar air of that particular room, as history's dare to the pioneer, the Puritan's dare to the future. The past hadn't claimed the future, but the past was alive with temptation and portent, a kingdom anyone could rule.

Where the past is, in the basement recordings, in the mood of any given performance, is the question to ask the music and the question the music asks. This question raises the frame of reference that each performance passes through as if it were a door. In the chronology remade in the Catskills in 1967, the basement was an omphalos and the days spent within it a point around which the American past and future slowly turned. The music suggests one of those queer theaters-in-the-round built and soon demolished in the 1970s, where a circular platform actually moved as a band played, the musicians catching only a glimpse of faces as they circled past the audience, the audience catching distorted fragments of the sound the band was making as the band approached and for a moment hearing the music whole, then turning as if they could see what they were ceasing to hear, the sound dimming and leaving an echo as the musicians disappeared around the bend. In the basement theater, nothing was exactly clear and nothing was obviously wide open. There were doors all around the room, a door for every worry or imagining; all you had to do was find the key. Each time a new key opened a door, America opened up into both the future and the past—and it is perhaps only a progressive notion of time that leads one to presume that when Dylan spoke of an America that was wide open, he meant open to what was to come, not to what had been, open to the question of who and what Americans might become, not to the question of who and where they came from. There is no nostalgia in the basement recordings; they are too cold, pained, or ridiculous for that. The mechanics of time in the music are not comforting. In the basement the past is alive to the degree that the future is open, when one can believe that the country remains unfinished, even unmade; when the future is foreclosed, the past is dead. How the future depends on the past is more mysterious.

As a nation at war both at home and abroad, the U.S.A. was a faith and a riddle in 1967, Washington's monument facing Lincoln's sphinx. The country was a threat and a plea, a church and a scaffold. It took faith to solve the riddle: in the basement you could believe in the future only if you could believe in the past, and you could believe in the past only if you could touch it, mold it like the clay from which the past had molded you, change it. You could believe in the past only if you could reenact it. The present, the historical present, was meaningless; Dylan and the others had already enacted the present, as it was elsewhere in the republic in 1967, in their onstage wars of a year or two before. In 1967 that was a long time ago; except perhaps in the basement, time moved fast then.

"Time like a scorpion, stings without warning," the Wailers sang in Kingston in 1966, in their cool, rock-steady revision of "Like a Rolling Stone," Dylan's huge hit of the summer before, the chorus intact, new verses written as if straight from Old Testament apocrypha. A year after that the musicians in Big Pink took the Wailers' spirit out of the air and put the sting on time, and so the biggest questions were also the smallest. What was folk music?—Did it even exist?—was also the question of whether Richard Manuel or Robbie Robertson should play drums on "This Wheel's on Fire." The question of why such transparently rock 'n' roll basement tunes as "All American Boy" and "I'm in the Mood" felt more like "historical-traditional music" than other people's folk songs was also Dylan calling out to Garth Hudson between versions of two old Johnny Cash tunes, "Big River" and "Folsom Prison Blues," asking if any tape was left on the tape recorder. (There was, so the singer shot a man in Reno just to watch him die, and with just the right air of still not giving a damn.) The question of the existence of the republic was also the question of how to pass the time on a given rainy afternoon—"On a Rainy Afternoon" being one of the first original songs Dylan and the refugee Hawks set down.

. . .

The five of them began playing again not in the Big Pink basement but in Dylan's house in Woodstock, in a room a previous owner had painted red and called the Red Room; the room was no longer red, but the name stuck. The equipment used was catch-as-catch-can, the sound rough, the material mostly borrowed or new tunes so generic as to be all but indistinguishable from anything old. Soon enough they moved into the basement, where Hudson set up a first-class home recording unit, using a full set of microphones from Peter, Paul & Mary and a tape recorder and two stereo mixers on loan from Albert Grossman, then Dylan's manager. Over the summer and into the fall sets of songs came that saw Comedy and Tragedy sitting down for a long bout of arm-wrestling, a drunken mob cheering them on, bets flying, then sudden silence when the game got rough. Late in the year Levon Helm arrived from Arkansas to rejoin the Hawks' fold; with a laconic, musing sense of lowered stakes and time winding down—a feeling that, in Paul Nelson's words, "If there are tests, they've all been passed"—the basement days eased to an end.

In the Red Room there is most of all a tentativeness, a vagueness in the sound, a lumbering toward the end of a line that in places can't even be called a rhythm. Vocals fall short of any angle of attack or point of view. A singer is looking for the blues in the wrong places, spots that turn him into a crooner: in Ian and Sylvia's "Four Strong Winds," say, or Eric von Schmidt's "Joshua Gone Barbados," Hank Williams's "You Win Again," the sea shanty "Johnny Todd," the chestnut "Spanish Is the Loving Tongue," Elvis's corny "I Forgot to

Remember to Forget," the hoary "Cool Water." It's a meandering in blind search of what the combo—or, really, Dylan alone—occasionally stumbles on: the scary, no-good-can-come-of-this melodies that kick off a drifter's adventures on the whaler "Bonnie Ship the Diamond" or in the Comanche-ridden "Hills of Mexico." "The Bells of Rhymney" calls up a passion that lets Dylan change Pete Seeger's protest song about mine disasters into a nightmare that could be about anything—and without changing a word. "They have fangs, they have teeth," he sings; with Seeger it was plain this is what mine owners were like. For Dylan it's an ugly wonder that anyone can be like this, and a glimpse of the horror that if someone can be like this, so can anyone else. "Even god is uneasy," Seeger sang, seeing the right. Drawing the words out, Dylan is uneasy with the thought. If the Old Testament god he knows is uncertain then there is no right.

You begin to sense people digging deeper, bored with the obvious. Someone excavates an obscure Johnny Cash number—lifelong Cash fan Dylan, or perhaps Hudson, who with Paul London and the Capers, his Ontario-based teenage rock 'n' roll band, backed Cash in Detroit bars in the early 1960s. It is in fact the first song Cash ever wrote, in 1950 or '51, serving in the Air Force in Germany, playing with his own little band, the Barbarians: "Belshazar." Cutting the tune in 1957 for the Sun label in Memphis, Cash and the Tennessee Two gave it the same clippity-clop beat they were using for most of their hits; now a hipster Daniel reads "MENE, MENE, TEKEL, UPHARSIN" off the Babylon wall to the new Memphis beat of Rufus Thomas's "Walking the Dog." The song turns into an amusement park ride, and the quintet smashes the verses together like kids and old ladies in bumper cars.

Along with a breaking humor comes a sliding back and forth between languor and action, as such hazy, shapeless numbers as "The French Girl" and "I Can't Make It Alone" yield to the shock treatment of "900 Miles" and "Under Control." "900 Miles" is just a fragment of the folk song—and the sound of a curtain ripped back to reveal a long-vanished world. Usually the tune is done as a lament; now it's a scream, a riverboat whistle blowing itself out. Danko's fiddle leads the music when it isn't fighting off Dylan's keening vocal, so desperate it's as if he knows he has only the poor forty seconds the tape lasts to sing his way across the nine hundred miles from here to home. Scratchy, out of tune, the fiddle does the singer's crying for him. Inside his singing there's such musicality, the melody as familiar to him as the sound of his own voice, that the real time of the performance is suspended, and you get the feeling that for all the singer's fear of not making it home before his time runs out buttonholing you right here and making you listen to his story is more important. The rush of the music is only backward. As the current pulls the singer farther south his boat gets smaller and it moves faster, passing keelboats and river rafts, runaway slaves and slave hunters, none of whom pay the singer any mind as the miles on his journey are not shortened but lengthened.

"Under Control," a new song, half written but fully formed, might be the only truly violent performance on the basement tapes. Robbie Robertson slashes guitar notes down at the singer's feet; Dylan picks them up along with words and phrases that litter the floor like pieces of a broken vase, fits words to notes and then throws them back, storming, the whole sound caught between panic and attack. What hesitations and pauses that survive the whiplash of the beat are the worst of all. "She's—under control," Dylan sings through gritted teeth, making you feel she's either tied up or pointing a gun as if it weighs less than a feather. "Watch out!" he says again and again. You're in a house that's going up in flames. You're flinching, but you can run. The singer knows he has to wait the fire out. He's the witness. It might be his fault. He's not telling. He may not know.

One night Hudson, Danko, and Manuel tested the equipment in the basement of Big Pink with a round of foolery they titled "Even If It's a Pig Part I"; pleased with the results, they called Robertson over the next evening for "Part II." The sense of people playing with no accounts to settle—the sense that everything is possible and nothing matters—defines the basement tapes once they get rolling, and it might have started here, on these nights. "Reefer run amok," Robertson remembers fondly.

In a thin, effete, Wally Cox/Bob Newhart voice, Hudson emerges from the opening chaos of the first session as a dithering professor, his speech coming from far off and swathed in echo. It's a lecture program on a station a thousand miles away, picked up as you spin the dial in the middle of the night. Hudson: "Some forms of American music, while *limited* in the very simple aesthetic coherencies, meet more beautifully bred and ethnically heart-rending requirements of the cunning, ah, *men*tally figuring voices of the *greater* composers, by the *all-too* apathetic public *ear*."

A piano comes in atonally, then tinkles cocktail jazz as a hurried cool-school bass follows. A tambourine stops the music. A clarinet plays "Stardust" out of tune, putting 1940s high-school sweethearts on a front porch, then sweeping them onto a hay wagon as the tune changes to "Blue Moon." The piano coughs up only drunken triplets, the bass replays Lesson #1 of How to Play the Bass. It's the kind of distortion you'd get in a 1950s sock-hop dream sequence by David Lynch.

There's echoed applause, as if from the few sodden customers left in this after-hours bar. There are some groans. Manuel responds. Reverently, with high horn notes—or high comb notes—coming up, he puts a candelabra on his piano with a half glissando: "And now, kind people, Farnsworth Foundation presents—" And what it presents is "Gloria, gloria, gloria"—from the heart of a cathedral, though somehow it could also be Them's G-L-O-R-I-A "Gloria" with a fancy intro. Manuel offers it his all: "Gloria / Gloria / In excelsis Deoooooooh—" And then he's shouting, as if shocked at what the hymn is about to give up, at how it demands a leap from the Mass to Harry Belafonte. "In excelsis Deeeeooooh—"

> DAY-OH
> Day-ay-ay-OOOH!
> Daylight come and me wan go home

For "The Banana Boat Song" you can only say the singer goes bananas. It was 1967, after all; Donovan's "Mellow Yellow," instantly decoded as a promise that the fine products of the United Fruit Company could get you high, had topped the charts just months before.

> I smoke the banana
> WHILE I WORK! HUH!
> Daylight come and me wan go home

Here everything falls apart. Hudson is the rescuer, in a comforting, simpering Rod McKuen voice: "Some of my, uh, *original* poetry, we sing with our soft, sarcophagus of insight: 'Our truant members' fondest pagings, reach for the brim, but catch only the offerings, tossed on paper's kinships' attachment, learning' "—and Hudson suddenly gets very agitated—" 'our problems' unique, tidy scribblings! Leaving, dead leaves, that crack! When dagger-feet tripping! Pigskin-lined womb! Exit light out!' " This is even more like David Lynch—Lynch as a bad beatnik—and close enough to Burroughs or, here and there, Bob Dylan. " 'All round for reason has told us, but—brutus force, the dealer blowing her tongue. So close to cactus, a stymied rejoinder, found us all within us, we knew, tout les *environs*, et al., taking each other for a harmless' "—Hudson sniggers as a mandolin goes berserk with irritating high notes—" 'lie.' " He turns philosophical: "As for the nearest that *anyone* has ever come, to printing this side of the leaf"—and for a moment he is desperate—"well, find it easier, to turn it again. Out with the past, to reroute the news, toward the end of each line."

The band starts up again, playing with their feet: taps, ooommms, banging, Futurist bruitism, then a piccolo, drums, and bass, soon enough the iconic fife and drum trio of 1776 tumbling facedown into a march. It's an alcoholic variation on "Yankee Doodle," wordless, but with a cracked and stretching sound that might call out of memory the oddest words the tune ever carried: "Corncobs twist your hair / Cart wheels run round you / Fiery dragons take you off / And mortal pestal pound you." The music shifts with a quack and a bark back to jazz, then into Twilight Zone effects from Hudson's organ, protoplasm music, silly-putty feedback, then a harrumphing tuba, the band climbing down from the bandstand and chasing an ice-cream truck, ending up on a merry-go-round. There is applause. "Damn good!" someone says. "Very hot damn good!"

" 'Even If It's a Pig Part II'!" comes the cry the next night, highlighting an ensemble—scratchy sawed fiddle, nearly random drums, a flute lead—trying to find a rhythm, or lose one, rising out of a terrible mess with "A Bicycle Built for Two," essayed by Hudson on concertina. There's a break, and a slow Richard Manuel entry to tuxedoed piano: "Oh, Caygwood barn / And the bin was shallow / And the cheese came / From / The ground." This is the lead-in to "Stagger Blee," surely the worst version of "Stagger Lee" ever committed to tape. Rather than the usual tale of the black bad man and his cool, killer's eye for pose and flash, "Stagger Blee" is the story of a man who goes upstairs, then downstairs, then upstairs—as if already chronicling the daily routine of Bob Dylan, who upon arriving at Big Pink would sit at the typewriter upstairs writing, then head down to the basement with the Hawks to record, then perhaps hit the typewriter again. "Stagger Blee, he went upstairs," sings Richard Manuel, a half-dead beat pulling against the exasperation already in his voice. "Then he goes downstairs / He gonna come upstairs." There are five more verses of this, plus a horrendous guitar solo, and yet by the third verse—

> Stagger Blee
> He went back upstairs
> Saw we're all just sittin' round
> Say you gotta stay here with me
> We goin' into town

—the performance is beginning to build on its own blank mania. The idea of one of the most fearsome characters in American folklore—"Stag" Lee Shelton, killer of Billy Lyons on Christmas Day, 1895, in Bill Curtis's saloon in St. Louis, legend almost immediately after that—devoting his life not to dispatching his enemies, humiliating white sheriffs, or dethroning the devil but rather to going up and down the stairs, more or less in pursuit of whatever he left up here or forgot down there, becomes fascinating for its equation of repetition, oblivion, and discovery, or anyway finding what you're looking for. Soon enough, the joke turns onto the road so many of the basement tunes will follow, opens the road and cuts the ribbon.

It's a road where a certain nihilism lies within the freedom and hilarity of a perfectly written, perfectly arranged song—"Million Dollar Bash," say—that casts off all meaning. There's a gruff verse—

> I took my potatoes
> Down to be mashed
> Then I made it on over
> To that million dollar bash!

—with the last word waving in the air like a happy good-bye, the first two lines so playfully alive to talk and metaphor as to suggest setting up a whiskey still, taking your ashes down to be hauled, or suiting up for the hottest new dance of 1962 as easily as a place where they mash your potatoes for you. There's a smiling, drawn-out chorus that lasts just long enough for you to hear the smile begin to fade—

Ooo
Baby
Ooo-wee
Ooo
Baby
Ooo-wee
It's that
Million
Dollar
Bash

—a fade that just barely undercuts the song's rolling promises with doubt, the basement road now coming up on a hard turn into a swamp where the singer can no longer pretend his nihilism promises anything but death, a road where the memory of a good joke is not even a bad one.

On pig night the joke only gets better, more absurd and more believable. "Stagger Blee," Manuel sings seriously, half awed and half bored by the remarkable exploits of the legendary outlaw. "Goin' back upstairs / Well, you been downstairs too long / I'm goin' back upstairs / You can stay down here . . ." This brings applause and whoops. "Wonderful concert," someone says politely.

After this the evening went off the rails. Professor Hudson returns: "Too many of us are ignorant of the vast, untamed wilderness to the north, and the *odd* graces of Canadians that have contributed to the *scene*, if you'll pardon the expression, in their own, inimitable fashion. Here, is a *flower song*, a veritable prayer dance for mushroom sauce, invented by the *Sasquatches*, a great beautiful tribe of more than a dozen happy"—and

Hudson sticks on the word like a nick in vinyl—"happy—happy souls, completely covered with hair, if you can imagine." The Bigfoot aria that follows—and sustains itself—features a chorus of preverbal grunts and squawks and a lead that sounds as much like a vocal recorded underwater as a tape played backward. As the creatures strain toward words, you realize they don't need them.

The finale is "He Is Gone," a eulogy notable mainly for hysterical weeping and the whitest organ playing imaginable—circa 1900 Episcopal funeral music so palely genteel it could lighten the skin of the janitor. In its utter perversity, it too catches you up. A rinky-dink piano steals the theme away, circles a skating rink a few times, then fades out. "Bye," voices cry, happy and proud. "Bye, bye, bye . . ." As "Even If It's a Pig" set the scene, revelation was almost as likely as idiocy, and telling one from the other perhaps less likely than either.

The sound, as it is on the original tapes of the best-known basement songs, is clear and intimate, full of air, the shape of every note plain—a sound that makes you feel you're in the room, that places the room around you as you listen. It's a room, as it reappears in sound, you can almost picture: low ceiling, dim corners to hide in. A room to fool around in; a place where anything can happen, but where nothing happening would make as much sense as anything else. From here on come new tunes carefully arranged and rehearsed or made up on the spot. There's the rambling, random, often obscene humor—all in the delivery, in the slyness, in the leer—of "Yea! Heavy and a Bottle of Bread," "Please Mrs. Henry," "I'm in the Mood," "Tiny Montgomery"—and the harsh, biblical warnings of "This Wheel's on Fire" and "Down in the Flood." There is the frantic nonsense of "Amelita (The Spanish Song)," a cut-rate flamenco nightclub act diving into its big number so deliriously—cackling, shouting, crossing Marty Robbins's "El Paso" with Sam the Sham and the Pharaohs' "Wooly Bully," they do it twice, as if they can't get enough of it—that by the end you know not even the bartender is left in the place. There is the greater nonsense of a rough version of "You Ain't Goin' Nowhere" ("Look here, you buncha basement noise," Dylan addresses the Hawks, grasping for a lyric), "Next Time on the Highway," and "All American Boy," a gravely lunatic parody of Bill Parsons's already impossibly cool 1958 hit of the same name (nothing in rock 'n' roll quite matches the way Parsons, actually country singer Bobby Bare in a record-company snafu, lets "He's a squ*are*" drift out of the side of his mouth). And there is "The Big Flood," where Dylan rewrites—or unwrites—John Lee Hooker's "Tupelo" from the inside out. With the Hawks making trouble behind him, his voice deep and reflective and not caring if Sunday is Monday or Suzie is Fred, Dylan turns a dank, still blues about death and ruin into a spelling bee. And somehow it's still a blues; maybe that's what happens to a story when it's the only one you've got to tell. The singer could be sitting across from Junkie Bill in that Kansas depot, the two of them talking right past each other as the regulars stand around and place bets on whose throat will dry up first. It was in Mississippi, Dylan is saying, "that's MI, MISS, ISS, IP . . . PY. *Mississippi*," he says firmly, glad to have gotten that out of the way. "I'se just a little boy at the time; twenty-two years old. I was just walkin' around at the time. Mindin' my own business: M, M, MI, MISS, MISSIPPI. Big flood. Happened long time ago. *I was there.* I was there but I didn't want to be there.

Tupelo. Tupelo, Mississippi. That's T, TU, TUO—Toop-lo. Big flood. Terrible . . ." It's more convincing with every line—more convincing that you can describe the world this way, more convincing that the man who's talking *was* there—and it's increasingly creepy. You begin to get the feeling the fun could break wrong at any time, like Joe Pesci in *GoodFellas* burning your eyes out with his stare just when you're sure you've got the joke: "You think that's *funny*?"

You don't know whether it is or not with "Sign on the Cross." It begins in a Primitive Baptist church, empty except for the man who's singing, trying to explain, worried, sick at heart, loving god and doubting god is real. Then he breaks off and turns into a crafty old man rocking on his porch: someone who's seen it all before and is impossibly amused to hear the first singer hasn't. As the old man rattles on, his voice all singsongy and happily cruel, he turns into a radio evangelist hawking his prayer rugs with a shit-eating grin on his face, a grin you can feel through the speakers. Images of prison, of homelessness fade in and out of the song, as near the end the huckster's monologue alternates with the confusion of the penitent; finally resolution is out of the question. Hudson's organ and the piety in Dylan's voice have made a church, but the uncertainty of god's existence produces only mockery and nervousness, ridicule and isolation, speech the first singer is sure no one will hear, god least of all.

The stronger the songs get, the older they feel—that is what people have always heard in the miasmic, unplaced, floating dramas, Gothic or comic, of "I'm Not There," "Clothesline Saga," "Get Your Rocks Off," "Million Dollar Bash," "Lo and Behold!," and "You Ain't Goin' Nowhere," in "Tears of Rage" perhaps most of all. But in pieces, this uncertain feeling, deepening into vertigo, is present throughout the music: the sense that the past is rushing forward, about to sweep all the conceits of the present away for good, to take away its knowledge, deprive its deeds of value, as if the past holds chits on the present and is ready to call them all in.

You can hear this mood of warning, and fear, and delight—a relish for destruction—anywhere on the basement tapes, most powerfully not as any kind of narrative, in a moment a song has prepared, as in "This Wheel's on Fire," but as invasion, coming out of nowhere. In "Baby, Won't You Be My Baby," a seduction song with a broken beat, a tune so languid the singer can hardly be bothered with his task, it's the listener who's seduced—into drifting away from the music, even as portents float to the surface like corpses and the singer steps on his own pickup line.

East and west,
The fire will rise, baby
East and west,
The fire will rise, baby
East and west,
The fire will rise
Shut your mouth
Close your eyes
Baby
Won't you be my baby?

I hear this sense of debts coming due—this wish for an ending—most plainly in "Apple Suckling Tree," a half-written ditty about almost nothing but a country beat that swings and a drawl that would be at home anywhere in the South any time in the last couple of centuries. The group is looking for that beat, the second time through the tune they find it, they push it, Dylan letting out "Underneath that tree, oh, there's just gonna be, you and me" with an anticipation it's impossible not to smile over, and then the song turns hard, mean.

> Now I wish to my soul I had seven years, uh huh
> I wish to my soul I had seven years, uh huh
> Yeah, if I die on your burying ground

—and a crushing bitterness takes over the next line, final, deadly—

> Ohhh, catch you name, buddy, hang a hound

—with the last line thrown away, fading out in disgust, as if the singer could care less—

> Bad on down the avenue, oh yeah

That's where I hear a mood that can open up in any direction, or close them all up. Reviewing a book on bootlegs, Howard Hampton heard it in the lovely, gentle, stymied "I'm a Fool for You."

> It's no more than a ragged, unfinished rehearsal, stopping and starting, Dylan calling out the chord changes to the Band and then

fumbling them ("D . . . wait, uh, no, D, not D, E . . ."). Yet it has a floating melody like no other he has found, sung in a voice of rapture and engima he has sought ever since. The music-box piano of Richard Manuel and the frontier-church organ of Garth Hudson lift "I'm a Fool for You" out of time: the words are like some bootleg gospel of Christ, ellipsis as parable. It's a vision of transmutation: Christ returned as both supplicant and unbeliever, as in folk legends where he escaped with Mary Magdalene to exile in France or assumed the form of King Arthur. As partners in myth and maybe crime (self-apostasy?), he and the singer merge. "When I come back, when I don't make my return," he proclaims, as his first (or last) dispensation, "A heart shall rise and a man shall burn."

Except to say that I hear "A man shall burn" as "Every man shall burn," this is not an interpretation I would ever think of or that anyone else would likely think of—or rather it is not an interpretation at all. It's not an attempt to define or decode what a singer meant when he sang what he sang, but a response to a certain provocation. It is an attempt to catch what the singer took out of the air of a particular time and place, to catch what the singer and the musicians with him put back in the air.

What they took out of the air were ghosts—and it's an obvious thing to say. For thirty years people have listened to the basement tapes as palavers with a community of ghosts—or even, in certain moments, as the palavers of a community of ghosts. Their presence is undeniable; to most it is also an abstraction, at best a vague tourism of specters from a foreign country.

FOUR

THE OLD, WEIRD AMERICA

As it happens, these ghosts were not abstractions. As native sons and daughters, they were a community. And they were once gathered together in a single place: on the *Anthology of American Folk Music*, a work produced by a twenty-nine-year-old man of no fixed address named Harry Smith. Issued in 1952 on Folkways Records of New York City—as an elaborate, dubiously legal bootleg, a compendium of recordings originally released on and generally long forgotten by such still-active labels as Columbia, Paramount, Brunswick, and Victor—it was the founding document of the American folk revival. "It gave us contact with musicians and cultures we wouldn't have known existed," John Cohen of the New Lost City Ramblers, an archivist guitar-fiddle-and-banjo band that formed in 1958, recalled in 1995 at a gathering to mark the fourth anniversary of Smith's death. The *Anthology* introduced Cohen and hundreds, then thousands of others to performers from the 1920s and '30s—artists, Cohen said, "who became like mystical gods to us." The "*Anthology* was our bible," singer Dave Van Ronk wrote in 1991 of the Greenwich Village folk milieu in the mid-1950s. "We all knew every word of every song on it, including the ones we hated. They say that in the 19th century British Parliament, when a member would begin to quote a classical author in Latin the entire House would rise in a body and finish the quote along with him. It was like that." In 1959 and 1960, at the University of Minnesota, in Dinkytown, the *Anthology of American Folk Music* was Bob Dylan's first true map of a republic that was still a hunch to him.

From its first number, "Henry Lee" (which as "Love Henry" Dylan used to open *World Gone Wrong* in 1993), to its last, Henry Thomas's "Fishing Blues" (which Dylan tossed off in a New York studio one day in 1970), Smith's *Anthology* is a backdrop to the basement tapes. More deeply, it is a version of them, and the basement tapes a shambling, twilight version of Smith's *Anthology*, which was itself anything but obvious. "In Elementary Music The Relation Of Earth To The Sphere of Water Is 4 to 3, As There Are In The Earth Four Quarters of Frigidity to Three of Water," ran one of four "quotations from various authors that have been useful to the editor in preparing the notes"; in this case the author to whom editor, compiler, and annotator Harry Smith turned was Robert Fludd, seventeenth-century member of the London College of Physicians, pantheistic theosophist, a translator of the King James Bible, and devotee of the Swiss physician-alchemist Paracelsus. A more modern quotation, slightly twisted, might make at least as good an entryway.

Once the poet Kenneth Rexroth was looking for a phrase to

describe the country he thought lay behind Carl Sandburg's work—the poems and folk songs, the Lincoln books and the clean face framed by straight white hair—whatever it was that, say, led Bob Dylan to knock on the old man's door one day in 1964, looking for a blessing or a legacy. Rexroth came up with "the old free America."

When I first ran across those words they almost made me dizzy. "The old free America"—the idea, the words themselves, seemed all but natural, coded in the inevitable betrayals that stem from the infinite idealism of American democracy. I don't hear any irony in those words. But while I respond helplessly to them, I also recoil—because those words cast Americans out of their own history.

They cut Americans off from any need to measure themselves against the idealism—the utopianism, the Puritans' errand into the wilderness or the pioneer's demand for a new world with every wish for change—Americans have inherited. By fixing the free America, the true America, in the past, those words excuse the betrayals of those Americans who might hear them. There's an alluring, nearly irresistible pull in the phrase—at least there is for me—and I almost took it to name the territory that opens up out of the *Anthology of American Folk Music*, but instead I only stole the cadence; as I listened to Smith's assemblage with the basement tapes playing before or after, the phrase rolled over. The old, weird America is what one finds here—not Rexroth's rebuke to his readers, but an inheritance Smith's listeners might prefer to claim had reached them by mistake.

There is a frame for Smith's U.S.A., his fashioned nation, in a book called *American Studies*—not a textbook, but a first novel published in 1994 by Mark Merlis. The narrator of the novel is a sixty-two-year-old man named Reeve; he lies in a hospital bed after being beaten nearly to death by a boy he picked up. He is remembering an English professor he once studied with, a man named Tom Slater. Slater is transparently based on F. O. Matthiessen—the great Harvard scholar, author in 1941 of *American Renaissance: Art and Expression in the Age of Emerson and Whitman*, a troubled Stalinist, and secretly a homosexual. In the Red Scare of the late 1940s, Matthiessen heard the hounds baying at his door; in 1950 he killed himself. In the Harvard English department, debate over who might have been to blame went on for years.

As Reeve thinks through the past, he chases down its every vanity—of the left, the university, the famous book (here called *The Invincible City*), of the closeted, celibate professor and his salon of golden youths. But no matter how distant, evanescent, or false, the image of utopia the long-dead professor once raised before Reeve's eyes cannot be erased. In a dreamy passage that echoes back and forth from the present to the seventeenth century, Reeve remembers it all: Tom Slater has been driven from the university. "He sits in his living room and realizes that he hasn't read anything in weeks, he hasn't written anything," Reeve says, re-creating the time, imagining the scene: "he will never teach again. Everything he sank his energy into for thirty chaste years is gone."

The seminar above all, that famous seminar of his, that he first had the audacity to call "American Studies"—nowadays that means dissertations on "Gilligan's Island." But that wasn't what Tom meant at all. He never meant to study America, the whole shebang, in all its imbecile complexity. For him there were, perhaps, three hundred Americans in as many years. They dwelt together in a tiny village, Cambridge/Concord/Manahatta, Puritans and Transcendentalists exchanging good mornings, and Walt Whitman peeping in the windows. A little Peyton Place of the mind, small enough that Tom could know every byway and every scandal. I am not certain that Tom, in his life, ever uttered words like "Idaho" or "Utah." Not unless there was a strike there.

He had made a little country of his own. In those first few years during and after the second war, America was what we talked about in Tom's overheated seminar room. Every week someone came into the room with a chance notion or an off reading destined to become holy writ for the generation that came after. As Jefferson thought it would take a millennium to settle the continent, so we thought it would take forever just to cut a few paths through the forest primeval of nineteenth-century letters. Now it's used up, all of it, from Massachusetts Bay to Calaveras County. But while it lasted: even I was excited some days, though I hadn't quite done all the reading and was there only because this was the life Tom had laid out for me. Even I felt, with Tom and his real students, like a conquistador, staking my claim on the imagined America that lived in that little room where it was so hot my glasses fogged up.

There was the real exile, maybe, when they shut the door of that seminar room in his face, cast Tom out from the land that wasn't just his birthright but to which he had given birth and a name.

An imaginary home and a real exile: those might be the borders of the imagined America in Harry Smith's *Anthology of*

American Folk Music. It was no accident that the *Anthology* was issued in 1952, at the height of the McCarthyist witch hunt, just two years past the time Mark Merlis's real and fictional incident takes place. It was not irony that led Smith, near the end of his life, as shaman in residence at the Naropa Institute in Boulder, Colorado, to record every sound he encountered in the course of a Fourth of July, from speech to fireworks to crickets. In 1952, with the United States at war in Korea and resurgent at home, a world power and the envy of the world, seemingly complete and finished, Smith too made his own country, with about as many inhabitants as filled Tom Slater's village, those from the twentieth century conversing easily with those of two hundred years before.

That is Smith's *Anthology*. It was a collection of eighty-four performances on six lps in three hinged two-record sets—contraptions (soon replaced by boxes) that suggest less a likely mechanism for the delivery of recorded music than a cryptic homage to a lapsed patent that, dating to some time before the First World War, understandably failed to catch on. Each set carried the same cover art, in blue (air), red (fire), and green (water): from a Robert Fludd compendium on mysticism, Smith used an etching by one Theodore DeBry of what Smith called "the Celestial Monochord." Dating back to at least 400 B.C., said to have been invented by Pythagoras, the monochord was a protean instrument, a simple sounding box with a single string, not dissimilar from the diddley bow of the black American South, a piece of wire strung against a wall from floor to ceiling. The monochord was used for tuning and as a timer until the late nineteenth century; five hundred years earlier the word had entered the English language as a synonym for harmony, agreement—for the "acorde," the poet John Lyngate wrote in 1420, between "Reason & Sensualyte."*

On the covers of the *Anthology* volumes the monochord was shown being tuned by the hand of god. It divided creation into balanced spheres of energy, into fundaments; printed over the filaments of the etching and its crepuscular Latin explanations were record titles and the names of the blues singers, hillbilly musicians, and gospel chanters Smith was bringing together for the first time. It was as if they had something to do with each other: as if Pythagoras, Fludd, and the likes of Jilson Setters, Ramblin' Thomas, the Alabama Sacred Harp Singers, Charlie Poole and the North Carolina Ramblers, and Smith himself were calling on the same gods.**

Smith's twenty-eight-page accompanying booklet was just as unlikely. Visually it was dominated by a queer schema:

*From the *Oxford English Dictionary*, as is another quotation Smith surely knew ("There's no subject I haven't studied," he once snapped to an interviewer), this from John Bulwer's 1644 *Chirologia, or the natural language of the hand . . . Whereunto is added, Chironomia; or the art of manuall rhetoricke*: "Their cunning management of the Hand in time and tone, I have sometimes call'd the Horse-Rhetorique of Smithfield, which by calculation I have found to differ from the Fish Dialect of Billingsgate, in the monochord of motion."

**In the early 1960s, Irwin Silber of *Sing Out!* magazine took over the marketing of Folkways Records and replaced Smith's chosen art with a Ben Shahn Farm Security Administration photograph of a battered, starving farmer, effectively transforming Smith's alchemical allegory into Depression-style protest art. In the context of the time, when folk music was linked to protest, specifically in terms of the civil rights movement and the commonly invoked national shame of Appalachian poverty and backwardness, with poverty understood as ennobling and the poor themselves often perceived as art statements, it was a smart commercial move.

heavy, black, oversized numbers, marking each of the eighty-four selections as if their placement altogether superseded their content, as if some grand system lurked within the elements Smith had brought to bear upon each other. The booklet was decorated with art from record sleeves advertising "Old Time Tunes" (music that as first recorded in the 1920s was already old, even on the verge of disappearance, and was sold and experienced as such), with woodcuts from turn-of-the-century catalogues of musical instruments, and with faded, hard-to-make-out photos of performers. In 1952 fiddler Eck Dunford, blues guitarist Furry Lewis, the Eck Robertson and Family string band, bluesman Blind Lemon Jefferson, and Cannon's Jug Stompers were only twenty or twenty-five years out of their time; cut off by the cataclysms of the Great Depression and the Second World War, and by a national narrative that had never included their kind, they appeared now like visitors from another world, like passengers on a ship that had drifted into the sea of the unwritten. "All those guys on that Harry Smith Anthology were dead," Cambridge folkies Eric von Schmidt and Jim Rooney wrote in 1979, recalling how it seemed in the early 1960s, when most of Smith's avatars were very much alive. "*Had* to be."

Smith's notes were solemn jokes. Information for each recording as to performer, composer, label, master number, date of release, and so on was given precisely; comments on the sourcing or transmission of a piece followed in sober manner; and each song and ballad, hymn and sermon, was reduced to pidgin summary or newspaper headline, the latter running from screaming newsbreak ("JOHN HARDY HELD WITHOUT BAIL AFTER GUNPLAY . . . WIFE AT SCAFFOLD") to charming human-interest filler ("ZOOLOGIC MISCEGENY ACHIEVED IN MOUSE-FROG NUPTUALS, RELATIVES APPROVE" for a version of "Froggy Went A-Courtin' "). Again in 1995, John Cohen:

> Here's "The Butcher's Boy": "FATHER FINDS DAUGHTER'S BODY WITH NOTE ATTACHED WHEN RAILROAD BOY MISTREATS HER." Here's another song: "WIFE AND MOTHER FOLLOWS CARPENTER TO SEA: MOURNS BABE AS SHIP GOES DOWN." "GAUDY WOMAN LURES CHILD FROM PLAYFELLOWS: STABS HIM AS VICTIM DICTATES MESSAGE TO PARENTS." Now, I think it's terrific—it seems forceful and crazy and comical—but if you ever looked at the serious folklorists, [at what] they've written, *these are the Child ballads*, these are the *major tomes*, these are handed down from medieval times to ancient Britain, they're the great traditional ballads, and there's volumes and volumes of scholarship about them—and that Harry could get them down to one-liners is—unnerving.

The whole bizarre package made the familiar strange, the never known into the forgotten, and the forgotten into a collective memory that teased any single listener's conscious mind. There was, remembers the artist Bruce Conner, who encountered the *Anthology* in the early 1950s in the Wichita Public Library, "a confrontation with another culture, or another view of the world, that might include arcane, or unknown, or unfamiliar views of the world, hidden within these words, melodies, and harmonies—it was like field recordings, from the Amazon, or Africa, but it's here, in the United States! It's not conspicuous, but it's *there*. In Kansas, this was fascinating. I was sure *something* was going on in the country besides Wichita mind control."

As a document carrying such faraway suggestions, the *Anthology of American Folk Music* was a seductive detour away from what, in the 1950s, was known not as America but as Americanism. That meant the consumer society, as advertised on TV; it meant vigilance against all enemies of such a society and a determination never to appear as one; it meant what Norman Mailer, in words that in the 1950s could have been those of many other people, described as the state of mind of the republic: the coexistence of the fear of "instant death by atomic war" and the fear of "a slow death by conformity with every creative instinct stifled." This was boilerplate, no matter how true; a dead language the instant it was spoken. The *Anthology* was a mystery—an insistence that against every assurance to the contrary, America was itself a mystery.

As a mystery, though, the *Anthology* was disguised as a textbook; it was an occult document disguised as an academic treatise on stylistic shifts within an archaic musicology. This was in Harry Smith's grain. A polymath and an autodidact, a dope fiend and an alcoholic, a legendary experimental filmmaker and a more legendary sponger, he was perhaps most notorious as a fabulist. He liked to brag about killing people: "Maybe every three or four months," he said in 1972, "I'll think of somebody I've killed and wonder what their life would have been if they'd gone on." He was a trickster: "Magic Man," Robert Frank called him. Bruce Conner, who met Smith in 1956 in New York, when both were working for Lionel Ziprin's Inkweed Studios, an avant-garde greeting card company, was a skeptic (Smith, he says, once tried to kill *him*), but not Ziprin: " 'You know,' Lionel would say," Conner remembers, " 'you can't tell how *old* Harry Smith is—he might be thirty, he might be sixty.' " Sometimes Ziprin thought Smith was a nineteenth-century mystic: not a reincarnation, but the ageless thing itself, immortal, all mask.

He was in fact born in 1923 in Portland, Oregon, and grew up in and around Seattle; he died in 1991 in New York City, where he had become known as "the Paracelsus of the Chelsea Hotel." Devotees surrounded him at the end; at his memorial service, Lionel Ziprin told Conner, Smith's followers were mixing his ashes with wine and ingesting them. "What they're doing to Harry, these people are cannibals!" Ziprin said. "Look, Harry's gone," Conner said. "You should be concerned about what Harry's doing to *them*—sitting in their rooms, in their bodies." For a man who was raised on the notion of the transmission of souls and who as a young man sat down with a pile of old records to practice it, it would have been a fitting end.

Smith's parents were Theosophists; when he was a child, Madame Blavatsky, Annie Besant ("She had already been people like Christ and Leonardo," Smith said), and Bishop Leadbeater, dead or alive, were almost like family friends. Smith's great-grandfather John Corson Smith, who Smith claimed had been aide-de-camp to Ulysses S. Grant during the Civil War and later governor of Illinois, was one of many nineteenth-century mystics to refound the Knights Templar, the medieval order of crusader-monks believed by some to have possessed the Holy Grail, the Ark of the Covenant, or the secret of being. Smith's paternal grandfather was a leading Mason. "I once discovered in the attic of our house all of those illuminated documents with hands with eyes in them, all kinds of

Masonic deals that belonged to my grandfather," Smith said in 1965. "My father said I shouldn't have seen them, and he burned them up immediately." But, Smith said, on his twelfth birthday his father presented him with a complete blacksmith's shop and commanded that he turn lead into gold. "He had me build all these things like models of the first Bell phone, the original electric light bulb, and perform all sorts of historical experiments," Smith said; the *Anthology of American Folk Music* would be the most complete historical experiment he ever devised.

Smith's upbringing was a garden of confusions. His mother's family, he recalled, had left Sioux City, Iowa, in the 1880s, "because they felt it was becoming too contaminated by the Industrial Revolution"; his mother's mother founded a school in Alaska "that was supported by the Czarina of Russia," which led to his mother's sometime insistence that she was Anastasia, the last of the Romanovs. His father was once a cowboy and later worked in the Washington salmon fisheries—unless his father was, as Smith often said, the English satanist Aleister Crowley, whose motto "Do As Thy Wilt Shall Be The Whole Of The Law" was another of Smith's *Anthology* epigraphs. Crowley was yet another refounder of the Knights Templar, his sect being the Ordo Templis Orientis—in which, in 1985, Smith, without his knowledge, was ordained a bishop. His mother, Smith said, had had a long affair with Crowley, beginning in 1918, when she saw him "running naked down the beach" on Puget Sound. "We were considered some kind of 'low' family, despite my mother's feeling that she was the Czarina of Russia," Smith said. "We were living down by the railroad tracks."

Smith developed rickets, which left him stunted and humped. "The universal hatred I've stirred up against myself, it comes from being sloppy among a bunch of tidy people," he said near the end of his life—despite his common appearance as a derelict, he was speaking philosophically. By tidy people he meant certain circles of his parents' friends, followers of "the Transcendental philosophy that Emerson developed . . . [who] came to Concord to learn," but his own family "prided itself on its backwardness. You see, even when they had James Whitcomb Riley to listen to they still preferred Chaucer."

As a schoolboy, swirling in the irregular orbits of his parents' religion, their fantasies, their poverty and delusions of grandeur, Smith discovered the local Indian tribes. Living near Seattle in South Bellingham, he began to investigate the rituals, music, and languages of the Nootka, the Kwakiutl, the Lummi. A photo in a 1941 issue of *The American Magazine* shows a teenage Smith—with glasses, Pendleton shirt, and a look of calm concentration on his face as he sits before the feathered and horned elders of the Lummi tribe—"recording the drums and chants of the Lummis' annual potlatch, or winter festival. . . . Closest to the aboriginal form of any Indian dance in the U.S." "He hopes to study anthropology under University of Washington profs.," the article titled "Injuneer" concluded, "and they are hoping to study anthropology under him."

A turning point in Smith's life came about two years later, when he left his studies at the university and traveled to San Francisco. There and in Berkeley he entered bohemian circles. Already at work on abstract, hand-painted films, he met artists, poets, Communists, folk singers, and folklorists.

Writing in 1994 of that time and that milieu in *Utopia and Dissent: Art, Poetry, and Politics in California*, Richard Cándida Smith could be describing the auras of Smith's *Anthology*:

> The avant-garde on the West Coast had a preference for cosmological-theosophical over psychological-sociological understandings of art and the individual's relationship to larger forces. The sacred, which need not involve a personalized diety, was valued over the profane. . . . Historical "facts" served hierarchy, while tradition was liberating because it grew from a voluntary personal response to the repertory of the past.

I like that phrase, "the repertory of the past." I like Cándida Smith's description of response to it. Harry Smith might have as well. He drew on both his haunt-ridden boyhood and his own vast collection of 78s to assemble his *Anthology*—a collection that began around 1940, when he bought a record by the Mississippi bluesman Tommy McClennan. "[It] had somehow gotten into this town by mistake," Smith said of South Bellingham, speaking to John Cohen in New York in 1968. "It sounded strange so I looked for others." In a Seattle Salvation Army shop he heard Uncle Dave Macon's "Fox and Hounds": "I couldn't imagine what it was." Carl Sandburg's *American Songbag* took him to the Child ballads so named for—and famously numbered by—the Harvard English professor whose 1882–96 *English and Scottish Popular Ballads* catalogued a legacy that by the 1920s persisted more readily in the southern Appalachians than in the British Isles. Other books and directories took him to southern fiddle music, Cajun chansons tristes, cowboy laments. The war was a boon: warehouses were cleared for military supply, putting thousands of forgotten discs from the 1920s and '30s on sale for next to nothing. Smith found scores of old records—gospel, blues, parlor tunes—by the Carter Family, the beloved trio from the Clinch Mountains of southwestern Virginia; not long after, in a Calaveras County trailer camp, in the California Gold Rush country, he found autoharpist Sara Carter herself. Though devout in her retirement, barring all music from her door, Carter nevertheless regaled the young collector with tales of Jimmie Rodgers, the Blue Yodeler, who like the Carter Family first recorded in 1927 at the prophetic Bristol Sessions on the Tennessee–Virginia line: tales of how in his days as a railroad brakeman, "everywhere Jimmie Rodgers went he threw marijuana seeds off the back of the train so that you could tell where he had been." "I was looking for exotic music," Smith told John Cohen. "Exotic in relation to what was considered to be the world culture of high class music."

As Smith searched for the hillbilly classics and primitive blues made in the commercial half-light of the Jazz Age, he found himself in the first years of his own childhood. He might have heard what people have always heard in strange music: the call of another life. He might have imagined that, going back to his first years with his oldest records, he was reliving and rewriting his life from the start. It would have been only a first step; the history of the republic, the story the country told itself, was just as vulnerable. As Smith learned the contours of old styles, as he tracked melodies and phrases through the Chinese boxes of folk etymology, he found himself in the 1800s and then back further still, decades tumbling into centuries, ghost lovers and backwoods crimes replacing the great personages and events of national life.

It was a quest, and not merely personal. "I felt social changes would result from it," Smith said of his *Anthology* in 1968; he meant to provoke an instinctive response on a plane of social magic. In the scared and satisfied reactionary freeze of the postwar period, the *Anthology* was meant to distinguish those who responded from those who didn't, to distinguish those who responded to themselves. "Told with 'cunning,'" Susan Buck-Morss writes of Walter Benjamin's ambitions for his *Passagen-Werk*, his unfinished study of Paris arcades, in words that fix what Smith completed, "[it] would accomplish a double task: it would dispel the mythic power of present being . . . by showing it to be composed of decaying objects with a history"; "it would dispel the myth of history as progress (or the modern as new) by showing history and modernity in the child's light as archaic." Cunning was the last thing Harry Smith lacked.

Smith's definition of "American folk music" would have satisfied no one else. He ignored all field recordings, Library of Congress archives, anything validated only by scholarship or carrying the must of the museum. He wanted music to which people really had responded: records put on sale that at least somebody thought were worth paying for. Though Smith noted that folk songs had been commercially recorded as far back as the 1880s and that markets for blues and hillbilly records took shape in the early 1920s, he restricted himself to the commonly held music of traditional and marginalized American cultures as it was professionally recorded between about "1927, when electronic recording made possible accurate music reproduction, and 1932 when the Depression halted folk music sales."* These years comprised the high point of a time when northern record companies suddenly realized that the spread of rail lines and the emergence of radio on a mass scale had opened up self-defining and accessible audiences throughout the South for church and dance music, regionally distinctive blues, melodic allegories handed down over generations; as a commercial proposition, those years were a window opening onto a seemingly infinite past. As a historical period, they were an economic opportunity to capture ritual, and it was the scent of ritual Smith pursued.

*By 1933 record sales had fallen to a bare 7 percent of what they had been in 1929; in the rural South, a cash economy, never firmly established, all but ceased to exist. Sales revived in the mid-1930s, partly because of the introduction of 78s selling for as little as twenty-five cents and, in fields of vernacular music, the replacement, in the main, of itinerant or community-based recording artists by full-time professionals. Older, traditional material was dropped for recording purposes; the commonplace banjo, with its limited vocabulary, was replaced almost completely by the guitar, which allowed for greater virtuosity and in the more competitive milieu of the period led to a demand for it.

Smith programmed a fourth, brown-covered (earth) volume of his *Anthology*, based on a "content analysis" of the post-1932 Depression period. "My essential interest in music was in the patterning that occurred in it," Smith told John Cohen. As he had noticed that 1880s recordings of "Victorian ballads" were full of "children freezing to death . . . a great many of these songs on the records were in a snowstorm, some poor kid peddling the papers at the Ferry Slip in order to get medicine for the father who is at home dying of Asiatic Cholera or something," for the Roosevelt era he was fascinated by the plethora of brother acts, the profusion of songs with the word "food" in their titles, and "how many times the word 'Railroad' was used during the Depression and how many times during the war." The set was never issued because Smith never completed the notes.

Dressed up as a good pedagogue, and arming his selected old discs with complex, cross-referenced discographies and bibliographies, neatly attaching story songs to the historical events from which they derived (the mythical historical events, sometimes), noting changes in approaches to voicing, instrumentation, tunings, and the like, Smith divided his eighty-four choices into three categories, his three sets of two lps each: "Ballads," "Social Music," and "Songs." Within his five-year span, he paid no attention to chronology as he sequenced the numbers; for all of his painstaking annotation, he never identified a performer by race, determinedly sowing a confusion that for some listeners persists to this day. "It took years," Smith said happily in 1968, "before anybody discovered that Mississippi John Hurt wasn't a hillbilly."

Very carefully, Smith constructed internal narratives and orchestrated continuities. He moved tunes about homicide into those about suicide. Or he placed a performance so that it would echo a line or a melody in a preceding number—so that the repeated line might deepen its power of suggestion, or the doubled melody intensify the gestures of the actors on its stage. Linking one performance to another, he ultimately linked each to all.

Out of such arrangements Smith made a world, or a town: Smithville. In this town Clarence Ashley's "The House Carpenter," a tune once known as "The Demon Lover," a ballad in which earthly lust is ended with unearthly punishment, is as suffused with religious awe as the Reverend J. M. Gates's sermon "Must Be Born Again." Here Bascom Lamar Lunsford's "I Wish I Was a Mole in the Ground" is more otherworldly—less at home in this world—than the Memphis Sanctified Singers' "He Got Better Things for You."

Smith opened his first volume, "Ballads," with Dick Justice's "Henry Lee," the story of a knight's murder by his spurned lover, as witnessed by a talking bird ("Not a good record," Smith said with numerological certainty in 1968, "but it had to go first because it was the lowest numbered Child ballad [of the set]"). He followed it with progressively spookier versions of the often supernatural English and Scottish love tales that since the late eighteenth century had functioned in mountain hollows as what in blues language would be called a second mind: tales of murder and suicide in which love is a disease and death the cure. With the air over his town growing heavier, Smith moved to numbers about more prosaic, homegrown killings. The blind fiddler G. B. Grayson—a descendant of the man who arrested Tom Dula in 1866 and who as both a singer and a player sounds at least as old as the story he is telling—describes how in 1807, in Deep River, North Carolina, a pregnant woman named Naomi Wise was drowned by her lover, who escaped justice and disappeared into the West. The sense of age in the performance is displacing. It's not as if the event is being recalled by an ancient witness; it is as if the event, as it happened, has made the witness old. The actions described are all will, the performance is all fate, and the rest of "Ballads" follows its path. Cole Younger goes down after the James Gang's 1876 bank robbery in Northfield, Minnesota. President Garfield falls to hobo evangelist, con man, and would-be ambassador to Brussels Charles Guiteau in 1881, and President McKinley to anarchist Leon Czolgosz twenty years after that. In 1894 a coal worker hangs for killing a man over a crap game in West Virginia; in 1895 Stackalee shoots Billy Lyons in St. Louis. Four years later, in the same neighborhood, Frankie shoots her lover Albert (unless it was thirty years earlier, and somewhere else).

Murder is superseded by disaster. Craftsmen are thrown out of work by machines. "TECHNOLOGICAL UNEMPLOYMENT HITS SHOE INDUSTRY IN THE YEAR OF 18 AND 4" is Smith's headline for the Carolina Tar Heels' "Peg and Awl": the band is so comically pathetic, as if it's all their own fault but they can't figure out how, you can see Laurel and Hardy acting out what they're singing. So people go where the work is, and in a refrain that runs all through American song and past the borders of the country, from "Canadee-i-o" to "The Hills of Mexico," they find themselves tricked out of their shoes. Stranded in the American version of hell on earth—Arkansas—a "DITCH DIGGER SHOCKED BY EMPLOYMENT AGENT'S GROTESQUE DECEPTIONS" repeats his name again and again because he's not sure he still owns anything else.

Then the hammer comes down. In the years after the Civil War, John Henry dies in a race with a steam drill. The *Titanic* sinks. Trains are wrecked; across six minutes, Furry Lewis wonders over Casey Jones's last ride as if it is a story his mother told him, holding every lesson he will ever need, if only he could plumb the story to its depths. Farms fail; the boll weevil dethrones King Cotton. "Ballads" ends with "Got the Farmland Blues," which really is a *farm*land blues. "I woke up this morning," Clarence Ashley sings with the Tar Heels, "between one and two . . ."

Though roughly tracing a chronology of British fable and

American happenstance, and in most cases tied to historical incidents, these ballads are not historical dramas. They dissolve a known history of wars and elections into a sort of national dream, a flux of desire and punishment, sin and luck, joke and horror—and as in a dream, the categories don't hold. What Smith's ballads dramatize is action; passivity; regret; sardonicism; absurdity; fear; acceptance; isolation; the wish for mastery running up against forces no one can understand, let alone master. After this—after Kentucky banjoist Buell Kazee's disappearance into "The Butcher's Boy," in which he becomes a young woman reading from her own suicide note ("Over my coffin place a snow-white dove / To warn this world I died for love")—Smith's two lps of "Social Music" are a respite, a place of simple pleasures where the most troubled heart is filled only with a gentle yearning.

A dance is under way. Fiddlers play waltzes and reveries, reels and stomps. There is drinking and merriment, time for brazen shouts and fond words. Home is venerated, a beloved dog is recalled, and then—then god, in the person of the Reverend J. M. Gates, asking, like a man making the cruelest joke last as long as he can, "Oh! Death Where Is Thy Sting?" Chanting in a fashion that Smith dated to the spread of the Great Awakening to the Georgia territory in the mid-eighteenth century—chanting against a chorus that seems constantly on the verge of breaking up into pieces—the Atlanta preacher is fearsome and implacable. His voice is deep, harsh, impatient; impatient with the weaknesses of the spirit and the flesh—impatient with human nature. Suddenly you're trapped. The party wasn't supposed to end this way, in the middle of a Jonathan Edwards sermon reincarnated as a 1926 gospel hit and an ineradicable aspect of national memory, transmitted to all Americans as if it were a gene, but now, in a church that changes shape and color with each new performance, the party is just starting. It's as if, now, the whole community has to pay for the solitary crimes of the first two lps and for the revelry of the third—and as if everyone knows that this is fitting and proper, that this is right. But by the time "Social Music" ends, it is not only the shape of the church but god's face that has changed. Against all odds, it is smiling. The Reverend F. W. Moore celebrates "Fifty Miles of Elbow Room." The Reverend D. C. Rice and His Sanctified Congregation take their place in a great army. "I'm on the Battlefield for My Lord," they sing, and they make you want to join them. The pleasures of the dance, the wallow in drink, now seem very distant, and worthless. In this place is a great spirit of freedom: the freedom of knowing exactly who you are and why you are here.

You leave "Social Music" in the arms of certain knowledge. Instantly, on "Songs," you're ripped from that embrace and cast into a charnel house that bears a disturbing resemblance to everyday life: to wishes and fears, difficulties and satisfactions that are, you know, as plain as day, but also, in the voices of those who are now singing, the work of demons—demons like your neighbors, your family, your lovers, yourself. The first side of "Songs" is a panorama of the uncanny. It's not that here nothing is as it seems; as Buell Kazee feels his way through the dimming haze of "East Virginia" and in "I Wish I Was a Mole in the Ground" Bascom Lamar Lunsford pictures himself as a lizard in the spring, as Rabbit Brown wanders the one-block labyrinth of "James Alley Blues" and Dock Boggs smiles

"Sugar Baby" 's death's-head smile, it's as if nothing that seems even is. "Who'll rock the cradle, who'll sing the song?" Boggs asks, as always it seems, twisting the words until they're scratching off each other's vowels, and Brown answers, his guitar all foreknowledge, his voice all suspicion, the gonging of his strings making a hall of echoes: *Are you sure we really want to know?*

Now tricksters rule, sharps who can guess your weight and tell your secrets. The carnival has arrived in Smithville, just as it does in Smith's *Heaven and Earth Magic*, the sixty-six-minute animated film he made between 1957 and 1962. There he set dancing countless images clipped from the same sources as the illustrations in the *Anthology* booklet; as on the opening side of "Songs," every image was less a representation of the real than a symbol of the imaginary, of the notion that the imaginary could become real at any time.

"Step right up, win a kewpie doll, ladies and gentlemen, eight shots for a quarter," you hear on the soundtrack, along with lots of talk, the noise of crowds moving eagerly down the midway, rifles cracking in the shooting gallery. Set before you is the Theatre of Illusion, assembled from cutouts of old advertisements, Sears catalogues, instructional manuals, religious tracts, and the likes of *Epilepsy and the Functional Anatomy of the Human Brain*: an array of mechanical devices, including klieg lights, a boiler, and instruments less easy to name, all topped by a rotating wheel.

In the foreground of the machines, a homunculus opens a valise. A man removes mannequin stands as pieces of the valise are sucked into the lights by an unseen force. The mannequin stands turn into mannequin shapes, then into dresser's models with rounded, Lillian Russell busts, which are replaced on the stands by giant eggs. A skull emerges and goes into the lights, a carp appears and goes into the boiler as the crowd laughs, a hand materializes and disappears into the lights with the eggs, followed by a whiskey crock. A huge mallet appears; the crowd roars. A head like that of an old-time baseball player drops onto a dressmaker's shape, changes into the head of a woman, and floats off. You hear hurdy-gurdy music and the pitchman again; the mannequin stands reconfigurate as androgynous silhouettes.

The mallet rotates the wheel faster and faster. As the noise of the wheel moving takes over the sound, the mannequins are thrown back by the wind of the machine. A two-headed figure—a body with two circles for heads—is self-assembled out of detritus the wheel is casting off. The whole begins to swirl in a storm of its own making, sweeping up confused and frightened noises from the crowd until all is sucked up, all is swept away, the carnival gone, the landscape bare. You hear crickets, a train whistle; for a moment there is no movement.

This is the mood of the first side of "Songs." The streets of Smithville have been rolled up, and the town now offers that quintessential American experience, the ultimate, permanent test of the unfinished American, Puritan or pioneer, loose in a land of pitfalls and surprises: Step right up, ladies and gentlemen! Enter the New Sensorium of Old-Time Music, and feel the ground pulled right out from under your feet!

The two lps of "Songs" continue on from this first side, maintaining a startling level of power and charm, on through suites of tunes about marriage, labor, dissipation, prison, death. Mississippi John Hurt quietly puzzles over John Henry's self-sacrifice, as if burrowing out from under the rubble he left behind. Blind Lemon Jefferson makes his guitar into a tolling bell for "See that My Grave Is Kept Clean." He stops time, stops Death, and then, as if he knows the pause is somehow less cheating Death than a cheat on life, lets the song move on. Uncle Dave Macon's foot-stomping exuberance, his long reach for good times, bursts through numbers beginning on a chain gang or in the midst of deadly labor strife. Born in 1870 in Tennessee, Macon died in 1952, the year Smith's *Anthology* appeared; before 1924, when he made his first records, he worked as a teamster. For "Way Down the Old Plank Road" he stands up in his wagon, pushing his horses, cracking his whip with a Babe Ruth smile: "KILL YOURSELF!" he shouts out of the hurry of the song. He sounds like he wants to watch and then go you one better. It's one of the truest, highest, most abandoned moments in American speech—as can seem every note of "The Lone Star Trail." With a passion words and melody can elicit but not account for, movie star Ken Maynard, "The American Boy's Favorite Cowboy," ambles out of the soundtrack of *The Wagon Master* to chant and moan, yodel and wail, stare and tremble, more alone, more stoic and more restless between heaven and nature, than anyone has been before. The shape of the land, its vast expanse, its indifference to who you are or what you want, looms up as this solitary figure says his piece: I am the first cowboy and the last. Here no one sees me, myself least of all, I am happy, I am free.

The whole long story is brought to a close when it is lifted out of itself, with the freest song imaginable, Henry Thomas's "Fishing Blues," played on panpipes, an instrument that blocks all possibility of tracing the historical origins of this song or that—the high, lilting sound of the panpipes goes back to the end of the Paleolithic. This sound is older than any surviving language, and so might be the message of this song from a railroad bum who crisscrossed the South from the end of the nineteenth century into the 1940s, a message he repeats over and over, as if it holds the secret of being: "Here's a little something I would like to relate / Any fish bite if you got good bait."

There is an almost absolute liberation in "Fishing Blues"—a liberation that is impossible not to feel, and easy to understand. Yet there is a liberation just as complete brooding on that first side of "Songs," breathing through Dock Boggs's nihilism, Bascom Lamar Lunsford's pantheism, the ghost dance of Rabbit Brown. This liberation—or this absolute—is not easy to comprehend, but for just that reason it is here, in Smith's most explosive collage of scavenged old records, that the *Anthology of American Folk Music* finds its center, or its axis; it is here that Smithville begins to shade into Hawthorneville, Melvilleburg, Poetown. Judgment Day is the weather here: in 1926 in "Oh! Death Where Is Thy Sting?" Judgment Day was an event, but in Smithville it is also a way of life, present in the smallest details of landscape and language, gesture and the passage of time. Its presence makes all these things into symbols and charges them with meaning that cannot be enclosed. "I have seen the task which God hath given to the sons of men to be exercised therewith," one of Smith's preachers might be explaining, taking his text from Ecclesiastes. "He hath made every thing beautiful in his time; also he hath set the world in their heart, yet so that man cannot find out the work that God hath done from the beginning even to the end."

In an essay on the *Anthology* called "Smith's Memory

Theater," Robert Cantwell wrote about one of the songs in this sequence, but he might have been writing about almost any one of them, or all of them. "Listen to 'I Wish I Was a Mole in the Ground' again and again," he says. "Learn to play the banjo and sing it yourself over and over again, study every printed version, give up your career and maybe your family, and you will not fathom it." What he is saying is not that different from what Bob Dylan was saying about folk music in 1965 and '66, when to so many nothing he could have said about folk music could have been less than a lie. "All the authorities who write about what it is and what it should be," Dylan said, "when they say keep it simple, [that it] should be easily understood—folk music is the only music where it isn't simple. It's never been simple. It's weird . . . I've never written anything hard to understand, not in my head anyway, and nothing as far out as some of the old songs."

I have to think of all this as traditional music. Traditional music is based on hexagrams. It comes about from legends, Bibles, plagues, and it revolves around vegetables and death. There's nobody that's going to kill traditional music. All those songs about roses growing out of people's brains and lovers who are really geese and swans that turn into angels—they're not going to die. It's all those paranoid people who think that someone's going to come and take away their toilet paper—*they're* going to die. Songs like "Which Side Are You On?" and "I Love You Porgy"—they're not folk-music songs; they're political songs. They're *already* dead.

Obviously, death is not very universally accepted. I mean, you'd think that the traditional-music people could gather from their songs that mystery is a fact, a traditional fact . . . traditional music is too unreal to die. It doesn't need to be protected. Nobody's going to hurt it. In that music is the only true, valid death you can feel today off a record player.

Bob Dylan could have been talking about the first side of Harry Smith's "Songs": one quality that unites the singers here is that *they* sound as if they're already dead, though not because they have accepted that the meaning of the songs they're singing can be fixed in advance. It's as if they're lining out an unspoken premise of the old Southern religion: only the dead can be born again.

No performance captures this sensation more completely than the first number on this magical side, Clarence Ashley's 1929 Columbia recording of "The Coo Coo Bird." There is no more commonplace song in Appalachia; the song has been sung for so long, by so many, in so many different communities, as to seem to some folklorists virtually automatic, a musicological version of the instinctive act, like breathing—and therefore meaningless. Like scores of other coffeehouse folk singers, Bob Dylan was singing it in the first years of the 1960s; as Ashley sang and played the song, he paid in full every claim Dylan would make about traditional music. He pays as well the claims of the uniquely plainspoken argument the South African musicologist Peter van der Merwe makes about the sort of Appalachians who appear all across Smith's *Anthology*: Ashley, Lunsford, Kazee, Boggs, Eck Robertson, the Carter Family, G. B. Grayson, Uncle Dave Macon, Frank Hutchison.

When middle-class America first discovered these mountain folk there was a tendency to present their ways as even more primitive and archaic than they actually were. Nonsense was talked of their "Elizabethan speech," as though they had been preserved unaltered since the sixteenth century. As an inevitable reaction, it is now fashionable to point to urban influences on this isolated rural culture, just as it is fashionable to make similar observations about British country people. Taking all such reservations into account, I still believe that the biggest danger lies in *under*estimating the strangeness of these cultures. It takes a constant effort of the imagination to realize the isolation of their lives, the lack of canned music, the scarcity of professional musicians, the grip of tradition.

Clarence Ashley was born in 1895 in Bristol, Tennessee; as a teenager he traveled with minstrel troupes and medicine shows ("I was always crazy about the show business"). By the 1920s he was a professional itinerant musician, playing in string bands, at fairs, on the streets, to miners as they picked up their money or their scrip. He died in 1967. In 1929 he was in his mid-thirties; he sounded seventeen, or one-hundred-and-seventeen, as if he'd died seventeen or one-hundred-and seventeen years before. For "The Coo Coo Bird" he carried the tune as it appears throughout Lee Smith's 1992 novel *The Devil's Dream*, sounding down through the history of a Virginia mountain family (which in its sixth generation of filial and fiddler mystery turns up a young woman studying semiotics at Duke), every time a beckoning to the will and a warning against fate, a sign of lust and mortal danger. Ashley's performance made one thing clear: however old the singer was, he wasn't as old as the song.

Like many of the numbers on the third volume of the *Anthology*, "The Coo Coo Bird" was a "folk-lyric" song. That meant it was made up of verbal fragments that had no direct or logical relationship to each other, but were drawn from a floating pool of thousands of disconnected verses, couplets, one-liners, pieces of eight. Harry Smith guessed the folk-lyric form came together some time between 1850 and 1875. Whenever it happened, it wasn't until enough fragments were abroad in the land to reach a kind of critical mass—until there were enough fragments, passing back and forth between blacks and whites as common coin, to generate more fragments, to sustain within the matrix of a single musical language an almost infinite repertory of performances, to sustain the sense that out of the anonymity of the tradition a singer was presenting a distinct and separate account of a unique life. It is this quality—the insistence that the singer is singing his or her own life, as an event, taking place as you listen, its outcome uncertain—that separates the song, from which the singer emerges, from the ballad, into which the singer disappears.

Just as it is a mistake to underestimate the strangeness of the cultures that spoke through folk-lyric fragments ("I'd rather be in some dark holler, where the sun refused to shine"; "My name I'd never deny"; "Forty dollars won't pay my fine"), it is also a mistake to imagine that when people spoke through these fragments, they were not speaking—for themselves, as contingent individuals. What appears to be a singer's random assemblage of fragments to fit a certain melody line may be, for that singer, an assemblage of fragments that melody called forth. It may be a sermon delivered by the singer's subconscious, his or her second mind. It may be a heretic's way of saying what could never be said out loud, a mask over a boiling face.

Ashley's singing—high, a voice edgy with the energy of

musing, of wanting, of not getting, of expecting to get it all tomorrow—rises and falls, dips and wavers, playing off the rhythm his banjo makes like a tide eddying up to a bank again and again. There's a willful irascibility in his voice, a disdain for the consequences of any action the singer might take, or not take. The banjo could be from another song or another world. The music seems to have been found in the middle of some greater song; it is inexorable. The opening and closing flourishes on the banjo seem false, because the figures in the music make no progress, go from no one place to any other; the sound was here before the singer started and it will be here when he's gone.

In this mood, in this weather, the most apparently commonplace fragment in Ashley's "Coo Coo Bird"—the verse seemingly most unburdened by any shard of meaning—cannot be meaningless.

Gonna build me
Log cabin
On a mountain
So high
So I can
See Willie
When he goes
On by

It sounds like a children's ditty only until you begin to realize the verse is made to refuse any of the questions it makes you ask. Who is Willie? Why does the singer want to watch him? Why must he put aside his life and embark on a grand endeavor (in versions of "The Cuckoo" closer to its protean, British form, the log cabin is a castle) just to accomplish this ordinary act? The verse can communicate only as a secret everybody already knows or as an allusion to a body of knowledge the singer knows can never be recovered, and Ashley only makes things worse by singing as if whatever he's singing about is the most obvious thing in the world. The performance doesn't seem like a jumble of fragments. Rather there is a theme: displacement, restlessness, homelessness, the comic worry of "a people," as Constance Rourke wrote of Americans as they were when the Civil War began, "unacquainted with themselves, strange to the land, unshaped as a nation." "We Americans are all cuckoos," Oliver Wendell Holmes said in 1872. "We make our homes in the nests of other birds." This is the starting point.

As long as seven hundred years ago, the English were singing that the cuckoo heralded the coming of summer, and yet the bird was hated. Its cry was reviled through the centuries as oppressive, repetitious, maniacally boring, a cry to drive you crazy, a cry that was already crazy, befitting a bird that was insane. The cuckoo—the true, "parasitic" cuckoo, which despite Holmes's choice of it for national bird is not found in the United States—lays its eggs in the nests of other birds. It is a kind of scavenger in reverse: violating the natural order of things, it is by its own nature an outsider, a creature that cannot belong. Depositing its orphans, leaving its progeny to be raised by others, to grow up as imposters in another's house—as America filled itself up with slaves, indentured servants, convicts, hustlers, adventurers, the ambitious and the greedy, the fleeing and the hated, who took or were given new, imposters' names—the cuckoo becomes the other and sees all other creatures as other. If the host bird removes a cuckoo's egg from its nest, the cuckoo may take revenge, killing all of the host's eggs or chicks; in the same manner, as new Americans drove out or exterminated the Indians, when the cuckoo egg hatches the newborn may drive out any other nestlings or destroy any other eggs. As a creature alienated from its own nature, the cuckoo serves as the specter of the alienation of each from all.

If this is the theme of the song, then rather than the anti-narrative many find in folk-lyric performances, what is present in Clarence Ashley's performance—the axis on which Smith's *Anthology* seems to turn, or maybe the proud anthem of Smithville, sung every night at sundown—is a master narrative: a narrative of American willfulness and fatedness, a narrative implied but altogether missing, replaced instead by hints and gestures, code words and winks, a whole music of secret handshakes. Just as there is a certain historical impersonation on "Ballads," with Virginian Kelly Harrell singing as Charles Guiteau on the scaffold, recounting his assassination of President Garfield, and on "Social Music" there are no individuals, only townfolk indistinguishable from their fellows, on "Songs," where the premise is that one is singing as oneself, the mask goes on, the most profound mask of all, transparent and impenetrable. Who is singing? Who *are* these people? If you could put your hand through the mask you would feel nothing but air.

"The Coo Coo Bird" seems to assume a shared history among its listeners, to take in the countless volumes of what does not need to be said, and yet as Ashley sings the song it is almost a dare. That's how it feels; but who or what is being dared, or why, is completely unclear. "Oh, the coo coo / She's a pretty bird / And she warbles, as she flies," Ashley begins. "And it never / Hollers coo coo / Till the fourth day / Of July." It is usual to dismiss this as not even a metaphor, merely a rhyme. But that is because as a metaphor this verse can be understood but never explained; because it can place the listener, pull the listener's feet right out from under, but cannot itself be placed. Ashley's voice can be solemn, wry, crafty, and blank all at once; his song is not an argument, it is a riddle.

Imagine that in 1929 this was a riddle Clarence Ashley took pleasure putting before the country. Part of the charge in the music on the *Anthology of American Folk Music*—its reach across time, carrying such individualistic flair, in T. J. Clark's phrase such collective vehemence—comes from the fact that, for the first time, people from isolated, scorned, forgotten, disdained communities and cultures had the chance to speak to each other and to the nation at large. A great uproar of voices that were at once old and new was heard, as happens only occasionally in democratic cultures—but always, when it happens, with a sense of explosion, of energies contained for generations bursting out all at once. The story is in the numbers. When the first black vocal blues record, Mamie Smith's "Crazy Blues," was released, in 1920, it sold a million copies in its first year; it was the same in 1923, with the record that revealed what would soon become the hillbilly market. As Smith noted in the foreword to his *Anthology* booklet,

> Ralph Peer, of Okeh Records, went to Atlanta with portable equipment and a record dealer there offered to buy 1,000 copies if Peer

would record the singing of circus barker "Fiddling" John Carson. "The Little Old Log Cabin in the Lane" and "The Old Hen Cackled and the Rooster's Going to Crow" were cut, and according to Peer "It was so bad that we didn't even put a serial number on the records, thinking that when the local dealer got his supply that would be the end of it. We sent him 1,000 records which he got on Thursday. That night he called New York on the phone and ordered 5,000 more sent by express and 10,000 by freight. When the national sale got to 500,000 we were so ashamed we had 'Fiddling' John come up to New York and do a re-recording of the numbers."

Many copies of these records were bought by people without phonographs. They bought the discs as talismans of their own existence; they could hold these objects in their hands and feel their own lives dramatized. In such an act, people discovered the modern world: the thrill of mechanical reproduction. "Something that had survived orally for a very long time suddenly turned into something that Sears Roebuck sold," Smith said in 1968, "and you could order it from Pakistan or wherever you might be"—such as Deep River, North Carolina, or Bristol, Tennessee. Why was it inexpressibly more exciting to hear a song you could hear next door or at a dance next Saturday night coming out of a box? Precisely because you could have heard it next door, or even played it yourself—but not with the distancing of representation, which made a magic mirror, and produced the shock of self-recognition. What one saw in the mirror was a bigger, more various, less finished, less fated self than one had ever seen before. "We cannot escape our life in these fascist bodies," Camille Paglia wrote in *Sexual Personae*; as a black ten-inch 78 turned, for a moment one could. One could experience a freedom from one's physical body, and from one's social body—the mask you wore to go about in public among those who thought they knew you, an unchosen mask of nervousness and tradition, the mask that, when worn too long, makes the face behind it shrivel up and rot away. For some, a spinning record opened up the possibility that one might say anything, in any voice, with any face, the singer's mask now a sign of mastery.

For a few years, this possibility became a fact—and, exposing a hidden republic, a democratic event. The special energy of such an event must have been part of what Harry Smith heard in the commercially vital years of the late 1920s, when all but fifteen of the recordings on the *Anthology of American Folk Music* were recorded, and why he orchestrated the event as a conversation, the folk music of people attempting to connect to other people, to take their money, to feel their presence, to change their minds, even to change the music, to take it places—places in the nation, places in the heart—it had never been. "I don't think that you can say that folk culture was doing such and such, and that in popular culture these things became disseminated—although I used to think that was the case," Smith said to John Cohen in 1968. "I now believe that the dissemination of music affects the quality. As you increase the critical audience of any music, the level goes up." "Doesn't it also go down," Cohen said, "because it has to appeal to a more divergent range of people?" "I don't think they're that divergent," Smith said, changing from folklorist to democratic theorist. "There isn't that much difference between one person and another."

There is, though—and that is why the spirit of the democratic event dramatized in Smith's *Anthology* has its own peculiar, for some irresistible, cast. In the tension between the one and the many, that democracy reveals itself on the *Anthology*—because to a great degree the music Smith wove together was not exactly made by a folk. It was made by willful, ornery, displaced, unsatisfied, ambitious individuals (almost all of them men, because it was men and not women who were permitted to exhibit such traits in public): contingent individuals who were trying to use the resources of their communities to stand out from those communities, or to escape them, even if they never left home.

These were people who had summoned the nerve to attend auditions held by scouts from northern record companies, or who had formed bands and tried to get their fellow men and women, people just like them, to pay attention to them as if they were not quite just like them. These were people who, if only for a moment, looked beyond the farms and mines to which they were almost certainly chained. The stories they would later tell of journeying to New York to record are almost all the same. *How,* one singer after another would recall asking himself—as the singers spoke in the 1960s, when folklorists and fans and record collectors had tracked down the *Anthology*'s survivors, Ashley, Boggs, John Hurt, Sleepy John Estes, Furry Lewis, Eck Robertson, Buell Kazee, so many more—*how,* they remembered asking themselves, as they arrived in New York City in the 1920s like tourists from some foreign land, *how* could they keep hold of their pride, speak their piece as if they knew their neighbors would hear, but also as if they imagined the nation itself might actually acknowledge their existence: myself, Clarence Ashley, yes, but also everyone I know, and those I don't know, my ancestors, and those I'll leave behind?

It is this spirit—the pride of knowledge to pass on, which is also a fear for the disappearance of that knowledge and of its proper language, and, a step past that fear, a looming up of an imagined America one never dared imagine before, whole and complete in a single image—that makes a whole of the *Anthology of American Folk Music*. It is the suspicion that there is, somewhere, a perfectly, absolutely metaphorical America—an arena of rights and obligations, freedoms and restraints, crime and punishment, love and death, humor and tragedy, speech and silence—that makes kin of Mark Merlis's Tom Slater, F. O. Matthiessen, and Harry Smith, and all those he brought forth so long after they stepped forward to say what they had to say.

What is Smithville? It is a small town whose citizens are not distinguishable by race. There are no masters and no slaves. The prison population is large, and most are part of it at one time or another. While some may escape justice, they do not remain among their fellow citizens; executions take place in public. There are, after all, a lot of murders here—crimes of passion, of cynicism, of mere reflex—and also suicides. Here both murder and suicide are rituals, acts instantly transformed into legend, facts that in all their specificity transform everyday life into myth, or reveal that at its highest pitch life is a joke. Thus humor abounds, most of it cruel: as the citizens love to sing, "Roosevelt's in the White House, he's doing his best / McKinley's in the graveyard, he's taking his rest." There is a constant war between the messengers of god and ghosts and demons, dancers and drinkers, and, for all anyone knows, between god's messengers and god himself—no one has ever seen him, but then no one has ever seen a cuckoo either. The town is simultaneously a seamless web of connections and an anarchy of separations: who would ever shake hands with Dock Boggs, who sounds as if his bones are coming through his skin every time he opens his mouth? And yet who can turn away from the dissatisfaction in his voice, the refusal ever to be satisfied with the things of this world or the promises of the next?

This is Smithville. Here is a mystical body of the republic, a kind of public secret: a declaration of what sort of wishes and fears lie behind any public act, a declaration of a weird but clearly recognizable America within the America of the exercise of institutional majoritarian power. Here the cadence of Clarence Ashley's banjo is both counterpoint and contradiction to any law; here everyone calls upon the will and everyone believes in fate. It is a democracy of manners—a democracy, finally, of how people carry themselves, of how they appear in public. The ruling question of public life is not that of the distribution of material goods or the governance of moral affairs, but that of how people plumb their souls and then present their discoveries, their true selves, to others—unless, as happens here often enough, the fear of not belonging, or the wish for true proof that one does belong, takes over, and people assume the mask that makes them indistinguishable from anyone else. But in Smithville that mask never stays on for long.

God reigns here, but his rule can be refused. His gaze cannot be escaped; his hand, maybe. You can bet: you can stake a probably real exile on a probably imaginary homecoming. Or you can take yourself out of the game, and wait for a death god will ignore; then you, like so many others, already dead but still speaking, will take your place in the bend of a note in "The Coo Coo Bird." It's limbo, but it's not bad; on the fourth day of July you get to holler.

FIVE

KILL DEVIL HILLS

. . . street by street, block by block, step by step, door by door, all that's left of the old America is under siege. I catch sight of it from time to time: a fleeting glimpse at the top of the stairs, or outside rustling in the bushes. This is the old America of legend and distant memory, that invested no faith in the wisdom of history and no hope in the sham of the future, the old America that invented itself all over from the ground up every single day. . . . the America where no precaution is sufficient and nothing will protect you, no passport or traveling papers, no opportune crucifix or gas soaked torch, no sunglasses or decoder box or cyanide capsule, no ejector seat or live wire or secret identity or reconstructed tissues or unmarked grave or faked death. It's the America that was originally made for those who believed in nothing else, not because they believed there *was* nothing else but because for them, without America, nothing else was worth believing.

—Steve Erickson, *Amnesiascope*, 1996

"I could really believe in god when I heard Bob Dylan on the radio," Harry Smith once told Paul Nelson. Some years later, in 1976, an NYU student who had just seen *Heaven and Earth Magic* called Smith at the Chelsea Hotel, asking for an immediate interview ("I have to do a paper"); he caught Smith in a particularly unbelieving frame of mind. "When I was younger," Smith said, rambling, lonely, "I thought that the feelings that went through me were—that I would outgrow them, that the anxiety or panic or whatever it is called would disappear, but you sort of suspect it at thirty-five, [and] when you get to be fifty you definitely know you're stuck with your neuroses, or whatever you want to classify them as—demons, completed ceremonies, any old damn thing."

The basement tapes are not completed ceremonies. There are rituals forming, as bland tunes break out into a haze of jokes and doubt, but no rite takes a finished shape. Like the records Smith collected, the known and unknown basement tapes together make a town—a town that is also a country, an imagined America with a past and a future, neither of which seems quite as imaginary as any act taking place in the present of the songs. Erickson's old America is palpable here, because that country is defined solely by the way it can be made up, or can rise up, on any given day, whole and complete in a single phrase or metaphor, melody or harmony.

Smithville folk would recognize this place—the jail is full, and some people still remember when the Fourth of July was the biggest day of the year—but they might have trouble keeping up. For one thing, this town is more drunk. For another, while some people here say they see god as the children of Israel saw him, "by day in a pillar of a cloud," "by night in a pillar of fire," there are no churches, save for the church the man who recites "Sign on the Cross" inhabits in his own mind, a church with no address. The Bible is everywhere, but less invoked than tested against the happenstance of ordinary affairs or invasions of the uncanny. Though more blasphemous than Smithville—blasphemous in the sense of a refusal to grant god, or any force larger than appetite or inconvenience, the slightest claim on one's attention—comes with the whiskey—this town might be even more religious, because here people can read fate out of the weather. Fate is less suspended, as it is in those Smithville singalongs "Sugar Baby" and "East Virginia," than looming, rushing forward—unless, as occasionally happens, someone here is rushing to meet fate. Sometimes it can seem as if the whole population is made up of Casey Joneses and John Henrys: daredevil stoics, like the hard-luck wrangler in "Hills of Mexico," the half-bored, half-threatening character in "Apple Suckling Tree," the squinting mystic of "This Wheel's on Fire," or the map-hopper in "Lo and Behold!" People here are restless, but while the citizens are always hitting the road, they seem to carry the air over the town with them, to the point where the place-names that dot their songs—Wichita, Williams Point, Tupelo, Mink Muscle Creek, Blueberry Hill—soon enough feel as recognizable as street signs and as interchangeable as signposts.

People talk funny here. Instead of the language of allegory and home truth that rules in Smithville, the currency is the shaggy dog story, from tragic parable to slapstick sermon, sometimes the one hiding inside the other. Every time you turn your head, ordinary speech cracks into word play that makes fitting "Coo Coo Bird" verses together feel about as tricky as stacking baby blocks. The native tongue is close enough to English to give you the illusion you're following a story whether it makes sense or not, but often it's only the way a story is told—the way a suggestion of letting you in on a secret catches your curiosity, or the way a sly drawl makes you feel you've lived here all your life—that makes sense. Think the story through after the storyteller has passed by, fit one word to another, and it may make no sense at all.

For all of those behind bars here, and despite the sense of foreshadowing that murder can bring, it's unclear whether anyone has killed anybody, even the joker who says he killed someone just to watch him die. While Smithville murderers always chant "My name I'll never deny" as they confess on the scaffold, here prisoners don't necessarily know what they've done or even who they are, only that they've been condemned, by others or by themselves. There is no guilt in Smithville; here it's second mind. There are no executions. If crimes instantly become legends in Smithville, and with such drama that the drowning of a pregnant woman can emerge as more significant, more central to the town's sense of what it is than the assassination of a president, in the town made by the basement tapes no crime comes sufficiently into focus for it to become more than a rumor—or for justice to be done. In the tongue spoken in "This Wheel's on Fire," "Sign on the Cross," "Apple Suckling Tree," "I'm a Fool for You," "Tears of Rage," and "I'm Not There"—the words rushing or coming one by one as masks seem almost to dissolve before they seem almost bolted down—you can sense the town on the verge of a collective confession to a crime far greater than any simple murder. The whiskey comes with it.

Smithville has its suicides and its homicides; this town can appear full of village idiots, like those bearded geezers set up on the corner, harmonizing on what sounds like a 1957 Dell-Vikings B-side they can't remember. "I am a teenage prayer," the leader offers, a dirty old man lost in contemplation of his own good looks, crooning with the perfect composure of the absolutely plastered, standing straight until he falls right over. In lieu of the drummer, who's having too much fun to worry about a beat, the organist keeps time as the guitarist plays sock-hop triplets and doo-wahs fill the air. "Take a look at me, baby, I am *your* teenage prayer," the leader insists, as if stating a philosophical proposition, or maybe running for office. "No, take a look over here at *me*, baby," demands a second voice—a deeper, more addled voice, the voice of a syphilitic trolling for fourteen-year-olds, the voice of a man who says what he means, means what he says, and doesn't care about either—"*I* am your teenage prayer." As a body of pure lust he makes a better case, but the leader is not dissuaded. As the boys around them raise their voices like glasses, the two men happily wrestle over the song until they're singing to each other, the leader finally lost in a joyous reverie. "Any day or night just come to me when you're in fright," he grins, as if she, or he, already has.

A woman passing by calls out for Gid Tanner and His Skillet Lickers' "You Gotta Quit Kickin' My Dog Around"—"They cut it in 1926, the year I was born," she crows, as others in the street cheer her on—a tune the band essays as if it were Tanner's "You Gotta Stop Drinking Shine," which is reasonable, given how much the musicians have already drunk. Now the singer summons a great stillness, as if, for the first time in the last few minutes, true mysteries present themselves:

Every time
I go to town
The boys keep kickin' my dog around
I don't know why
I'm goin' to town
I don't know why they kickin' my dog around

"DOG, DOG, DOG," the rest reply craftily. "WHY, WHY, WHY." Still upright, the group jumps ahead thirty years for Bill Haley and His Comets' "See You Later, Alligator," which a stray shout from one of the musicians turns into "See You Later, Allen Ginsberg" ("After 'while, croc-a-gator," he adds helpfully), just like that.

These are priceless moments—that is, they're free, they cost you nothing. The crowd that has gathered for these ditties breaks up and moves on down the street. But the weather changes all the time here—if you don't like it, just wait—and sometimes you can't tell when it does. Just like that, everything is the same and everything is different. The blank questions in "You Gotta Quit Kickin' My Dog Around" can yield blurred images of mobs chasing men and women suddenly exposed for what they really are—dogs exposed as people, people exposed as dogs, the pious exposed as the reprobate, whites exposed as blacks, dog dog dog, why why why—and the woman who asked for the song may begin to suspect that as she called the tune, sooner or later she will have to pay the piper. In their happy, querulous abandon, "I Am a Teenage Prayer" and "You Gotta Quit Kickin' My Dog Around" are not so far from the fragmentary, chiliastic rehearsal of "I'm a Fool for You," its voice of rapture and enigma not so far from the judgment hidden in its lover's sighs and slow cadence: the single cemetery this town keeps, that place where every heart shall rise and every man shall burn.

Here the streets are even less well marked than the streets in Smithville. The citizens are even more adept at disguises. They change their faces as easily as they change their clothes, a hooked nose flattening, rubbery lips going thin and pursed. Ben Franklin could pass for Groucho Marx, George Washington for Aaron Burr, Abraham Lincoln for either Ishmael or Ahab, Emily Dickinson for Sojourner Truth, Jonathan Edwards for Jimmy Lee Swaggart. That drunk singer on the corner is now preaching. As in a film running in reverse, the crowd is pulled back up the street and regathers itself at the speaker's feet. "Mem'ry serve well," he mutters, though it also sounds like "Mem'phis town"; the words come from a distance, weighted with tiredness and defeat, a breath for every bare syllable. As the men and women before the preacher crane their heads to place his words, to mouth them with him, he traces a rolling, deliberate rhythm, with his voice, with his hands, stepping into his famous sermon on the Book of Revelation, a soliloquy the crowd knows as "This Wheel's on Fire." It's a story the preacher has told for years, but his listeners are rapt and still, because neither he nor they have ever gotten to the bottom of it. As the man nears his peroration, urging the people in the crowd to bring forth their memories, or daring them to, reminding them of promises he has remembered and they have forgotten, his back hunches, his clenched fists open, and in a gesture no one can read his fingers wave raggedly in the air.

This town and Smithville are congruent, in the way they match the unknown to the obvious, in the high stakes the citizens of both towns place on a bet that may not be legal anywhere else—the bet that anything can be transformed. The towns are like outposts on the same frontier, perhaps even in sight of each other over some unmarked borderline. Each place might be a tall tale to the other, people in Smithville laughing over the confusions of life on the other side, people on the other side baffled by the certainties of life in Smithville. Even a riddle like "The Coo Coo Bird" can feel like certainty in the town the basement tapes make.

Feeling the ground beneath your feet, as you likely would listening to "You Ain't Goin' Nowhere," "Million Dollar Bash," "See that My Grave Is Kept Clean," or for that matter "I Am a Teenage Prayer," you might call that town Union, after the town in Connecticut, or the one in Nebraska, Oregon, Maine, Mississippi, South Carolina, West Virginia, Kentucky, Tennessee. Feeling the ground pulled out from under you, as you can listening to "Hills of Mexico," "The Bells of Rhymney," or "Lo and Behold!" you might call the town Kill Devil Hills, after perhaps the most ambitiously named spot in the U.S.A., a North Carolina hamlet a few miles down from Kitty Hawk, where the Wright Brothers first found their wings. If the balance tips to Kill Devil Hills, it might be because you can imagine that no place with a name like that could fail to deliver the visions demanded in "Lo and Behold!"—or deny anything.

Associated Press dispatches, February 21, 1995:

SUSAN SMITH WAS MOLESTED BY STEPFATHER

Union, S.C.—Susan Smith, who is accused of drowning her two young sons, was molested by her stepfather when she was 16, the man admitted in court papers unsealed yesterday. . . . According to court papers released yesterday, Beverly Russell abused Smith by "participating in open-mouth kissing, fondling her breasts and by the stepfather placing the minor's hand on him in and about the genital area." Russell was never charged with a crime.

TOWN STUNNED BY SLAYINGS OF THREE CHILDREN

Kill Devil Hills, N.C.—Residents left flowers and notes on the blackened spot of pavement where the bodies of three slain children were found in a burning van. Their father committed suicide nearby.

Even Police Chief James Gradeless, a 20-year law enforcement veteran who also served with Special Forces in Vietnam, was shaken by what he saw this weekend.

"It's not a Kill Devil Hills story," Gradeless said yesterday. "It's an American story. It bothers all of our consciences because somewhere, some place, society has failed to prevent this kind of thing from happening."

The question of why some crimes once instantly turned into legends while in our day, as for years now, the most irreducible crimes seem to disappear from consciousness as instantly as they appear in the news is also the question of what spirit it is that animates the basement tapes—the way they seem to float in time. Turning on elemental, symbolic incidents of transcendence and transgression, primal dramas were enacted in the sort of songs, dances, ballads, sermons, and hymns out of which Harry Smith made a nation; they were enacted in the languages he brought together. By definition, these primal dramas—acts of founding, acts that founded not merely a nation but a local version of the human condition—remained unfinished. The basement tapes can be heard as an attempt to reinhabit this dramatically unfinished world, as if sparked by a suspicion that the languages of the time in which the basement tunes were fashioned—the political languages of right and left, the aesthetic languages of corruption and purity—were by comparison to those Smith gathered impoverished, unable to describe the crimes that were making the time, which is to say incapable of preserving their memory.

Recognizing that there might be such a thing as a primal drama, you might find yourself drawn away from the events of your own time—the war abroad, the war at home—even if, opening the day's paper, you could read the Constitution and the Bible as truth or lie between every other line. Accepting that such a drama must remain unfinished, you might find yourself less impressed by the crimes of your own time than you once were, and drawn to the possibility of fashioning a country of your own—a country where both you and the old voices that spoke to you might converse and feel at home. To fashion such a country would not make the crimes that might have driven you out of your time less burdensome; it might make them more so, just as dreams can weigh more heavily on the soul than events.

In such a venture, the cost of vision is ambiguity. An old language is suddenly alive with imagery, but while it can name anything for what it is, it can no longer hold narrative. In the country where this language is spoken, crimes will no longer vanish as soon as they occur, as with, say, "HIGHWAY BEHEADING"—

USA Today, July 24—Eric Star Smith, 34, is to be arraigned today on charges he stabbed and beheaded his 14-year-old son on an

Estancia, N.M., roadside Friday while the boy's brother and passing drivers watched. Smith, of Parker, Ariz., was on a weekend fishing trip with his sons when he decided they were possessed by the devil, authorities said. Police chased Smith for 40 miles, during which he threw the head of son Eric Jr. out the window. The chase ended when Smith crashed his van into a retaining wall in Albuquerque.

—but in their constancy they will carry neither names nor faces. They will not turn into legends; they will turn into myths.

"A myth is a public dream," Joseph Campbell once said. Not so long ago, in the rural South and the farm states of the Midwest, the most common form of myth was the weather report—because whether it was a question of a good year for wheat or cotton, or getting caught out of doors at the wrong time, the weather was a matter of life and death. Because it was also a question that had to be talked over every day, there was little point raising your voice over it. Take that beloved American story, that Gothic weather report, about a girl swept off a Kansas farm by a tornado and dropped down into another world as the killer of a witch. There is a way in which Dorothy's adventures in the land of Oz are really about the frustrations of a young woman who wants more than anything to escape from a language in which every vocal sound has been so polished in taciturn mouths that neither a laugh nor a scream can be made, let alone heard, let alone paid any mind.

Such a way of speaking, or not speaking, gives rise to a belief that something is being left unsaid—or denied. Recounting a conversation he overheard one day as a small boy growing up in McPherson, "The Biggest Little Town in Kansas," Bruce Conner might be telling Dorothy's story as a negative image of itself, as if it truly was only a dream: in Campbell's phrase, only "a private myth." "I learned to distrust words," Conner says, remembering his father out in the front yard, then a neighbor coming by: "Hi, Joe." "Hi, Nick." "How're you doing." "I'm doing fine." "Great day, isn't it." "Sure is." "Think we might get some rain?" "Could be." "How's the wife?" "Real good." "Well, gotta go now." "Well, see you." "See you." "I was amazed," Conner says. "I was *suspicious*. I thought, kids don't talk like this! They've got to be hiding things from us! Conversations like this have got to be a *code*."

Cracking the code of any Gothic language, especially one as flat as the plains, can be like cracking open the earth. "I took back the night," writes Sarah Vowell. "And it's all mine until I get stabbed, raped, mugged, shot. I've walked alone the darkened streets of tough towns from Palermo to New York, but the congenial Midwest makes me tremble. I know for a fact that the steam rises from the gates of hell in downtown Fargo and the Antichrist, laying low, shovels snow off the streets of Dubuque for extra cash. Forget the Big Bad Wolf, the fear of God, the hands of time—they can't stand up to Minnesota Nice."

Such a vision is usually buried in a muttered curse—a curse even the one who makes it may not quite catch. On the basement tapes, you can hear a trace of this displacement—the displacement of the familiar into nowhere—in the way Dylan snaps off a verse in "Yea! Heavy and a Bottle of Bread." "It's a one-track town," he says. "Pack up the meat, sweet, we're headin' out." Against the chopping, hesitating beat of his own acoustic guitar—a beat full of misgiving, even an escapee's remorse—riding the bright highlights of Richard Manuel's piano, ignoring the steady steps of Garth Hudson's organ, a sound that is all longing, like the song's second mind, Dylan doesn't so much sing the line as get it over with. His voice is direct, plain, determined, vaguely bitter—and nearly bored with the action even as it happens.

As if hidden in its own flat, brittle sound—so brittle you can almost hear the words breaking off each other—this is one of the most intense and cutting incidents in the hundred or so known basement performances, an incident that maps the basement town and opens into a seemingly complete ambience of speech and gesture, a whole world: the absolutely flattened world of "Clothesline Saga." Queer things happen here in Kill Devil Hills; this song, which Dylan, Hudson, Manuel, Danko, and Robertson recorded as "Answer to 'Ode'," slowly walks you through one of the ways people have learned how to talk about these things, and not talk about them.

"It was the third of June / Another sleepy dusty Delta day"—in fact it was late July 1967, midway through what some Americans were calling the Summer of Love and the rest were calling the Long Hot Summer, when "Ode to Billie Joe," written and performed by Bobbie Gentry, born in Mississippi, schooled there and in Los Angeles, first made itself heard across the U.S.A. Within a week it was inescapable. By August 26, when the record hit number one, it was as if every state had stopped to listen to this quiet, unsolved mystery, and the quiet might have been the hook, the special noise that caught the nation's ear. It was a season of loud noises. On July 11, the day after Gentry recorded her song in Hollywood, the death toll for violent black protests in Newark, New Jersey, came in: twenty-six. Two weeks later the historic black riot that tore Detroit apart left a count of forty-three. In the movie theaters, people watched transfixed as former Dallas waitress Bonnie Parker, twenty-three, and one-time Texas layabout Clyde Barrow, twenty-five, by 1934 famed Dust Bowl bank robbers and killers, now irresistibly incarnated as Faye Dunaway and Warren Beatty, were shot to pieces in a police ambush. On the screen hundreds of rounds smashed into metal and bone. In the theater you could hear every one of them, and with the sounds bouncing off the datelines of the newspaper you carried in your head you could hear every echo: Newark, Detroit, Saigon, Hanoi. On television, as August 1967 ended, David Janssen, as the Fugitive, finally caught the One-Armed Man—but everywhere else in the land everyone was going down or getting away. In the theater, Bonnie and Clyde stopped on a country road. Just before the police opened fire you heard birds singing, then like Clyde you heard them flutter off in fright. The day was so bright you could almost hear the sunlight. With the execution over, the police emerged from the bushes, their faces set; the silence was so complete it was as if what you saw had made you deaf. That was the end of the movie. People walked out disgusted, angry, exultant, thrilled, scared, unsure if they had heard a warning or a call to arms. The movie cast back more than three decades to bring forth what could not be felt as the past, and for many the movie did what the historical events of the day could not do; as Pauline Kael wrote that season, it "put the sting back into death."

This was the national train wreck that for the four minutes and thirteen seconds it lasted "Ode to Billie Joe" brought to a halt.

A young woman—she could be twenty, she could be fourteen—is telling the story of the day she and her family, gathered around the table for their midday farmers' dinner, heard the news that Billie Joe McAllister jumped off the Tallahatchie Bridge. The family knows the boy, of course, everybody knows everybody else in this little corner of the Mississippi Delta, but the singer knows him best of all; as her mother remembers, the new preacher mentioned he saw Billie Joe and a girl who looked like the singer throwing something off the same bridge. Mother and brother and father recall what they can about Billie Joe as they pass food across the table. The mother notices that her daughter hasn't lifted her fork but then moves on to something else.

Bobbie Gentry's voice has an ache in it, but while she will go down low at the end of a line, she stays away from high notes. She counts the song off on her guitar, sometimes staggering the dialogue, as if to keep the story from gaining on itself; violins and cellos seem to come from a long way off, less orchestration than signs that a memory is being kept. The singer is like the woman who walks the hills in "Long Black Veil": *she* knows why Billie Joe went to his death, she knows what they threw into the black water, but not only will she not tell, no one around the table even thinks to ask. There's a meal to get over with; there's work to be done. So not a voice is raised or even inflected. Billie Joe's suicide rests on the same moral plane as the black-eyed peas on the table. Everything is flat. Everything is quiet. Outside the kitchen window camped an entire country, listening in.

"The song is sort of a study in unconscious cruelty," Gentry told *Billboard* writer Fred Bronson years later. "But everybody seems more concerned with what was thrown off the bridge than they are with the thoughtlessness of people expressed in the song—and what was thrown off the bridge really isn't that important."

> Everybody . . . has a different guess about what was thrown off the bridge—flowers, a ring, even a baby. Anyone who hears the song can think anything they want . . . but the real "message" of the song, if there must be a message, revolves around the way the family talks about the suicide. They sit there eating their peas and apple pie and talking, without even realizing that Billie Joe's girlfriend is sitting at the table, *a member of the family*.

Well, her sister got married and bought a store in Tupelo, the singer sums up. "There was a virus going round, papa caught it and he died last spring," she says, putting no more feeling into his story than he or anyone else around the table put into hers. The record topped the charts for a month. I remember driving then with the song on the radio, trying to follow its sliding phrases, drifting into its miasmic trance, and plowing straight into the car in front of me.

In the grand tradition of rock 'n' roll answer records—from Etta James's 1954 "Roll with Me Henry" (her hit reply to Hank Ballard and the Midnighters' number-one R & B classic "Work with Me Annie") to the Spokesmen's 1965

"The Dawn of Correction" (their patriotic retort to then new-Dylan Barry McGuire's number-one protest anthem "Eve of Destruction"—despite its unintentional hilarity the Spokesmen disc did no better than Johnny Sea's forgotten "Day for Decision"), or for that matter Bob Seger's obscure "Ballad of the Yellow Berets" (his left-wing draft dodger's lampoon of Sgt. Barry Sadler's 1966 number one "Ballad of the Green Berets")—the idea was for a nowhere artist to catch the tail of a star and ride it to fame and fortune, or more likely notice and the price of a round of drinks. More than that, though, the answer record was a game, a fan's game, like making up new words to a song you can't understand or arguing about a record that refuses to explain itself. The great public conversation about "Ode to Billie Joe" was in its way the ultimate answer record.

As "Answer to 'Ode'," the song that was finally released as "Clothesline Saga"—in 1975, on the sole official *Basement Tapes* album—was part of that conversation, but in 1967 and after it was also its opposite: a secret answer record, which contained a kind of secret public. Ignoring the rules of answer-record making, which required that for would-be hit purposes one focus directly on the original's lyric theme or story line (the proper title for an answer to "Ode" would have been something like "I Know What Billie Joe McAllister Threw Off the Tallahatchie Bridge"), "Clothesline Saga" applied the language and the tone of voice of "Ode to Billie Joe" to a whole nation; like Don Siegel's *Invasion of the Body Snatchers*, it masked a whole town. Or maybe the effect was simply a perfect illusion, the private joke of Dylan's narrator, his teenage-boy double for Bobbie Gentry's teenage girl—the narrator's ability to make anyone speak the language of nothing, nowhere, never was, never mind.

"Clothesline Saga" opens in Bruce Conner's childhood front yard. The boy's family goes out of the house, gets their clothes off the line, brings them back into the house. The father asks a question; "What do you care?" is the answer. "Well, just because," the father says, and the shame in his voice, his embarrassment at having violated the boredom everyone treasures, makes it plain he won't be saying anything else. The family takes the clothes back out and hangs them on the line again. Everything in the music is circular; Robbie Robertson plays a lazy guitar so slowly only Garth Hudson's organ, coming in after the narrator as if what he's describing might actually turn out to be interesting, someday, keeps the song from coming to a complete stop. "It was January the thirtieth," the singer says, looking back on himself. "And everybody was feeling fine." Suddenly it feels like this was all a very long time ago, then that it was just the day before the song's next day, but the question barely asks itself; there might be deep memory in the singer's voice, but there is no time in the song. Everybody is feeling fine because in the town the song has so quickly called up it is a moral certainty that absolutely nothing can happen. That certainty, that prophecy, that pleasure, is what the song is about, what it describes the way ordinary songs describe events, but that certainty is also the song's Tallahatchie Bridge. If nothing can happen here, why does the singer remember the date?

The next day everyone in the family gets up to see if the clothes are dry—this will clearly be the day's adventure. But then Bruce Conner's father's neighbor comes by. The singer's mother says hello. "Have you heard the news," the neighbor asks, grinning, a hint of satisfaction in his voice, though in this story the idea of "news" is so odd the word seems part of a foreign language. "The vice-president's gone mad."

For a split second in the lassitude of the music—music in which the actors move and speak like people who have absorbed so much alcohol there is no longer any need to drink it, their cells produce all they need—the town in the song is Washington, D.C., where in 1967 Minnesota's Hubert Humphrey is vice-president. It is a prize he was awarded in 1964, for his work at the presidential nominating convention, where he turned aside his party's rules on racial justice—rules he helped make—refusing the Constitutional claims of Mississippi's black and white Freedom Democratic Party out of fear the tribunes of White Democracy, jealous of their right to keep black southerners from voting, might walk out of the hall; now he stands for Lyndon Johnson's crusade in Vietnam. In a fraction of time within the split second, the town is Minneapolis, in 1948. Here Hubert Humphrey is the crusading reform mayor, founding the Democratic-Farmer-Labor Party, fighting the Ku Klux Klan and its secret rule of the state Democratic Party regulars, then in this same year carrying the first civil rights plank in the history of the national Democratic Party to the floor of the convention, standing for it even as Strom Thurmond, governor of South Carolina, led the South out of the hall and, this year, out of the Democratic column in the Electoral College—and then on this day, January 31 of its unnamed year, the town is just Kill Devil Hills. The vice-president has jumped off the Tallahatchie Bridge, the neighbor is saying, and common courtesy requires some kind of response, just as "Think we might get some rain?" must be followed by "Could be."

"Where?" says the mother.

"Downtown," says the neighbor.

"When?" says the mother.

"Last night," says the neighbor, the pace of the exchange sharpening to the point where you can believe the talk might be going somewhere. "Hmm, gee, that's too bad," says the mother, dashing those hopes, the narrator putting her words across so flatly the mother is either amused or dead. "Well, there's nothing we can do about it," says the neighbor, as if looking at a few clouds moving in. "It's just something we're going to have to forget." "Yes, I guess so," says the mother, as if she already has, and then she asks the singer if the clothes are still wet. With more urgency than he used to relate the tale of the now-disappeared vice-president—which is not much urgency—the neighbor turns to the boy, listening all this time, standing at the clothesline: "Are those clothes yours?" The boy knows how he's supposed to answer, he knows how to talk weather, he knows how to turn Judgment Day into weather. (Everybody talks about it but nobody does anything about it.) "Some of 'em, not all of 'em," he says.

Rising imperceptibly throughout, Hudson's organ now looses the song from its moorings, spinning it, giving it the same movement you make when you twirl your finger at your temple, looking at someone who is looking at the person the motion is meant to describe: the person the organ is looking at is you, the song's secret public, whose vice-president is simultaneously in his Constitutional chair and at the bottom of the Tallahatchie River. Listening in like the narrator, the music says that what the words describe is a world upside down, cuckoo; the neighbor, standing in the yard, doesn't notice. "You always help out around here with the chores?" he asks. "Some time, not all the time," says the boy.

Then the neighbor blows his nose; as the boy describes the event—the way the singer's voice hesitates over the words, then floats them in strangeness—he just barely opens an invisible door in the song. The vagueness of the song is now sinister—so much so that for an instant the neighbor is not human. But then the father calls, the boy has to bring in the clothes, so he does. "And then I shut all the doors," he says.

That old American mask—that covered voice, hiding the way Frank Hutchison rolls into town, leaves crêpe on every door, and moves on—has all but sunk into the flesh here, at least on this day. Here in Kill Devil Hills people understand that these things happen, even if not all of them understand why they happen, or care. Grab for the mask, try to tear it off, and on this day you might find your fingers covered in blood, people staring at you as they pass by. But on another day, cracking the code of the talk in "Clothesline Saga," you might find something even harder to take. You might find a mask beneath the mask, and the language to go with it. You might find the beginnings of a true picture of the crime on which the town was founded—founded perhaps so that someday the crime could be discovered, along with the language to make it speak.

Were that to happen, the language of "Answer to 'Ode' " would be a finished thing. This shaggy dog story would be a completed, no longer necessary ceremony, though were that to happen, the people of Kill Devil Hills might find it impossible to sit through "This Wheel's on Fire" even one more time.

For then, in the shifting humors of the old Americas that loom up in the songs, neither a secret identity nor a faked death, more or less what has been acted out in "Clothesline Saga," would be worth a dollar or a dram, and anyone listening would have to answer for which song he liked best, for who she really was.

S I X

GET INTO THE GRAVEYARD

Of all the rounders in Smithville, the one most often spotted in Kill Devil Hills is Dock Boggs. You might find him walking alone, staring straight ahead, stonefaced, like a man ashamed to admit he ended up in the wrong place because his money didn't run out before the booze did. Or you might find him playing on a corner, people around him, dollars in his hand, a glint in his eye that says—what? That, this day, the time is right to go all the way into the songs he's sung for forty years, songs that, somehow, he's less sung than listened to, less loved than feared? Or that what the people who are giving him money are purchasing is a treasure, a memory he will be permitted to keep long after they have forgotten they paid for it?

You know, a lot of these people now, used to be over there in Jenkins. Used to be the *hottest* place in town—if you go too far, if you needed a little money, you see . . .

It is December 1969, in Needmore, Virginia, just over from Norton, in the mountains in the southwest corner of the state, and Boggs has been drinking all night. Mike Seeger, Boggs's friend and collaborator, has had the tape recorder on, taking down Boggs's stories as he has for years; now Seeger is trying to get Boggs to go to bed, but this night, though Boggs has forgotten the tape recorder, he has many stories left to tell. He is seventy-one; he'll be dead in little more than a year.

I'm up to Jenkins once, me and a fellow in a A-model Ford, and we—that's before they got this road graded, down, this side of the mountain. You had to go up the old road to get to the top of the mountain, you get to the top of the mountain, you was all right, you see, come on to Norton, everything was paved up. We went down, stayed all night, with my brother-in-law, Lee Hunsucker, lived in Mayking, we went down to stay all night with Laura and Lee, visit with 'em a night. He didn't have no money and I didn't have none, and so we come back, we drove back—down below Jenkins, about eight or ten miles. He said, "Dock, my gas tank's runnin' kind of dry," and he said, "I gotta have oil in this 'fore it runs—how in the world are we gonna get back 'cross that mountain?" I said, "You just be right quiet." I said, "This thing hauls us to Jenkins, that's all I want, just haul us to Jenkins." And that used to be one of the biggest, poorest places—what I'm talking about, they was the most freest givers I ever saw.

We got up to where we get into a parking lot. I walked out there . . . that's when I had that Silvertone. He said, "What we gone do, Dock?" I said, "Just be quiet." I said, "Things'll turn around—don't be uneasy." We hadn't had dinner, either. He said, "My gas tank ain't got but a couple gallons in it." I said, "Just be right quiet." We walked out there, and they had some park benches, settin' out there by the side of the street. They's a whole group, 'bout ten or twelve there, I guess, settin' on the bench. "Waaaaaaallll," some of 'em cursed—"Damned if there ain't old Dock!" Said, "Where that banjer at, Dock?" I said, "Banjer is out there in that little old A-model car." Said, "Well, God, don't you come out here with that, you go get it, and you bring it down here and play something for us." I said, "Banjer is plumb sick. And that there car, gas tank's about empty. My stomach's about empty." And I said, "If you fellas got some money, that you want to put out, for pick a few pieces, I'll set down on one of these benches here and play a piece or two for you."

They give me about three or four dollars 'fore I even started up on my banjo. That's a long time ago, when a dollar was worth a dollar. I went and got my banjo, come out there, get it out of the case, set it down on the bench. I never paid no attention to the traffic, people. Before I played a piece, I'd already took up a second collection. I had over ten dollars in hand. First thing I know here come a group of flash buttons, police caps and so on, bust through the crowd, and I looked out there and—I had that town blocked. I had the street blocked, they was all around, I bet they had two hundred and fifty, three hundred people around there. And he come up to me, he said, "Dock," saying, "you blockin' the street here, and you can't do that, you mustn't do that," said, "Go over there on that bandstand if you want to play, play *all* you feel like playin'." Say, "I love to hear you play myself." I said, "Oh, chief," I says, "I hadn't paid no attention to blockin' the street, I had never looked out there, all I'se doin' is takin' up a few quarters here." So I went over to the bandstand, followed me over there, and I don't know how much money they give us—hardly anybody give you less than a quarter, a half, or a dollar bill. I played about an hour, hour and a half, and I had plenty money to fill up the gas tank, plenty money to eat dinner on, plenty money to buy extra oil and get to the top of the mountain. I know that's about the best time that guy ever had in his life—his name was Sam. He's dead now. He used to brake on the L&N. You get to the top of the mountain, it's *easy* to get down.

Dock Boggs returned to stories like this one—stories about the chord his music struck in other people—again and again in the last years of his life. He talked around and through the deep and helpless manner in which his fellow Appalachians had responded to his songs: the way they responded to his traditional tunes and his refashioned, radio-borne blues as if they'd never in their lives heard anything like them, as if the land, the history, and the airwaves they shared with him had left them unprepared for what he had to offer.

As Boggs spoke into Mike Seeger's tape recorder, he was not embellishing these memories but fully retrieving them, spinning a tale until he could almost balance it on the palm of his hand and watch it spin of its own accord, like a top. In 1927, Boggs had traveled from Virginia to New York City to make his first 78s, then disappeared back into the history of the anonymous—but now, in 1969, Boggs had for six years known a second public life. In 1963, at the height of the folk revival, Seeger—who along with John Cohen founded the New Lost City Ramblers to play the music such abstract, all but incorporeal *Anthology* legends like Boggs once played—located Boggs in Norton. Though Boggs had not performed in public since the early years of the 1930s, within weeks he appeared at the American Folk Festival in Asheville, North Carolina. After that his voice could be heard throughout the nation, at folk festivals from Newport to Berkeley and on three new albums, if one knew where to look, or cared to.

Many responded from the heart—but not that many, even in the country of the folk revival. As Peter Guralnick wrote of Skip James—the great blues singer who after making eighteen unique recordings in 1931 vanished like Boggs, only to reappear at Newport in 1964 immediately following his discovery by blues collectors in a Tunica, Mississippi, hospital—on bad nights Boggs could feel "that he had been snatched from obscurity only to be returned to an obscurity just as profound," from nowhere to nowhere, here to back again. Weirdly, as he had sung in the 1920s in the Virginia and Kentucky mountains or as he sang before college audiences in the 1960s, it was all in the music: at both borders of his career Boggs sang like a seer, standing outside of himself as the prophet of his own life, the angel of his own extinction. Young or old, he sang as if he could see his life as something that had already passed. The sensation, boiling in the music as he received it himself, was irresistible and unclear, like religion. Sometimes, as on that day in Jenkins, the performances were the ceremonies and the songs, "Country Blues," "Down South Blues," "Sugar Baby," "Danville Girl," "Pretty Polly," the mysteries; sometimes it was the other way around.

Dock Boggs made primitive-modernist music about death. Primitive because the music was put together out of junk you could find in anyone's yard, hand-me-down melodies, folk-lyric fragments, pieces of Child ballads, mail-order instruments, and the new women's blues records they were making in the northern cities in the early years of the 1920s; modernist because the music was about the choices you made in a world a disinterested god had plainly left to its own devices, where you were thrown completely back on yourself, a world where only art or revolution, the symbolic remaking of the world, could take you out of yourself. Modernist, really, because in 1923—one year before André Breton published the first surrealist manifesto in Paris, four years before Dock Boggs cut "Country Blues" and "Pretty Polly" in New York—D. H. Lawrence's pronouncement on the subject in his *Studies in Classic American Literature* could have applied as readily to the music Boggs was then contriving as to *The Scarlet Letter*. "The furthest frenzies of French modernism or futurism," Lawrence wrote, "have not yet reached the pitch of extreme consciousness that Poe, Melville, Hawthorne, Whitman reached. The European moderns are all *trying* to be extreme. The great Americans I mention just were it. Which is why the world has funked them, and funks them today."*

Boggs's music accepted death, sympathized with its mission, embraced its seductions, and traveled with its wiles. "Always the same," Lawrence said. "The deliberate consciousness of Americans so fair and smooth-spoken, and the underconsciousness so devilish. *Destroy! destroy! destroy!* hums the under-consciousness. *Love and produce! Love and produce!* cackles the upper consciousness. And the world hears only the Love-and-produce cackle. Refuses to hear the hum of desperation underneath." With Dock Boggs that hum is right on the surface—and still he sounds more subterranean than anything else. He sounds like the mask behind the mask, even if the feel-

*The phrase "primitive-modernist" is that of Memphis bandleader Jim Dickinson.

ing is strong that the mask behind the mask is a face, and that if it is a face, if the way this man sounds is the way the face looks, one might prefer it were a mask after all.

A story about what sort of world is possible when this is so—about what sort of town surrounds the actors and the acts such a world sparks—is told complexly in Dock Boggs's songs. Hesitation shades into madness: as a coal miner, a bootlegger, and a churchgoer in his ordinary life and a killer in his art, Boggs told a story of estrangement and sorrow, crime and no regret. That story lies behind what might be the most bottomless of the basement performances, "Tears of Rage" and "I'm Not There." Without Boggs's presence in Bob Dylan's field of vision—less as a musical influence than as a talisman, an artistic and moral example, someone Dylan spoke of always with awe and blunt distance, as if Boggs were aesthetically and physically unapproachable—those songs are really unthinkable. But the tale of the mask behind the mask, the mask that may also be a face, is also a story that can be told simply, as in *The Deadly Percheron*—a 1947 novel by the Cincinnati mystery writer John Franklin Bardin.

A psychiatrist has been confined for months in a mental ward without mirrors as someone he knows he is not. He is a partial amnesiac; he knows who he is, he just doesn't know how he got where he is. By carefully eliciting from his doctors hints about the nature of their diagnosis, he succeeds in conforming to their expectations—after all, he's treated scores of patients just like the one he's supposed to be. He exhibits the proper symptoms, makes the proper recovery, and wins his release. On the streets again, he enters a soda fountain and takes in the reflection of the customers in the mirror behind the counter, settling on one grotesque:

He was not old—about my age now that I studied his face—although he seemed older at first glance. This was because his short-cropped hair was grey streaked with white and his jaw, that showed the remains of strength, trembled spasmodically. But what made him really fascinatingly ugly was the wide, long, angry red scar that traversed his face diagonally from one ear across the nose and down to the root of the jaw at the base of the other cheek. It was an old scar that had knit badly and in healing had pulled and twisted at the skin until the face it rode had the texture of coarse parchment and the grimace of a clown. One cheek, and the eye with it, was drawn sideways and upward into a knowing leer—the other drooped, and with it a corner of the mouth, as if its owner were stricken with grief. The skin's color was that of cigar ash, but the scar's color was bright carmine. I pitied the man, then was embarrassed to look around at him; surely, he must have seen me staring at his reflection! But as I had this thought I noticed that his glass emptied itself of coca-cola just as I sucked noisily at my straw.

That is Dock Boggs's sound. In 1929 he had a band, Dock Boggs and His Cumberland Mountain Entertainers, with a fiddler and guitar players, featuring Boggs's own flamboyant buck-dancing, and one tune Boggs favored then was a kind of profane spiritual, a plea not for grace but for more time on earth, a song blacks and whites had known forever as "Oh Death." Whenever Boggs called for it his guitarist Scott Boatwright said the same thing: "Get out of the graveyard, Dock." "What is this that I can see, with icy hands taking hold on me?" Boggs would sing, the words jerking in his throat like the limbs of a marionette. "I am death and none can excel / I'll open the doors to heaven or hell."

In 1994 I was driving west out of Norton, in Wise County, the farthest reach of Virginia before it meets eastern Kentucky, about seventy-five miles south of Frank Hutchison's territory, as far from Thomas Jefferson's Virginia as the other side of the world.

I was heading toward Whitesburg, just over the Kentucky line into Letcher County, like Wise shaped by the sudden hollows of the always looming landscape and marked by old coal mines, coke ovens, slag heaps, and the flimsy housing of company towns. The route was a back road through the woods, ordinary if somehow imposing, like almost any road in the area, until it began to seem odd.

It was completely quiet; nothing moved. No birds sang, no small mammals darted across the blacktop. In Louisiana, Mississippi, Alabama, Tennessee, Virginia farther east, the roads were a zoo, or anyway a natural history museum: dead raccoons, possums, squirrels, snakes, skunks, cats, dogs, armadillos. But here, plainly because a century of coal fires and coke smoke had driven off the wildlife—here, I would say later to a professor in Arkansas and to a friend in California, there was no roadkill. They both had exactly the same reply. "You know why there's nothing on those roads? Because as soon as those hillbillies hit something, they jump right out of their cars and eat it!"

This was only months after voters in Cincinnati, just over

the border from Kentucky, repudiated a civil rights measure so sweeping, according to numerous commentators, as to reveal the whole idea of legal protection against discrimination for the joke it had become: not only had the city's human rights ordinance prohibited discrimination in housing, employment, and public accommodations on the basis of race, gender, sexual orientation, religion, age, disability, or marital status, it deemed it necessary to extend the same protection to persons of "Appalachian origin." That was the joke—a law for Li'l Abner!—and be it the joke told by the voters of Cincinnati or by my friends, the message was the same. Places such as Wise County and Letcher County were scorned ground, part of another country.

In the mountains the radio was all country, and the radio version of this terrain—the seedbed of the music that had made Nashville a new, glamorous kind of company town—was all bland. The music didn't fit. Glimpsed whole and on high, the mountains around Norton, through the Jefferson National Forest, into Daniel Boone country, could make you think no place on earth looked any different: they were that implacable. Merely hills on a map—the highest peak in Virginia doesn't reach six thousand feet—on some days they can seem bigger than anything in Colorado, rising up so suddenly an unwary traveler can find herself staring into the likes of a tornado. From one vantage point, you can see the leavings of strip mining and human devastation of the crudest kind; from another, with no sign of smoke or cut trees, you can see an entire landscape of hideouts, a world where people will never be found if they want it that way; the same view can let you imagine the land was never inhabited, not by Indians and not by

Europeans. The huge upsurges of earth and the blue haze around them can seem to say that in some impenetrable way this country can never be claimed, can never be home; the cuckoo flies on for lack of a place to light. "Men can see nothing around them that is not their own image," Marx wrote. "Everything speaks to them of themselves." Here you could look a lifetime and not see your reflection.

Not far to the east, where 23S turns onto 58E, into the Clinch River Valley, is the sylvan glade, a diorama of harmony and reassurance. Cattle graze on hillsides, everything is green, everything is defined, clear, marked off. The landscape is a backdrop to people, homes, enterprise, and leisure; everything has been made over. In the mountains where Dock Boggs worked, outside of the towns, every structure, coal shed, shack, or house, looks like an outpost, temporary, holding out or merely granted a reprieve against the day when it will join the ruins all around it.

The radio offered a slew of performers milking the ruling formula of rural nostalgia, I'm-your-pal vocals, bright old-timey fiddles, and happy endings. The resentment and defensiveness—the embarrassment and shame—that is the other side of the roadkill joke or the Cincinnati law was there, but as a kind of winner's us-against-them sneer, the sneer around the edges of the smile of singers primed to sing the National Anthem at the Super Bowl if they hadn't already. The fiddles were the worst. After a bit they were semiotics, not music. Nothing was communicated but the sign of traditionalism. It wasn't that one fiddle part sounded like another, doing the same job in every tune. It was as if there were no people actually playing, as if each part came from the vault in Nashville where they keep the all-purpose fiddle sample. Leaving Whitesburg, rounding north through Jenkins, I turned back toward Norton and stuck a Dock Boggs tape in the car's cassette machine.

Named Moran Lee Boggs, after the local doctor—thus the nickname he always preferred—Dock Boggs was born in West Norton in 1898, the youngest of ten children. The household went back a long way: the year the Civil War ended, Boggs's father turned sixteen. Beginning with three hundred and fifty acres in Harlan County, Kentucky, he sold one farm after another, each smaller than the last, to coal buyers. "When he died," Boggs told Mike Seeger, "he never owned enough land to bury him on."

The senior Boggs ended up in Norton as a blacksmith and a gunsmith. The spot was first explored by a white man in 1750 and in 1785 named Prince's Flat, after William Prince, the first man to raise a house there; just four years before Boggs was born the town was renamed for Eckstein Norton, president of the Louisville and Nashville Railroad. It was a signal transition. From this point on, the life that people like Boggs's father carried into Norton lived on mostly in music, in styles and songs that in the 1920s were already called old-time. Real life was defined by coal and the rail cars that hauled it away.

Educated in a one-room school open three months a year—the town lacked the money to pay a teacher for more—Boggs went into the mines at twelve, in 1910, earning seven cents an hour for a ten-hour day; after that he taught himself with a dictionary, the Bible, and a speller. For most of the rest of his life he followed mine work back and forth between Wise and Letcher counties. In 1954 mechanization left him permanently unemployed and destitute, dependent on his wife's vegetable garden and their church, until Social Security and a United Mine Workers pension began when he turned sixty. Boggs had pawned his banjo in the 1930s; some time before Mike Seeger found him he retrieved it and began practicing.

It was in the 1920s, when Boggs was in his own twenties, that he first lived a life outside of common expectation and market determinism—that he discovered a kind of freedom, or mastery, that he would soon lose.

In 1918, with six hundred dollars saved, Boggs married; Sara Boggs soon took ill and Boggs found himself twelve hundred dollars in debt. These were large sums in their place and time: enough to buy a house, enough to place a lien on the future. Self-willed and ambitious, Boggs had thought he was set. He'd rented a farm, subcontracted part of a mine: "I was making as much as any foreman. Had a whole section of the mine under me, and me just twenty years old. I was drawing more money than five or six, eight men." His wife's illness forced them back to her family's home in Letcher, and Boggs lost his job; it was given to two men, both of whom quickly cleared enough to buy their own farms.

At the same time Boggs's music, first found as part of family life, was edging him toward public life. As a small boy he followed a guitar player called Go Lightening, who lived in the black settlement of Dorchester, above Norton; Boggs would beg him to play "John Henry." From a black string band that he watched as part of a Dorchester crowd, and from Jim White, a black banjo player with blue eyes, he got the idea of playing the banjo like a blues guitar, picking the notes separately; the white musicians he'd seen all claw-hammered the strings up and down, producing in comparison an undifferentiated flurry of sound. Letting the notes stand out from one another, you could speak more clearly; you could speak to others as others had spoken to you. You could pass it on: the "thrill," as Boggs remembered it, that shot "from the top of my head to the soles of my feet."

Boggs's sisters taught him ballads; his brother-in-law Lee Hunsucker taught him sacred songs and played him blues records. From one Homer Crawford, a traveling photographer, he learned "Country Blues." It was just an old song called "Hustling Gamblers" with a more salable title, Boggs always said—in the 1920s, the word "Blues" was slapped onto every sort of tune—really just a variant of "Darling Cory" or "Little Maggie." It was as commonplace as any piece in the mountains. Boggs performed it as if it were the story of his own life, as if it were coming out of his mouth for the first time anywhere.

He listened to the radio. He found himself especially in tune with women's voices. He loved Sara Martin, famous for her work with Fats Waller and the W. C. Handy Band; from her he took "Sugar Blues" and "Mistreated Mama Blues," probably never catching "Death Sting Me Blues," a record she made in 1928, just before quitting the blues for gospel. He heard Rosa Henderson's light, swaying, charming "Down South Blues," which went through him and came out unrecognizably harsh and sardonic, funny and cruel; Fletcher Henderson's piano accompaniment disappeared into Boggs's cantering banjo. In his family, Boggs said, "four, five, six maybe ten, twelve pieces is all they could play." Boggs was becoming a musician, a person who, if only in his own mind, still far away from any notion of professionalism, might pursue a secret calling. He played for family and friends, for neighborhood socials and dances; for a little money he took his banjo into pool rooms and barbershops.

For real money he went into moonshining. Sara Boggs could not have children and must have feared losing her husband; as a devout woman she hated Boggs's music as a road to a fast life, to hell, and bootlegging only made the road wider, but there was nothing for it. Boggs was determined to free himself from debt. Soon he was always armed, even in his own house. Conflict with his wife led to mistrust and suspicion between Boggs and her family. His own business was dangerous—on Guest River below Norton, where Boggs was living, whiskey men regularly went down in shootouts over bribes and turf.

Boggs's corner of Virginia was a place of violence, economically unstable, socially chaotic. "It was dangerous," Boggs said, just "to get on the highway. People a-shootin' in the road, shooting everyway, carrying guns, everybody carrying revolvers, and they'd shoot to hear 'em pop like you'd shoot firecrackers. I was standing in my own doorway, and a fella down the road, about a hundred and fifty yards, pulled out his pistol and shot, shot right inside of the door. One foot from where I was standing. I emptied my pistol right down toward where the shot came from."

One of Boggs's schoolteachers was killed, over nothing, he remembered; one of his brothers and two of his brothers-in-law were murdered. "I've had I don't know how many first cousins killed," he said, "and I've had some first cousins kill some, too." In 1928, when a lawman named Doc Cox broke into Boggs's house and grabbed Sara Boggs as a shield—

"Aiming to, I reckon, to push her between me and him so he could maybe kill me and me couldn't get a shot at him"—Boggs threw down on the man, drove him and his deputy out of his house, and was over the border and into Kentucky by nightfall, not returning to Virginia for more than three years, when Cox was killed: "One of my friends killed him." With the events of his own childhood shading back into the stories he had heard his father tell, Boggs grew up in the specter of notorious local feudists Clayton Jones and Devil John Wright, the famous killer Tad Hall, who shot the Norton sheriff dead in the streets of his own town, and Doc Taylor, a physician and quadruple murderer who escaped from Wise County into West Virginia by train—in a casket. He was hanged in Wise when Boggs was a boy; so were at least five others. Emry Arthur, who wrote "Man of Constant Sorrow," and who backed Boggs on guitar in 1929, "couldn't reach the chords," Boggs said. "He'd been shot through the hands. Bullets went through his hands."

A deep well of violence within Boggs himself opened; he began a war with himself that despite long interludes of peace would last the rest of his life. He was arrested for fights and beatings. He beat one of his wife's brothers nearly to death over fifty-two dollars: "The blood was just squirtin'—I guess sometimes squirtin' three feet high." When it was over an onlooker pronounced judgment in words Boggs never forgot. "Looks like Dock had a little mercy on Dave," he said. "He's part human."

Feeling overmatched by his wife's family—"They had a tendency to be overbearing and kind of run over me. . . . I didn't know what they might start something with me"—he determined to kill them all. "I had it all planned," he said. "How I was going to do it."

I done made up my mind that if I did it I was gonna kill all's in the house. The old man, the old lady, the boys, everyone's there, I swear, I gonna kill everyone of 'em. And tell my own tale about it. Go to court, give myself up. "Well, why'd you kill the old lady?" "Well, she got in the way of a bullet." Ha ha ha ha. That's the way people get killed, get in the way of a bullet, you know.

That's the way I had it figured out. It's a bad thing, a man to have it figured out in his mind—I'm talking about being *set on it*, I was set on it. And there wasn't no nervous stuff, I'm not braggin' about it or nothing like that—that's the kind of person *I was*, and if a person do enough to me today, they'd cause me to kill them. They'd have to do an awful lot to me because I'm more settled, I've got more understanding, and I know more about life, and I know more about what it's about than I did then. I was just a young fellow, hadn't read much, hadn't traveled much, only I just didn't want to be run over and walked on. I'd as much as kill someone as to be walked on. Today I'd let a fellow walk on me a little bit before I'd kill 'im.

So Boggs said as an old man, when he was sober. When he was drunk the old story came out. On that long night in December 1969, troubled by a legal dispute over a cesspool, he suddenly broke out: "I'm going over to the hardware and have them order me a snubnose .38 Special, Smith. The Smith grip. Don't want to kill nobody but if anybody fool with me, they encountering danger." Mike Seeger tried to turn the conversation in a different direction, but Boggs simply turned a corner and began ruminating over a traffic dispute: "If they hoodoo me too bad, I'm liable to end it pretty quick. If they try to take my driver's license away from me, and my rights, and my insurance, I may walk in that insurance office and clean it up, clean it out." "Don't do it, Dock," Mike Seeger said, sounding scared. "Don't do it." "If I do it I'm a dead man, I know," Boggs said, his words dropping like stones in a lake. "I know my life will be over."

All of this—it was not really about him, Boggs explained again and again. It was about the U.S.A. Patrick Henry no less than John Henry was in his testimony if you knew how to listen. He told the story in the language of a civics book, but with the pride and remorse he brought to his accounts of mayhem and jeopardy, because it was the same story.

I never did want to look at myself, or figure myself to be, to have a chip on my shoulder, or feel that I was better than anybody else, or anything like that, but I always felt this way about it: I felt that I'm just as good as the other person. We's all borned equal. Came into this world with nothin', we go out with nothin'. We all supposed to have the same chance, under our Constitution, in this world. And God give us that, too. Because some person has got a big bank account, fine home, and a lot of the world's goods, it don't make him no better than me, nary a bit better 'n me.

In its way, then, Thomas Jefferson's Virginia was not that far from Dock Boggs's; Jefferson's idealism made a true country, Dock Boggs's country or anyone's. To trace the line is simple enough, but the reality is all switchbacks. As Boggs invoked the Constitution—or, really, the Declaration of Independence—he locked into a strain of American individualism that on his ground in the 1920s had few outlets beyond outlawry, music, or unionism. To be a citizen, Boggs had to stand for himself; if he did so, he might directly risk his life or his reputation, but he might also achieve dignity, democracy's blessing on the ordinary man or woman. Thus, as a teenager, when he saw *The Standard Book of Etiquette* advertised in a catalogue, he saved the $1.50 it cost, ordered it, and read it over and over: "It helped me more than all the books in school."

People would ask me, "Why in the world are you studying stuff like that for, you just a coal miner? Why do you wants to know good English, or how to act at parties?" I said, "I think a coal miner ought to have a little sense, and know how to meet the public, and speak very good English if he's to meet the king, or the president of the United States, he ought to know how to conduct himself, and how to act, if he's figuring on going into the White House."

Thus, as a young man, he stood facing his enemies at the line that once crossed could not be erased.

I don't know why I ain't killed nobody. I just ain't got that in me. Mike, I've had a chance, people talkin' over my shoulder, telling me, "Pour it on, Dock," and me with a .38 Special in my hand, dead cocked. 'Bout the only person that— and they really needed killing. I mean if you count anyone needed killing. *"Pour it on, Dock, we'll swear you on, pour it on, pour it on."* I say no, no, I won't do it without he goes too far and they never went too far and I never poured it on. And I ain't got no blood on my hands.

Not yet thirty, brooding over his life as his desires came into focus and were blocked, as face-offs over life and death took place and were repeated, as his music began to take shape and win the hint of a response, Boggs found the curse of the sort of individualism, the sort of citizenship, by which he defined himself. His descriptions of studying for the White House and of drawing his gun make it plain: if Boggs truly did not feel himself to be better than anyone else, he felt different.

That was in the Constitution and the Declaration too—between the lines. On the fourth day of July you get to holler; like a cuckoo, you get to make a sound no one wants to hear, or so you might flatter yourself. That fantasy, the thrill within it, might be the very thing that leads you to open your mouth. But part of the charge of that thrill is a kind of terror, because the American fantasy of public mastery contains a fantasy of public suicide. "The land of the free!" D. H. Lawrence wrote, opening his little book on what he called "the old American art-speech"—"speech that contains an alien quality, which belongs to the American continent and nowhere else," an alien quality, a strangeness, that even at home made it strangers' speech—speech that, just because it belonged to the American continent, was not necessarily speech most inhabitants of the American continent wanted on it. "This is the land of the free!" Lawrence crowed. "Why, if I say anything that displeases them, the free mob will lynch me, and that's my freedom. Free? Why, I have never been in any country where the individual has such an abject fear of his fellow countrymen. Because, as I say, they are free to lynch him the moment he shows he is not one of them." Like the apprehension of the face in John Franklin Bardin's mirror, that event too is in Dock Boggs's sound.

Boggs was twenty-nine when agents of the Brunswick company—a major New York label with separate lines for "hillbilly" and "race" records—arrived in Norton to audition mountain talent. Boggs showed up at the Norton Hotel on Kentucky Avenue with a borrowed, second-rate banjo. Even with a half pint of Guest River whiskey in his stomach he was intimidated by the crowd of pickers and fiddlers: "I stood around and pitched them high as a dollar, dollar and a half at a time—I mean nickels, dimes, and quarters—to hear them play. They wasn't doing nothing but playing and I was working on a coal machine." A. P. Carter of the Carter Family failed the audition; Boggs passed.

He cut eight sides, four 78s, in New York City; the company wanted more but he demurred. Before traveling out of the Virginia mountains for the first time, Boggs went to the Norton haberdashery for a new suit, shoes to hat, socks to underwear; determined to walk the city streets with pride, he insisted on clothes that would draw no northern smiles. Unlike his father, he would not play the country fool. He'd see how those eight sides did. He'd see, it is clear—as one listens to him tell the story to Mike Seeger—if he could make the Yankee pedlar understand he couldn't take him. Perhaps it didn't occur to Boggs that the people at Brunswick realized they might never hear his like again, just as he would never again get half as good a chance.

"I thought that I might get started," he said. "That I might make, happen to put out a record that would make a hit, that I might—to where I have an opportunity, I maybe never have to work in the mines no more." It all floods back as he speaks nearly forty years later, his words breaking out of their sentences, the story caught in his throat, along with all the stories untold and lives unlived. In the late 1920s Dock Boggs and Bascom Lamar Lunsford were two mountain singers recording traditional songs for the same New York record company, and a quarter century later Boggs's "Sugar Baby" and Lunsford's "I Wish I Was a Mole in the Ground" would appear side by side on the *Anthology of American Folk Music*; in between, in 1939, Lunsford sang in the White House for President and Mrs. Roosevelt and King George VI.

Boggs quit the mines after his records were released, drew crowds to schools and houses, formed the Cumberland Mountain Entertainers, and signed a booking agent, but the records sold mostly where he carried them. Boggs recorded only four more songs in the 1920s—generic blues and sentimental parlor lyrics written by a Richlands, Virginia, variety store owner named W. E. Myers. Myers would send his ballets, or poems, to musicians he liked, hoping they would put his words to music. He'd release the results on his own Lonesome Ace label, which featured both a picture of *The Spirit of St. Louis* and the slogan "WITHOUT A YODEL," because Myers loved Charles Lindbergh and he hated yodeling. Boggs cut "Will Sweethearts Know Each Other There," "Old Rub Alcohol Blues," and two other Myers efforts in Chicago in 1929; then the Depression destroyed the southern economy and Myers went bankrupt. Boggs pressed on, writing to record companies, traveling to Atlanta for a session with Okeh, which shut down just before he arrived, finally surrendering when a recording date with Victor in Louisville fell through because Boggs, knocking on the doors of his now-penniless friends and relatives, could not raise the train fare. He drank hard, leaving home, even leaving the state for a week at a time, running to where no one would recognize him on the last day of a ten-day drunk, always returning home, where his wife looked right through him. Days like the one in Jenkins became less frequent, more precious in memory and less valuable as life. Again and again his wife gave him an ultimatum: she refused to sleep with him unless he gave up his music, and finally, not long into the 1930s, he did.

Already, though, he had set down a handful of performances so strangely demanding as to lead a listener to measure what he or she knew of the American voice—any emblematic American voice, Huckleberry Finn's, Robert Johnson's, Franklin Roosevelt's, Barbara Jordan's—against Boggs's, to see if what one knew could pass his test. Already, he had created a small body of work so dissonant that like black gravity it can seem to suck into itself whatever music might be brought to bear upon it. Already, as Nathaniel Hawthorne wrote of a Shaker elder nearly a hundred years before, he "had joined in the sacred dance, every step of which is believed to alienate the enthusiast from earth."

In "Country Blues," a Brunswick disc that first reappeared as the seventy-third selection on the *Anthology of American Folk Music*—a Smithville password that presses and pulls inside such Kill Devil Hills standards as "Hills of Mexico" and "This Wheel's on Fire"—a wastrel antes up to pay the piper one last time. As he looks back across the ruins of his life he is guilty but distant even from his sins, let alone their punishment, and there is more foreboding in the distance than in the guilt. Perhaps that is what makes the singer's testimony even more convincing than it has to be.

> . . . a-drinking and a-shooting and a-gambling
> At home I cannot stay

In the singer's detachment, there's an anticipation of Willie Dixon's satisfied monologue in Howlin' Wolf's otherwise desolate 1961 version of "Going Down Slow" ("Now, I did not *say* I was a millionaire," Dixon deadpanned, gold tooth gleaming. "But I have spent more *money* / Than a millionaire"). There is also the cold terror of a man who knows that though he lives he has already drunk himself to death. "All around this old jailhouse is ha'nted," he says, but the claim is nothing to the image he finds to seal it. "Corn whiskey has surrounded my body," he says, wiping out the happy blues fantasy of a river of whiskey and the singer a diving duck; the jail cell fills with whiskey, and as the singer reaches for the last layer of air at the ceiling, he treads his own water.

Judgment Day is coming—but the singer will judge nothing, not the world and not himself. In some part of his soul he knows that if the citizens of his town even notice his death, as decent people they will have to conceal as much envy as delight.

> Go dig a hole in the meadow, good people
> Go dig a hole in the ground
> Come around all you good people
> And see this poor rounder go down

The great Irish tenor John McCormack once defined the element that separated the important singer from the good one: "You have to have the yarrrragh in your voice." What Boggs has is similar, but less physical, more moral, more secretive: a yowl. It is a smaller, fluttering presence, a creature darting out of a mouth and into the words of a song like a tiny, magical bird; it draws attention not to the singer, as a real person, but away from him, so that he too becomes a presence, a specter, his own ha'nt. The sound seems loosed from any singer's intentions, any lesson in the song. It is an imp that disorganizes all that is held together by rhythm and melody; it confuses performance with visitation, spinning words away from their lines, mere vowels into huge syllables their words do not recognize and can barely hold. "The whirligig," the English musicologist Wilfrid Mellers captioned a photo Boggs posed for in New York in 1927, and the word brings up lines Alexander Pope wrote in 1728, in *The Dunciad*: "whirligigs, twirl'd round by skilful swain / Suck the thread in, then yield it out again." That's the sound Boggs makes in "Country Blues." Time and again, a word—"people," "money," "buried," "empty," "troubles"—is cast out, reeled in, the word rolling and then violently bucking like a patient in a mental ward convulsing in restraints. The words break as their unwieldy new phonemes drag the listener out of whatever life she might have flattered herself to have inhabited and into the air—

burrrerrrrrreeeeed

—while some words, seemingly harmless, dive right out of the song.

One could speak of Boggs accompanying himself on his banjo, but that's not how it feels. The banjo creates a tremendous internal drive in "Country Blues," carrying the storyteller not forward, to his certain appointment, but elsewhere. Small notes, blues notes weighted down with a kind of nihilistic autonomy, a refusal to recognize any maker, any master in the music, barely rise to meet descending vocal phrases, and they don't make it all the way up—rising, at first, as if to support what's being said, then dropping away as if the music, so much older than the words, has heard it all before. Here the banjo can seem to take over the song, racing across the heroic peaks and valleys its quickening pace has revealed, until a ragged word appears to meet it and turn its course. But always, the sound the banjo makes pulls away from the singer, discrediting him as a fact, his performance as an event: the sound is spectral, and for seconds at a time a specter is what it turns the singer into. When this happens, to the degree that he has made himself felt before you, it's as if you can see right through him, as a physical fact, to a nowhere beyond.

The banjo leaps the hollows of the singer's voice, as if to bear him away, pressing a queer sort of fatalism: death is looking him in the face and it is in a hurry. But the singer is telling his own tale and he has dug his own grave. The face of death in his song is his own face, and so, for a last moment, the singer stands his ground against himself. Here the masks he has worn—the banjo's implacable solipsism in the face of the singer's wish to tell his tale to others, the singer's heedless solipsism in the face of the world that will not listen—fall away. The mask ceases to function, there is no longer any protection it can offer, and everything is revealed, even if this must be an incident without narrative, a breach in time that cannot be denied any more than sound and words can describe it.

At the close of the song ("When I am dead and buried / My

pale face turned to the sun"—Boggs worms you into the old, common lines, traveling from tune to tune from decade to decade, until you sense the racial transformation they hint at, the distant promise of a man shedding his skin, like a snake, like a lizard in the spring), everything moves faster, as if to say *Get it over with.* "Can't you spare me over till another year?" Boggs would ask in "Oh Death," and you can imagine Death's reply: *Sure thing, Jack, what the hell. It's no skin off my back. Anyway you sound like you checked into this hotel a long time ago.*

Across the street from the Norton Hotel, boarded up and scheduled for demolition (a move blocked by a citizens' effort to preserve it as a working landmark), I bought a copy of the *Coalfield Progress*: "A progressive newspaper, serving our mountain area since 1911." The paper announced a lecture by Virginia writer Sharyn McCrumb called "Keepers of the Legends," which was fitting, since keeping legends is what McCrumb does for a living. Born in North Carolina, she started out writing comic mysteries set in England and moved on to "The Ballad Books"—serious, complex mysteries set in the Appalachian highlands, each taking its title from one of the murder ballads that cling to the mountains like smoke. These are painful, historically ambiguous books, where legendary characters take on flesh and modern-day men and women lose layers of their personalities to mythic avatars—as with the third of the series, *She Walks These Hills*. Named for a line in "Long Black Veil," a 1959 country hit for Lefty Frizzell that the Band revived for their first album, *Music from Big Pink*, in 1968—"an instant folk song," said co-composer

Danny Dill, and the tune did feel too old to date—the book was about mountain women who killed their children, in 1993 and in 1779. Published in the fall of 1994, when the story of Susan Smith's drowning of her sons was breaking, as House Minority Leader Newt Gingrich announced that it was only the welfare state and the ruling Democratic Party that had brought the country to such a pass where a crime so unthinkable was possible, famously declaring that in the face of such a violation "The only way to get change is to vote Republican," McCrumb's tale threw the national orgy of pious incredulity over Smith's crime into ordinary light. In McCrumb's pages, both "Long Black Veil" and her characters make it plain that what most distinguished Smith from the countless Americans who each year kill their children was her wish to dramatize herself—claiming, before confessing, in a plea that reached every corner of the republic, that her children had been ripped from her arms by a mysterious black stranger—her wish to become, if only for a moment, precisely the sort of mythic figure the old ballads were made for.

In *If Ever I Return, Pretty Peggy-O*, the first of McCrumb's mountain mysteries, a folk singer is talking to a sheriff about one of the old ballads, "Knoxville Girl," which turns out to be a clue to a present-day murder. "It's a local variant of 'The Wexford Girl,' an English broadside," she says.

It dates from around 1700, but people have always changed the words to fit whatever local crime is current. "The Oxford Girl." "The Cruel Miller." There's always a new dead girl to sing about. Always a dead girl. . . . Isn't it funny how in the American versions, they never say why he kills her. She's pregnant, of course. . . . So many songs about that. "Omie Wise." "Poor Ellen Smith." . . . So many murdered girls. All pregnant, all trusting.

"Pretty Polly" was another: the story of young rambler Willie, who one night leads Pretty Polly to her already-dug grave. Perhaps the oldest of the songs in its family, it might be McCrumb's basic text; in English versions Polly's pregnancy is part of the tale. Yet whatever was stripped from the tune in America, something more, perhaps Bob Dylan's harried insistence on mystery as "a fact, a traditional fact," came into play. Take away the fact on which a story turns, and other stories, carrying new wishes and fears, take its place; as they become new facts, the story's characters may begin a great migration, to all the corners of the heart.

As "Pretty Polly" sailed off from its origins as "The Gosport Tragedy" or "The Cruel Ship's Carpenter," Polly could still appear after her murder as a ghost, carrying her baby in her arms; when the ship of the song reached the new world, Willie began to move back and forth between Polly's tune and the cuckoo's. Passed along in many different forms for centuries throughout the South, in the late 1950s and '60s "Pretty Polly" was being sung in all the folk enclaves of the northern cities. Bob Dylan sang it in Minneapolis in 1961; two years later in New York he took the melody for his "Ballad of Hollis Brown," where following a newspaper report of mass murder in South Dakota, Willie changes his name, marries Polly, becomes a farmer, sires five children, and when his farm fails shoots his family and fires his gun into himself. In 1991, in "Polly" on Nirvana's *Nevermind*, the murdered girl and murdered wife return as one, clinging to life as she is raped and tortured. "Polly want a cracker," Kurt Cobain sneers as one of the rapists. As the rapist sneers, in some collective unconscious of the tradition itself—in that spot where all the victims in all the ballads plot their revenge—he seals his guilt. Singing so idly, he has opened the window for the talking bird that so long before witnessed the crime in "Henry Lee," the ballad that in 1993 Dylan recorded as "Love Henry." "Hush up, hush up, my parrot, she cried," Dylan sang of the bird that in many variants takes the name "Pretty Poll," "Don't tell no news on me—"

Fly down, fly down, pretty parrot, she cried
And light on my right knee
The doors to your cage shall be decked with gold
And hung on a willow tree

I won't fly down, I can't fly down
And light on your right knee
A girl who would murder her own true love
Would kill a little bird like me

And always a new dead girl, the song always finding room for her. In 1995 the Chicago country singer Cindy Norton, who performs as Ninnie, saw the brother of a childhood friend on the evening news, with the report that he had killed his wife and was found holding their baby, chanting "I didn't mean to do it" over and over. Thus in Ninnie's "Pretty Polly," a dirge so slow each word seems to scrape the ground, Willie has become Gary, who now carries in his arms not a baby, as Polly did in the beginning, but Polly herself: " 'I didn't mean to do it,

Polly' / Was all that he could moan / Was all that he could moan / Was all that he could moan."

For all of that, there is no sense of pass-it-on in the peculiar aura of Dock Boggs's 1927 recording of "Pretty Polly," and none in the version he recorded in 1963. What one hears is a mythic occurrence, but an occurrence nonetheless: two people, appearing before you, one of whom kills the other, and no myth bears the crime away. There is a supernatural tinge to the song as it emerges from Boggs's performance, even though nothing unearthly is named or even hinted at; the sulfurous odor comes up because as Boggs tells it there seems to be no will in the story, only fate, or ritual.

Bang, bang, bang, the song starts, each note standing out on its own, the banjo tolling its bell, everything slow; as the song moves on Boggs drags out his vowels, this time every one on a flat plane. The man who is telling this story is in no hurry to finish it; he knows what is waiting at the end of every line. There are no surprises, there is no possibility of surprise. That's what is so murderous about the performance.

Boggs's "Pretty Polly" is a killer's confession, queered away from its narrator. "I used to be a rambler, I stayed around in town, I used to be a rambler, I stayed around in town," the singer begins in the first person; he disappears from the story, then reappears in the fourth verse in the third person, where he remains, farther and farther from his own crime with each spadeful of dirt on Polly's grave. Within that remove is a hint of the catacombed archives of utopia and morbidity beneath American highways of practical enterprise and manifest destiny. The small, circular pattern the banjo traces around each breath of the rambler's tale reaches deep into the nineteenth century for the single ancestor of its cadence. It is an echo of the great chant of the Shakers, "Come Life, Shaker Life."

The Shakers were like one of the old British ballads come to life and seeking death—seeking deliverance. With dim origins in the Brethren of the Free Spirit of medieval Europe and the Ranters of mid-seventeenth-century England, they emerged in about 1769 as a tiny dissident sect in Manchester. Led by a young charismatic called Mother Ann Lee, they traveled to America in 1774, and despite constant, virulent persecution by both officials and the public at large—"More than once," the historian Stephen J. Stein writes, "Ann Lee was dragged from her bed, abused by mobs, and examined physically to see if she was a man, a woman, or a witch"—began to flourish in the years after the Revolution. Of all American perfectionists, they were the most severe. The heart, a follower remembered Ann Lee saying, in words Emily Dickinson could have used, was "like a cage of unclean birds"; to the Shakers, the world was evil, and god in heaven was waiting for true revelators to end it. Judgment was no day but history seeking its final curtain, and judgment was under way. To do god's work, the human race, corrupted beyond grace, would have to end itself. Thus the Shakers came together to wait out their time on earth in forebearance of all desire. The sect would bring more and more of god's creatures into its fold, and humankind would begin to dwindle, until that time "when," as Hawthorne had a Shaker elder say, "the mission of Mother Ann shall have wrought its full effect,—when children shall no more be born and die, and the last survivor of mortal race, some old and weary man like me, shall see the sun go down, nevermore to rise on a world of sin and sorrow!"

A death that pure is in "Pretty Polly," with Boggs's hard count—"Pretty Polly, Pretty Polly, come take a walk with me / Pretty Polly, Pretty Polly, come take a walk with me"—matching the count of the Shaker plea, taken fast, the high voices of Shaker sisters reaching, reaching, shaking, whirling:

Come life, Shaker life
Come life eternal
Shake, shake out of me
All that is carnal

But while there is a wholeness in the Shaker chant that makes it shine, a wholeness that folds the attainment of the last trump into the wish for it, in "Pretty Polly" the singsong cadence pits each phrase of words or melody, voice or rhythm, against whatever phrase precedes or follows it. An irrational, insoluble opposition is established, and it becomes the premise of the entire performance.

As clearly as the narrator sees, the listener, like Polly, is given only haze. You can imagine that Polly's pregnancy is missing from the American song not because of Puritan prudery but because of the secret Puritan recognition of those places in the heart that cannot be reached, wishes that can't be explained, not even explained away—you can imagine that the motive has been removed from the song because that way the song is scarier. Or is it that the tension between the singer's foreknowledge and his victim's trust, his second sight and her blindness—a gap that only death can close—makes a mystery that is the song's true subject? The evil in Boggs's singing, its psychotic momentum, far outstrips any need to do this to achieve that; its only purpose, you can believe, is the announcement of its own existence, a revelation that is its own reward. *"Love and produce! Love and produce!" "Destroy! Destroy! Destroy!"* Given the chance to destroy, Boggs's performance asks, who wouldn't take it?

Boggs's drama is sadistic in its pauses—the pauses of a man who, with his lover waiting at the end of Kentucky Avenue, admires his reflection as he passes the store windows of his town, the narrator stepping back from his story to gaze upon his own loveliness. It is preordained; that is the beauty of it. He will lead her over hills and valleys so deep. Taking her by the hand, he will walk her through the woods, until they are near the banks of the river, and show her her grave. But before that he will pause, and watch the story begin. "Oh, where is Pretty Polly?" he asks, as if he doesn't know, as if already there isn't blood on his hands, the hands he already rubs together, not to rub away a stain, but in anticipation: "Oh, yonder she stands."

The mask—whatever its practical uses, as it is assumed upon waking, before it is removed for sleep, by the Puritan or the pioneer, or their shades lurking in any American—emerges from the dynamic of the new world. It is the face of a new nation where all are presumed free to invent themselves, to make themselves up out of nothing, just as, with each unspoken wish or finished act, all are making up their country. That is the credo, and no matter how many are at any time forbidden to utter it, American women, American blacks, and on, and on, sooner or later it will shape them all, and all will say it out loud, as blessing or curse: the presumption of self-invention is the presumption of beginning with nothing, which is the presumption of equality. As a credo it is an argument you have with yourself far more than with others, to convince yourself, since no one would publicly profess disbelief: "We's all borned equal. We all supposed to have the same chance, under our Constitution." "Negroes were not less American than anybody else," the omni-American critic Albert Murray said to interviewer Tony Scherman in 1995. "They expected the same thing." "But there was—is—a huge contradiction between the ideology of equality and the reality," Scherman said. "That's not as important as you might think," Murray said. "We got all those Negroes segregated? That's unimportant, compared to the fact that they shouldn't be. It's not the fact that they're segregated but the fact that if they were segregated in another society, it wouldn't even matter. Can't you see that?"

The old America of the founders, of the Puritan, the pioneer, and the lawgiver, was always present, Murray said—it was all about "free enterprise. Don't reduce it to economics; I'm talking about free endeavor: an experimental attitude, an openness to improvisation. The disposition to approach life as a frontiersman, you see, so piety does not hold you back. You can't be overrespectful of established forms; you're trying to get through the wilderness to Kentucky"—and the point was not "that if something doesn't work for everybody, it doesn't work. The important thing is that the official promise existed. 'All men are created equal.' Now you had something to appeal to."

This was the America shared by a Harlem jazz theorist and

an Appalachian banjo stylist; its ideal was the birthright of both. The trap set by this ideal, though, was made especially for people like these, for the person who had something to say, for the artist, for whoever used the common tongue to speak what in any given place or time might sound like a foreign language. Lived out, among one's fellow citizens, in one's town—in Smithville, Kill Devil Hills, or Norton, Virginia, each of them, in its own way, Murray's town as well as Boggs's—the presumption of equality can freeze into the presumption that all are the same, that all see the good in the same way, that all want the same things for the same reasons. Because this can never be true, the presumption that all are the same becomes the need of each uniquely perverse individual—the black intellectual preaching Jeffersonianism in Cracktown, the white Virginia miner hoarding the claims of death against life's blandishments—to appear as if he or she were just like everybody else. Thus the mask of equality covers subjectivity, and the masked voice that issues from it, speaking quietly, reasonably, without affect, turns all other voices into those of cranks, and so when the reasonable person one day becomes a crank and begins to rant, when he kills his family and himself, when he walks into the place of work where those who have troubled his life stand and kills them all, he says no real thing. He has simply removed himself from the community; giving speeches that make no sense and performing acts that have no meaning, he is at best part human.

The mask that turns others into cranks is the mask Dock Boggs removed to sing "Pretty Polly" or that the song as he felt it dissolved as he sang. "Nothing will protect you" in "the old America," Steve Erickson writes, no "secret identity or reconstructed tissues or unmarked grave or faked death." All of those things are present in Boggs's deepest performances; "Country Blues," "Danville Girl," "Sugar Baby," and "Pretty Polly" are nothing if not faked deaths. But they were not made for protection—they are the faked deaths of the defiant sinner, the unwilling killer, the determined flagellant, the rounder too smart for his own good, Arthur Dimmesdale and Susan Smith together placed on the confessor's block by a voice that in its Gothic tangle says what they remain afraid to say.

Driving around Norton, one can see the marks of a cultural war, the war between the likes of "Country Blues" and the churches and signs that dot the landscape: "JESUS IS THE ANSWER," "JESUS IS WAITING," or, in a hollow, a modest, somehow implacable white frame house, with three stark crosses underneath the words "HOUSE OF PRAYER." Against the obvious and occult desires one can hear in Boggs's music—the wish for a private exile, the lust for an endless drunk, the secret fantasy of a public unmasking of the face no one wants to see—the church promised a world where all would stand unmasked in fellowship before god, in a gathering of scorned saints recognizable only by god and by themselves: the nihilist singer's final temptation, beckoning him to surrender his refusal. With his music far behind him, Boggs finally did. In 1942 he experienced conversion and joined his wife's church, the Old Regular Baptists, the fifteen thousand or so self-named "peculiar people" who range from Frank Hutchison's part of West Virginia to the Boggses' patch of Kentucky and Virginia.* Boggs became a community man. In the worst weather, in the worst times, he and others collected food and clothes for those who had none and carried them over bad roads in the dead of night; speaking of it, Boggs broke down weeping at the memory of the misery he served. In later years, when Boggs returned to his music, members of the Free Pentecostal Holiness Church of God on Guest River, his church then, would send him unsigned letters condemning him for his apostasy.

"He's going to sober up now, he said," Sara Boggs said in December 1969, the morning after Boggs's long night of drinking, when he could not stop talking. "I'm going to get him started back to going to church again," she told Mike Seeger. "He'll be a different man when you see him again." "I couldn't be much of a different man," Boggs said. "Whenever you're upright, honest, fair and square, what else can you be?" He began to rail against false prophets, preachers who took money from people whose faces they never looked into. "It's a lot worse, that preachin' is, than musicians," he said. "They do earn the money. They have to play for it."

"I want to get at peace with myself and the Lord, you see," Boggs said. "That there is the main thing that I want to do. I'm not wantin' to make no big showin' as I'm such a big Christian, or anything like that. But I want to live a life that

*"But ye are a chosen generation, a royal priesthood, an holy nation, a peculiar people; that ye should shew for the praises of him who hath called you out of darkness and into his marvelous light (I Peter 2:9). . . . Who gave himself for us, that he might redeem us from iniquity, and purify unto himself a peculiar people, zealous of good works" (Titus 2:14).

the people can see the sunshine shinin' through me. I mean, understand me. Not live in a shell, or live a hypocritic life." To make a living, he was still singing "Sugar Baby" and "Pretty Polly" in 1969, and though there was no shell on those songs or hypocrisy inside them, no sunshine could shine through them either. Around Norton twenty-five years later, there wasn't a song on the radio that would have dreamed of writing a check Jesus couldn't cash.

S E V E N

CITY ON A HILL

Kill Devil Hills is a place where symbols clash with metaphors; it's also a place where people simply go about their business. On Sunday the streets are busy. Mrs. Henry's boardinghouse has tipped the "NO" down on the "VACANCY" sign. The potato masher has a line out her door. The only year-round Halloween shop in the nation has its new mask shipment in the display window: the big sellers are Buster Keaton, Jonathan Edwards, Calvin Coolidge, Barbara Stanwyck (choose between the cardshark from *The Lady Eve* or the nurse in *Double Indemnity*), Jimmie Rodgers (in blackface), a reversible Natty Bumppo/Chingachgook, the Invisible Man (Ralph Ellison model), Dana Wynter and Sam Peckinpah (from *Invasion of the Body Snatchers*), plus Charles Bronson, Henry Fonda, and Claudia Cardinale (from *Once Upon a Time in the West*—Leone's been previewing the five-hour rough cut here for weeks). A three-card monte dealer drawls lines like a comic at a stag night to pull her marks: "Get your rocks off / Get your rocks off / Get your rocks offa *me*," ever more slowly.

Down the alleys, one can glimpse people leaning against walls, sitting on the sidewalk, standing in doorways, a woman talking to herself about lies told long ago on a riverbank, a man mumbling to himself about hidden lace and lost chances. A thin woman with a determined stride passes by, wrapped in faded blues and whites, with a scarf over her mouth and a sun bonnet drawn so tightly one can't make out more of her face than an angry pointed nose, a pallor, and wisps of gray hair. "If the ladies were squirrels, with them bright bushy tails," croons a red-eyed, red-haired layabout with an air of impotent detachment, with the opiated ease of a man with a lifetime of worthless self-reflection ahead of him, "why, I'd fill up my shotgun, with rock salt and nails."

On main street, a crazy man with a rusted sword and dressed in what once must have been a priceless coat of rich green cloth—one can still see the strange clasps, embroidered in the shape of frogs, holding the coat closed over his huge belly—says he is Matthias, Prophet of the God of the Jews, that he is the King of France, that he is Belshazzar, that he is Daniel, that he can read the writing on the wall. He draws a few onlookers; they soon drift off to join a small crowd under the jailhouse window. A dozen men and women stand rapt as the elegant lament of "I Shall Be Released" comes from inside. Words rest in the air, then dissolve as a stoic, seemingly all-knowing guitar solo transcends the ability of any words to say what they mean. "He sounds like Aretha Franklin," a woman says of the invisible lead singer, wondering at how his voice can carry forgiveness when his words refuse it. "I still think they did it," a man says, "but for playing like that we ought to let them out." "They're not Leadbelly," says a second man. "They're not the

Prisonaires either," says the first man, "but they're the best this place has got." The crowd follows the local custom of slipping books through the bars in lieu of coins in the cup the prisoners aren't allowed to dangle: dog-eared paperbacks of *Peyton Place* and James Baldwin's *Another Country*, the Classic Comics edition of *Absalom, Absalom!* and Michael Wigglesworth's "God's Controversy with New-England" in its original 1662 broadside. It comes back shouted almost as soon as the paper has gone in:

> But hear O Heavens! Let Earth amazed stand;
> Ye mountaines melt, and Hills come flowing down:
> Let horror seize upon both Sea and Land;
> Let Natures self be cast into a town.
> I children nourisht, nurtur'd and upheld:
> But they against a tender father have rebell'd.

At the west end of main street, you can hear a string band begin to play and harmonize. The fiddle and the banjo bring the music into perfect balance: a sunny lilt born of practice and sympathy, the sound of people at home with each other, the ambience of a small room here in the open air. "Clouds so swift, rain won't lift," the band sings, until the crowd picks up the old chorus, crowing "Ooo-wee, ride me high" with a sway that in an instant has the whole town pitching back and forth like a single ship.

At the east end of the street, Rabbit Brown and Frank Hutchison, over from Smithville and looking for change, begin a duet on "The Titanic." Few pay them any mind, even though Rabbit Brown is an oddity—though blues can seem like a second mind in Kill Devil Hills, you don't see many black people here. "Tomorrow's the day, my bride's gonna come," the town sings with the string band, drowning out the two bluesmen, but the song ends when it runs out of verses and when it does the doomed passengers at the stern of the *Titanic* are just getting into "Nearer My God to Thee"; nobody knows how many verses "The Titanic" has. "Neeeeerrrraaaarrr my gwww*aaaaad* to thee," Brown croaks, strangling the tune with a satanic glee, crocodiles crawling from his eyes, cold revenge on all those going down—in 1912, black Americans knew as well as any others that for its maiden voyage, the *Titanic* was promoted not only as unsinkable but, from stateroom to steerage, from its captain to its lowest scrubber, whites-only. "Captain Smith, how's your machinery?" Frank Hutchison says directly, just like a reporter. "All right," he has the captain answer. "How's your compass?" "Settin' dead set on New York."

The song changes the mood of the town. As it fades, finally, the string band, rolling a pump organ on a flatbed, carry a dirge through the street as if its weight has bent them double. Despite the muted horns they're now playing, they move less like the second line at a New Orleans funeral than a line of flagellants. People watch but keep their distance; under the dank, forbidding tune, perhaps from just outside of town, you can hear a cuckoo. "And it never, hollers cuckoo, till . . ." someone says instinctively, and the rest of the crowd automatically finishes the line.

"Mom," says a girl, "what's 'The fourth day of July'?"

There is less at stake in Kill Devil Hills than in Smithville. The town is far more playful. There is loss and there is guilt, but little if anything is final—as opposed to Smithville, where whatever doesn't seem completed seems preordained.

That is how the music feels—and all that begins to change with a series of songs set down in August and September of the basement summer. They're taken slowly, with crying voices. Dylan's voice is high and constantly bending, carried forward not by rhythm or even melody but by the discovery of the true terrain of the songs as they're sung. Richard Manuel's and Rick Danko's voices are higher still, more exposed, though for everyone in the basement, with these songs—"Goin' to Acapulco," "Too Much of Nothing," "This Wheel's on Fire," "I Shall Be Released"—the only mask between nakedness and the invisible public of the secret songs is one of knowledge, craft, and skill.

In two of the basement songs that are part of this series—that emerge from the shifting ground laid by all the other songs—the stakes may be higher than they ever are in Smithville. In "Tears of Rage" and "I'm Not There," you can sense the presence of something that can't be found in Smithville, unless it's the keen wishfulness and utter abandonment of Ken Maynard's "Lone Star Trail," and that is tragedy. This is the sung and played embodiment of crimes that float in terms of argument and evidence but are immovable as verdicts, in their weight: sins committed, perhaps even without intent, that will throw the world out of joint, crimes that will reverberate across space and time in ways that no one can stop. What language do you speak when you speak of things like this?

You speak the language, as Bob Dylan would say in the fall of the year, recording *John Wesley Harding* in Nashville with Nashville musicians, of not speaking falsely. How do you do that? You go as far into your song as you can. When Bob Dylan asked himself how far you could go with a song—with words and melody that on paper or in your head said next to nothing and in the air made a world suspended within it—Dock Boggs always had an answer: this far, and maybe no farther.

"where i live now," Dylan wrote in the mid–1960s, for a book that would be published in 1971 as *Tarantula*, in a voice one does not have to push very hard to hear as Dylan's idea of something Boggs might have written, or wanted to, "the only thing that keeps the area going is tradition—as you can figure out—it doesnt count very much—everything around me rots . . . i dont know how long it has been this way, but if it keeps up, soon i will be an old man—& i am only 15—the only job around here is mining—but jesus, who wants to be a miner . . . i refuse to be part of such a shallow death."

Bob Dylan knew better than most that the death in Boggs's music was no shallower than the hole the singer puts Pretty Polly in. "I dug on your grave two thirds of last night," Boggs's Willie tells her, brazenly, drunkenly, proudly, as he leads her to the sacred spot, hallowed by the countless pilgrimages lovers before them have made to this shaded grove. Speaking his life to Mike Seeger, Boggs called up a context, a setting, but the tension in his story is all in his will not to be reduced to his setting, not to be taken for anybody else.

The death Boggs made wasn't shallow but faked, and it was faked because it was art, not life. As a folk-lyric song, "Country Blues" was a mild, ritualized version of the everyday life Boggs described over the years, a celebration of certain choices, a dramatized refusal to take them back. As a ballad older than any family legend, "Pretty Polly" was a mythic version of the desires Boggs felt welling up within himself, the wish for vengeance that all his life diffused into nothing here focused on a single anagogic object. In the culture of which Boggs was a part, that was what songs like these were for, if you could rise to them, or past them. Boggs could, and probably no one ever sang these songs as he did, or took them as far. As a primitive modernist, he accepted their invitation to transform commonplaces into unique emotive events, where the performer draws out what he or she has—what he is, or what she is afraid she could become—and measures it against the artifact of the occasion: the song and all the past lives that it contains. What results is not a reflection of real life for the singer any more than it is for the listener, but a vision, a *lo!* and *behold!* of possible life—lives the singer and the listener may have ahead of them, to realize or lose, lives that may already be behind them, deprived of oblivion only because of what the singer does with the song.

This is the territory of "Country Blues" and "Pretty Polly," and it's the territory of "Tears of Rage" and "I'm Not There." The difference is that the words and sounds in Dylan's new songs only seem commonplace, borrowed, transformed, resting in an aura of somehow having always been present, not made up one summer when the country was burning and five people in a Catskills basement were looking for a good way to pass the time.

"That's the sound he's got now," Bruce Springsteen said of Dylan in 1995, when he heard Dock Boggs for the first time. Springsteen was speaking of Dylan's early 1990s embrace of old music, of *Good as I Been to You* and *World Gone Wrong*. Was Springsteen hearing sound or aura? For sound—for pitch and intonation, for the unstable flatness, for the yowl—there is more of Boggs in "Like a Rolling Stone" as Dylan recorded it in 1965 than there is in "Little Maggie" as he recorded it in 1992 or "Delia" as he recorded it in 1993. In the aura, though, was the peculiar intensity of absence, and here the intensity of a vanished culture making itself felt, like a Rayograph turning up on a roll of Kodachrome you bought last week, the old America rustling in the drawers of any mall's Fotomat. "That world!" as Denis Johnson shouts in his novel *Jesus' Son*. "These days it's all been erased and they've rolled it up like a scroll and put it away somewhere. Yes, I can touch it with my fingers. But where is it?"

In 1993, two years before Bruce Springsteen heard Bob Dylan in Dock Boggs, Dylan played shows that included the new/old material of *Good as I Been to You* and *World Gone Wrong*: the Appalachian standard "Jack-a-Roe," the blues "Ragged and Dirty," the Memphis street song "Blood in My Eye." Here critic Dave Marsh heard Bruce Springsteen in Bob Dylan, and after one show he asked Dylan about that: about the question of Springsteen's then-stalled career, caught between an established audience that could produce huge sales for a greatest-hits package and an unknown audience that might have as little to say to Springsteen as they thought he had to say to them.

People like Springsteen had missed something, Dylan said, with Springsteen only eight years younger and still born too late: "They weren't there to see the end of the traditional people. But I was." What was he saying? He might have been saying that as in 1963 he watched Boggs, Mississippi John Hurt, Skip James, Clarence Ashley, Buell Kazee, Sara and Maybelle Carter—"the traditional people," standing on the Newport stage, for Dylan's cryptically perfect phrase, both as themselves and as a particularly American strain of fairy folk—he had learned something about persistence and renewal. Or he might have been saying something simpler, and harder: I saw a vanishing. He was present to witness an extinction, to see the last members of a species disappear. Thus it was left to him to say what went out of the world when the traditional people left the stage.

Where the past is in the basement tapes—what the past is—has more to do with this sort of question than with the question of any direct transmission of style or manner from one performer to another. In the basement tapes, an uncompleted world was haphazardly constructed out of the past, out of Smith's *Anthology* and its like, out of the responses people like Bob Dylan, Mike Seeger, and so many more brought to that music, its stories, and to the world—another country—implicit within it. The uncompleted world of the basement tapes was a fantasy beginning in artifacts refashioned by real people, dimly apprehended figures who out of the kettle of the folk revival appeared in the flesh to send an unexpected message. The vanished world they incarnated—as history, a set of facts and an indistinct romance; as a set of artifacts, as a work of art, complete and finished—was going to die, and you were going to be the last witness. Through your own performance, whenever it might take place, in 1963, 1965, or 1966, in 1967, 1992, or 1993, through its success or failure, you were to sign your name to the death certificate. You were to certify that a certain race of people had vanished from the earth, which was also a way of testifying that they once had been at large upon it—and as a result of your witnessing, what traces these people might have left behind were to be lodged in you.

It's a possibility that instantly raises its own question. What will go out of the world with *you*? This is the sense of loss and finality that is a bridge to the sense of tragedy in "Tears of Rage" and "I'm Not There." The past that drives these songs is this past.

The playfulness, the lowered stakes of Kill Devil Hills when measured against Smithville, is the only right backdrop for tragedy here: an arena where tragedy can be discovered and yet not claim the whole of life. It will throw the rest of life into relief: only tragedy can justify a place with a name like this, can give its pleasures memory, its drunks true sleep.

Smithville is definitively settled, and in Smithville there is no tragedy because there is no guilt. Fatalism overshadows everything else. Kill Devil Hills is not only unfinished, it is transitory. At times it can feel less like a town than a depot, a stopping-off point, like so many earlier American towns—not the utopian seventeenth-century Puritan communities, with so many masked against their inability to live up to their word to follow god's, or the scattered, multiplying perfectionist settlements of the late eighteenth and early nineteenth centuries, but the frontier towns, with the guilt and doubt of utopians and perfectionists no less present in their air than the free rapaciousness of traders, con artists, and killers, all walking streets where a mask was just part of the wardrobe. Here fatalism is nothing to the daredevil. Everything seems open, any turn can be made at any time—at least until a certain dead end is reached, and then no mask, no secret identity, no change of name or face will protect you, and for a moment all masks come off.

. . .

There is nothing like "I'm Not There"—called "I'm Not There, I'm Gone" when Garth Hudson wrote down basement titles, later retitled "I'm Not There (1956)"—in the rest of the basement recordings, or anywhere else in Bob Dylan's career. It was only recorded once; unlike others of the new basement songs, which Dylan rerecorded or continued to feature on stage thirty years later, it was never sung again.

The song is a trance, a waking dream, a whirlpool, a "closing vortex," as on the last page of *Moby-Dick*: "When I reached it, it had subsided to a creamy pool. Round and round, then, and ever contracting towards the button-like black bubble at the axis of that slowly wheeling circle." Very quickly, a listener is drawn all the way into the sickly embrace of the music, its wash of half-heard, half-formed words and the increasing bitterness and despair behind them. Just as quickly, the sense that music of this peculiar nature has no reason to end, a sense that this music can have no real exit, comes into focus and fades away; for this music a sense of time is almost vulgar. It's a Memphis blues, kin to Noah Lewis's 1930 "New Minglewood Blues" or the Memphis Jug Band's 1929 "K.C. Moan," which means the precision of the rhythm is hidden in a stagger, a slide. It's a dark hollow prayer, like Buell Kazee's 1929 "East Virginia," which means it is a love song the premise of which is "I courted a fair young lady / What was her name, I did not know."

She fell into conversation with the first fat man she saw.

"What do you do?" he said, fitting two potato chips into his mouth.

I go to parties and only talk to the fat guys, she thought.

Owen was home writing. She thought of it as an act of fidelity to talk only to the unattractive guys.

She started to tell him about her jobs. She was talking on automatic pilot, hardly listening to what she was saying—instead, she was listening to Dylan. Going through the host's record collection, she'd found a bootleg album that included "I'm Not There," a legendary, never-released, never-completed song from the Basement Tapes sessions—a song that she'd heard just once, the summer after high school, and that she'd been searching for ever since. It came on as she was talking; it was even more haunting than she remembered.

She touched the fat guy's wrist. "This," she said, "may be the greatest song ever written."

The woman speaking is the heroine of a 1991 novel by Brian Morton called *The Dylanist*, and it's a wonderful thing she says—because so many people have responded the same way, at the same time realizing that "I'm Not There" is barely written at all. Words are floated together in a dyslexia that is music itself—a dyslexia that seems meant to prove the claims of music over words, to see just how little words can do. "I *believe* that she'd look upon deciding to come," the singer says, if that is what he says through the fog of his own anguish; you hear the anguish, it doesn't matter if the sentence doesn't make ordinary sense. Here a sentence is an opportunity to find a word, here *believe*, that rescues the speaker from silence, the only real alternative you can credit as "I'm Not There" unwinds its ball of string. For every phrase that seems clear—"And I cry for her veil," "I dream about the door"—there are far more that make you doubt the apparent shape of anything you've heard: "By temptation less it runs / But she don't holler me / But I'm not there, I'm gone." In this music, where as you listen words are precisely as irretrievable as the plot of a fading dream, the moment of certainty offered by the title phrase when it occurs seems priceless; superseded in the next movement by a line that has no more shape than water in your hands, that certainty seems worthless. In the forest of this song, not only can a line of words you can identify not pierce the veil hiding words you can't, the line that speaks can't match the allure of words that don't. As if it were life, the song takes the measure of language and goes elsewhere. Sometimes the music reaches such a pitch of intensity the slightest turn of a word or a note can seem to tell the song's whole story. *"Well,"* Dylan sings to start the last verse. You can't make out what follows—not words but, as so often here, just slurs, there to fill up a line until the next one opens—but there's no need. In the darkness Dylan puts into this *well* there is foreshadowing and acceptance; in this moment, the singer is already looking back on the disaster.

The music makes you listen this way. "It's almost as though he has discovered a language," the composer Michael Pisaro said, "or, better, has *heard* of a language: heard about some of its vocabulary, its grammar and its sounds, and before he can comprehend it, starts using this set of unformed tools to narrate the most important event of his life."

For all of its insistence on miasma—for an unchanging weather indistinguishable from Judgment Day—there is no drift in the performance. The progression in the melody is unnoticeable and unbreakable, the sympathy between Dylan, Rick Danko, Garth Hudson, and Richard Manuel absolute. There is no hesitation in the way Dylan pursues his story through the thicket of his abandoned words—where vows are ripped apart and survive only as non sequiturs, where "She knows that the kingdom / Weighs so high above her" and "I daren't perceive her," lines barely separated in a verse, are not clues but warnings—and there is no doubt at all as to what the story is about.

In the last lines of the song, the most plainly sung, the most painful, so bereft that after the song's five minutes, five minutes that seem like no measurable time, you no longer quite believe that anything so strong *can* be said in words: "*I wish I was there to help her*—but I'm not there, I'm gone." There is a singer and a woman in the song; he can't reach her, and he can't reach her because he won't. They might be separated by years or by minutes, by the width of a street or a thousand miles; there are moments when the music is so ethereal, so in place in a world to come, that the people in the song become abstractions, lovers without bodies: "She's my own fare thee well."

The mood grows more awful as the song moves on. As Richard Manuel's piano waits behind Dylan's vocal, as Garth Hudson continues decorating the circle of the tune, as the muscle Rick Danko's bass puts behind every wail and moan of the singing demands that you not leave, you are listening to a crime, unspeakable as a physical fact of its description, more intolerable for the listener than, it seems, for the singer, more a tragedy for you than for him. *No one,* you say to the singer, can be left as alone as you have left this woman, can be as abandoned as finally as you have abandoned her—because it is plain that this is no mere love affair that has dissolved. As Dylan sings, as the shimmering northern lights in the sound Hudson, Manuel, and Danko are making rise to meet him, a phantom town gathers around the woman in the song, and like the phantom text of the song it disappears as soon as it is apprehended.

The song grows ever more desperate, and yet with the winding of stray and floating lines back to the sealing title phrase, more stoic, too—because the singer is not simply the only person who can reach the woman in the song, he is the last person who can reach her. The town has already abandoned her; by common will or her own, she is already outside of society, ostracized, banished, a self-made mute, a hermit—the cause can't be known, but her fate can't be questioned. The singer sings with such mortification because he knows the only way he can reach this woman is to place himself outside of society—but as in Geechie Wiley's unearthly "Last Kind Words Blues," that would mean there would be no one left to sing for him, and the circle really would be closed.

Recording in 1930, Wiley, of Natchez, Mississippi, sang a song of abandonment that only "I'm Not There" can match. She begins on guitar with a heavy minor chord; then she picks a small, circling pattern around it, pulling away from the doom in the first theme, not to deny it, but as if to say *not yet; don't rush me*. There is no hurry: everyone else in the song is already dead. She might be the last person on earth: every time she sings the word "I" or "me" or "my" it stretches out, takes over whole lines of meter, drowns the words around it, as if the singer believes she may never get a chance to say another word.

The story opens with the last kind words the singer's man told her before he went off to die in the Great War—the First World War, as we call it, though the man in this song just calls it "the German war," which means the song comes forth to us with prophecy in its history. Wiley's voice is as weighted as her first chord, dragging, then erupting and fading as quickly; again the refusal to be hurried curls her words, as if like Scheherazade she knows she may not outlive her tale. She lets the last word of each verse go like a whisper down a well. "If I die, if I die," her man says through her, somewhere back in the teens, when he left; now more than a decade has passed. She has already said these words to herself more times than she could count, if she bothered to.

'f I get killed
'f I get killed
Please don't bury my soul
Iiiiiiiiiiiiiii
Cried just leave me out
Let the buzzards eat me whole

And so she responds in the only way one can respond to a wish like that. She becomes a wanderer in her own song, as alone as Ken Maynard on the Texas plain, as scared and as at peace with herself. She becomes a visionary, and what she sees is so strong as to make her shake as she sings, or you shake as you listen; you can't tell which.

The Mississippi River
You know, it's deep and wide
Iiiiiiiiiiiiiiii
Can stand right here
See my face from the other side

This is what the singer and the woman in "I'm Not There" can't do. The singer in "I Shall Be Released" can do it; that is why compared to "I'm Not There," "I Shall Be Released" is a sentimental parlor ditty. Geechie Wiley can see her face from across the Mississippi River because hers is the only face to see; all those she loves are dead, and there is no hint of community or society, of town and fellowship, anywhere in her song. The country it makes is a wasteland. In "I'm Not There" all the other characters from the basement tapes surround the house where the woman lives, and then they turn and walk away. No one will ever speak to her again. That is how deep the abandonment is, and the question it raises is the question of what crime it is that is secreted in Kill Devil Hills. A town that can leave anyone so far outside of itself as "I'm Not There" leaves the woman in its every verse may be in and of itself a crime. It may be that when abandonment or exclusion as profound as that described in "I'm Not There" is present—present as a kind of civil death, like a public stoning without stones—there can be no real town, just a collection of individuals bound together by nothing at all. Or it may be a matter of the burden the town has taken upon itself with its name, a burden that has from one place to another defined the country from the time of the Puritans on down: when you can't find the devil, you kill someone else instead. In the words of the police chief, this isn't "a Kill Devil Hills story, it's an American story."

"Listen," Bob Dylan says just before beginning the first of three taped versions of "Tears of Rage." It's a hark! a raising of

the curtain; it could hardly be more dramatic, or portentous. It's a promise, and the song that follows pays it in full.

It is now, thanks to the recording that appeared on *The Basement Tapes* album, or that opened the Band's *Music from Big Pink*, a famous beginning: "We carried you / In our arms / On Independence Day." Singing slowly, letting the phrases pull him forward against his own fatigue and sorrow, Dylan rocks the words "Independence Day" like a cradle, into

In
de
Pen
dence
Day

stepping into a story of forgetting, rejection, betrayal, and, again, abandonment—he steps carefully, but without hesitation, because there is no other story to tell.

There is a vast and darkening sweep of history in the first images of the song: a party of elders carrying a child on a beach, to a naming ceremony. Her naming, certainly; perhaps also a naming ceremony for the nation, on this day, a reaffirming that it exists, that with each new member the nation is born again. But in the music—Robbie Robertson's milky notes counting off the rhythm, Rick Danko's bass heavy, only Garth Hudson's organ and Richard Manuel's harmony carrying Dylan over the high steps to the chorus—and in Dylan's singing—an ache from deep in the chest, a voice thick with care in the first recording of the song—the song is from the start a sermon and an elegy, a Kaddish. The procession on the beach is also, in the memory the music carries, given all that happens in the song—the father scorned by his daughter, the common lessons from the nation's founding ignored, the pull of justice and right broken by the lure of riches—a funeral procession, not for the child but for the country whose birthday is recalled so bitterly.

In the confines of this song, with Manuel's piano offering up notes that are sad and sentimental and Robertson's guitar placing a line that can regret its own disdain around Dylan's pleading, Independence Day is no longer celebrated. It's a story that can no longer be told. The Declaration of Independence itself is like a rumor, as if Jefferson's declaration of an irrevocable breach between past and future, mother country and colonies, parent and child, has erased itself with words that were expunged from the Declaration's final draft. "We must endeavor to forget our former love for them," Jefferson had written of England, of all the relatives and friends and ancestors who were to be left behind. "The road to happiness and to glory is open to us, too."

That is the road followed by the daughter in "Tears of Rage," a road paved with gold, as the daughter's heart is filled with it—"as if it was a purse," the singer says so painfully, shocked by the coldness of his own words, the old word-picture of a heart of gold now ashes in his mouth. As the singer knows, the road to happiness and glory is traveled only by the trusting and the faithless; in the only story on this road, the faithless prey upon the trusting. The father tried to tell the daughter this, she didn't listen, she prospered; she has crossed over, and she is now among the faithless herself. In the shame and guilt that all but possess Dylan's singing in the first recording of the song, in the singer's despair over his failure to pass on the ethics of place and loyalty, you can see Lincoln's face as it appears in bronze busts all through *The Manchurian Candidate*, more mute and saddened in each successive scene, forced to bear witness to plots to destroy the republic Lincoln preserved.

The emotion in the song is so deep, its reach so long, that it can remind you that a certain form of that republic was present almost from the beginning of the Old World experiment in what became the U.S.A. In 1630, on board the *Arbella*, in the middle of the Atlantic Ocean, John Winthrop, already elected governor of the Massachusetts Bay Company, addressed his fellow Puritans on what awaited them in the New World. "A Modell of Christian Charity," he called his brief lay sermon, along with Martin Luther King's address to the March on Washington the only American political speech that can be compared to Lincoln's Second Inaugural. Like those that would follow, Winthrop's talk was a prophecy of national salvation and a warning of national damnation, though it was not a nation the Puritans thought they had left England to found, but a town. In its quiet, burning sense of quest and mission, Winthrop's address can be compared to the greatest shipboard oration in the annals of American letters: Ahab's speech about the mask of the white whale.

Of their own free will, Winthrop told the men and women around him, they had joined in a covenant with god and with themselves to create a new society according to god's laws. Among those laws was that of inequality, or difference: god had made some high and some low, some great and some small, some rich and some poor, so "That every man might haue need of other, and from hence they might be all knitt more nearly together in the Bond of brotherly affeccion." It was in that knitting together, "in loue," in love, that would define the town in which they would live, where no individual could stand except as part of a whole: "for it is a true rule that perticuler estates cannott subsist in the ruine of the publique." The dangers were plain, Winthrop said to his huddled community of saints: in the bright light of the New World they might forget their mission and put their covenant behind them. Falling then "to embrace this present world and prosecute our carnall intencions seekeing greate things for our selues and our posterity, the Lord will surely breake out in wrathe against vs be revenged of such a periured people and make vs knowe the price of the breache of such a Covenant."

The "onley way to avoyde this shipwracke," Winthrop said,

> is to followe the Counsell of Micah, to doe Justly, to loue mercy, to walke humbly with our God, for this end, wee must be knitt together in this worke as one man, wee must entertaine each other in brotherly Affeccion, wee must be willing to abridge our selues of our superfluities, for the supply of others necessities, wee must vphold a familiar Commerce together in all meekeness, gentleness, patience and liberallity, wee must delight in eache other, make others Condicions our owne reioyce together, mourne together, labour, and suffer together, allwayes haueing before our eyes our Commission and Community in the worke, our Community as members of the same body.

Should they keep faith, Winthrop said, the tale of their endeavors would be a murmur on everyone's lips. Should they fail the same would be true.

For wee must Consider that wee shall be as a Citty vpon a Hill, the eies of all people are vppon vs; soe that if wee shall deale falsely with our god in this worke wee haue vndertaken and soe cause him to withdrawe his present help from vs, wee shall be made a story and a by-word through the world, wee shall open the mouthes of enemies to speake euill of the wayes of god and all professours for Gods sake; wee shall shame the face of many of gods worthy servants, and cause theire prayers to be turned into Cursses vpon vs tll wee be consumed out of the good land whether wee are goeing.

"A city on a hill" was an image often invoked by Ronald Reagan during his presidency, as a sign of American triumphalism; it was found more than three hundred years before as a warning, as a prophecy of self-betrayal. The depth of the possible betrayal measures the breadth of the possible achievement. What Winthrop's speech did do was lay the wish and the need for utopia in the American story; without it there is no American history.

The Puritans disappeared, their community shattered, their backs turned on god, as Michael Wigglesworth described in words so close to those Bob Dylan used more than three hundred years after, but the notion of a blessed society of right never disappeared. Just how completely it persisted is caught in Casey Hayden's "The Movement," a 1988 memoir that in its way rewrites Winthrop's call for the community of a single body and claims that for a brief time certain people lived up to it.

Hayden wrote about her life as a civil rights worker in the South, in 1963 and for a year or two after that, with the Student Nonviolent Coordinating Committee, the group then known on every college campus by its spoken acronym, SNCC as Snick. She was one of many white and black students brought together with "thousands and thousands of poor Southern blacks who were in fact the movement . . . they were there when we got there and they were there when we left. Many of them could not read or write and they could barely speak the English language. They will never see this writing."

With that harshness, that frankness, that will not to speak falsely, Hayden describes attempts to change a system of racist exclusion and public mendacity that many believed would never change, where black Americans who tried to assert their rights as citizens were murdered and white Americans who tried to assist them were murdered in their turn. And yet, as Albert Murray and Dock Boggs argued, those rights were guaranteed, they were in the Declaration of Independence and the Constitution, they were why the Fourth of July was celebrated, and so that perfectionist egalitarian echo of the Puritans' inegalitarian perfectionism brought black Americans and white Americans together.

We were protected by our righteousness. The whole country was trapped in a lie. We were told about equality but we discovered it didn't exist. We were the only truthtellers, as far as we could see. It seldom occurred to us to be afraid. We were sheathed in the fact of our position. It was partly our naivete which allowed us to leap into this position of freedom, the freedom of absolute right action.

I think we were the only Americans who will ever experience integration. We were the beloved community, harassed and happy, just like we'd died and gone to heaven and it was integrated there. We simply dropped race. This doesn't happen anymore. And in those little hot black rural churches, we went into the music, into the sound, and everyone was welcome inside this perfect place.

The archaism of the word "integration" makes it leap out of Hayden's testimony, and it puts the edge of betrayal on her calm and maddened insistence that American blacks and whites will never again meet without a consciousness of race superseding all contact, or even the common beliefs that might have shaped them. "For a brief time in history, in our very own lives," Hayden writes, "art, religion, and politics were the same."

We wanted to turn everything not only upside down, but inside out. This is not mild stuff. It is not much in vogue now. We believed, pre-Beatles, that love was the answer. Love, not power, was the answer. All the debates about nonviolence and direct action and voter registration

—and, Hayden might have added, about whether white Americans could remain in SNCC; they were expelled in 1966—

in my view, were really about whether love or power was the answer. And we did love each other so much. We were living in a community so true to itself that all we wanted was to organize everyone into it, make the whole world beloved with us.

"The movement in its early days," Hayden says, "was a grandeur which feared no rebuke and assumed no false attitudes. It was a holy time. This is, of course, just my personal experience," which means, *rebuke that, America, if you can*: "Our side lost. But we were right. Hierarchy could not replace the circle dance." *My America, the true America, which exists only in moments, like matches struck in a cave, rebukes you.*

In "Tears of Rage," the future rebukes the past, the treasure of wealth as found in the world rebukes the treasure of liberty as called up in the Declaration of Independence and, once, celebrated on Independence Day, the day of naming. In its sense of loss, though, the song beholds a country that is whole and true to itself. In its image of wholeness, the song asks if America even exists, and if the notion of Americans, or any people, as "members of the same body"—for that is what Hayden, like Winthrop, was talking about—is not some kind of lunacy or obscenity.

Certainly it would appear so three decades after "Tears of Rage" raised the question. "The framers," Justice John Paul Stevens wrote for a bare majority of the Supreme Court in *U.S. Term Limits v. Thornton*, which barred states from imposing term limits on national representatives, "envisioned a single national system, rejecting the notion that the nation was a collection of states, and instead creating a direct link between the national Government and the people of the United States. . . . In that national Government, representatives owe primary allegiance not to the people of a state, but to the people of a nation." In 1995 this was the voice of a civics textbook. The real national conversation, from ethnic activists and multiculturalist academics to the Republican congressional majorities to racist and military groups active in all parts of the country, went in the direction of Justice Clarence Thomas's dissent, which fell one vote short of carrying the shield of law and right. " 'The United States,' " Thomas wrote, quoting former Justice Hugo Black, " 'is entirely a creature of the Constitution. Its power and authority have no other source.' " But Black would not have recognized the strange and contemptuous language of the conclusion that followed: "The ultimate source of the Constitution's authority is the consent of the people of each individual state, not the consent of the undifferentiated people of the nation as a whole."

If the people of the nation are undifferentiated, then it falls to the people to differentiate among themselves. Speaking Thomas's language, David E. Whisnant, a professor from the University of North Carolina, writing about country music, decries the concept of, in his own scare quotes, " 'national' experience"—an idea, he says, "long since rendered useless by careful analyses of regional, gender, racial, class, and occupational differences within the body politic." This wasn't Winthrop's body. If there is no national experience there can be no such thing as a national voice—no notion that, say, when Dock Boggs, or Clarence Ashley, or Geechie Wiley, or, in certain hours in the basement, Bob Dylan sang, the contours of the country's aspirations and failures, shaped according to the particular hopes these specific individuals invested in them and the particular doubts those ultimately common hopes might have produced, could be heard. There could be no nation in Dock Boggs's voice; rather one could only hear a white male working-class Virginia miner. What one can hear in King's address to the March on Washington, with all of its invoking of national icons, landmarks, and songs, is no American voice but false consciousness.

Thomas's language was not altogether different from that

spoken by white supremacist groups founding their own sovereign nations as he wrote. Their language, presupposing true, "organic" Americans, white and male, who exist under the protection of the original, pre–Civil War Constitution—as opposed to those false Americans granted false rights by the post–Civil War Constitutional amendments, and who are in fact owned by the Federal government, its property—or presupposing true Christians, made by god, as opposed to blacks, Asians, Jews, and the like, made by satan, and whom god wills be exterminated like germs—is simply the language of action. It was the language of the self-named Freemen in 1996, members of an America comprised of such convictions, or rather of Justus Township, as they called their nation: a ranch occupied near Jordan, Montana, on foreclosed land. They were Puritans, they would have said, doing god's work, blessed by him. Standing as hardy frontiersmen, once their generous subsidies from the national government lapsed, they were the pioneer holding his ground against all odds. Surrounded by the FBI after months of intimidating state authorities with their arsenal, facing charges ranging from tax evasion to fraud to violent threats against public officials backed with cash bounties placed on their heads, the group recognized no god but Yahweh and no government but its own. On the first of May an intermediary announced that "Yahweh has placed an invisible barrier around their sanctuary that no foreign enemies"—those emissaries from another, false republic—"can penetrate." It was, one could think, the ultimate American mask, or perhaps just a rising memory of a 1950s toothpaste commercial, which also promised an "invisible shield" against germs: "Gardol."

"Why must I always be the thief?" Dylan asks in "Tears of

Rage," loss and distance now overwhelming everything else in the music. He shudders through the chorus, in that first run-through of the song, shaking the words, the music an ocean of calm around him. He is the thief because what others no longer want, he has kept; this places him outside of a society that no longer exists. In his voice, the words "Independence Day" still have grandeur, but no one knows what he's talking about. The words stand out alone in the last chorus, each one a negative place in itself: "rage," "grief," "alone."

In the beholding of this song, the town it makes with the other basement songs now turns its back on itself. There is no story its inhabitants need to tell each other. All bonds are dissolved, leaving only undifferentiated individuals: without a common charter, or a holiday that celebrates the birth of the town and, in that act, the special name of each town member, each is the same, faceless for all of his or her gaiety or gloom. The man in "Tears of Rage" looks out, and he sees only people who care only for themselves. To the singer they walk like they're already dead—not like the singers he loves, who return from a talk with death with a message for the living, just bodies without souls. The man looks out and bitterness consumes him, along with the notion that the town could ever be any different or that he is wrong. Sooner or later, he knows, with the quest for a single social body gone—with the end of the quest, really, to kill the devil in the hills, in each separate body—people will begin to kill each other, even their own children. Not yet—but he can see it coming.

"A Modell of Christian Charity" might still be in the library—after all, somebody got Wigglesworth's "God's Controversy with New-England" from somewhere, and

Smithville, if the man remembers correctly, doesn't even have a library—but it hardly matters. The crime hidden in the noise and bustle of the town is that the town has killed itself; singing in the string band as it moves down main street, the man finishes his song.

In Kill Devil Hills, Sunday is winding down. With the *Titanic* at the bottom of the ocean, Rabbit Brown and Frank Hutchison back where they came from, and the string band scattered, people on the streets move slowly back to their homes, not talking. "She sank in the war," as Lawrence said of the *Pequod*, "and we are all flotsam. . . . The *Pequod* sinks with all her souls, but their bodies rise again to man innumerable tramp-steamers and ocean-crossing liners." That's the feeling now.

Still, that hasn't stopped the wiry fellow strumming an autoharp in front of the bank, trying to brighten a few faces and catch a few coins with "See that My Grave Is Kept Clean." Tipped back in a chair and pushing back and forth against a telephone pole like Henry Fonda in *My Darling Clementine*, he puts a light trot in the rhythm, loosens the melody, sings easily and warmly, an uncle entertaining at a niece's fifth birthday party, your best friend ending an all-night stomp. The tune has almost nothing in common with the already-dead rendition Blind Lemon Jefferson left behind in 1928, or for that matter with the strident, self-mutilating version of the song Bob Dylan used to close his first album in 1962. Yet the longer you listen—if you're one of the few who's stopped to listen—the deeper the smile in the music seems to be. It's not a death's-head smile; it's the smile of someone who, happily looking death in the face, knows she or he has lived a good life.

Refusing to give up what started out as such a fine day, a striking man with long blond hair and a hooked nose sets up on a backdoor stairway, at his side an electric guitarist with a little amplifier and three cronies who both leaflet whatever crowd they can draw and sing harmony on the blond man's choruses. It isn't exactly clear what he's doing here. He's a con artist, that's for sure—the shit-eating grin on his face, the lazy, self-satisfied, what-me-worry? fall in his voice tell you that—but a brilliant one: stop for a moment and he's got you for an hour. He's selling something, but he won't quite let on what, as if the trick is to make you guess—Calico? Old Indian Liver and Kidney Tonic? Wa-Hoo Bitters? Aluminum siding? Amway dealerships? Breast implants? Penile enlargements? Freemen handbooks?

He's crooning down from the top stair, with a megaphone, just like Rudy Vallee, so plain-folks suave, talking about the high fuel costs farmers run up when they can't afford a silo—that's it, he's selling silos!—then about hog back scrapers, a modern kitchen with all the conveniences, cars for a nickel, but these are all, it seems, *metaphors* . . . maybe he's a preacher. Not at all changing his tone, the pitchman changes his story, from come-on to philosophy,

> But restriction causes damage
> And damage causes lust

which is probably just another come-on: loosen up, don't be afraid, don't hold back! When he reaches the end of his pitch he just goes wild, the other salesmen at his side, hearty and true, their ringing voices making it plain that what they're really selling is America, because in America the fantasy of the country sells everything else and everything else on sale sells the country:

ALL YOU
HAVE
TO DO
IS DREAM!

With their voices still floating, a few in the small crowd joining in in spite of the taste of death in their mouths, the guitar player opens up, reflectively, searching for blues lines to anchor the crazed optimism of his bandmates, then careening headfirst without warning into an anarchy of clatter and who-cares, his version of the chorus: why *not?* The salesman, the singer, the preacher, the philosopher, whoever he is, is already enraptured by his next tale, something about a sweet young thing and how to get her, just one time, he says, and he'll be gone, just like something that whatever it is he's calling a floorbird, which—and here he and the rest let go again, wish and delight altogether cut loose from meaning or utility, that is, getting the money. Now all that counts are floorbirds, so glorious, so free, just the spirit of this place, yes, the floorbird

Who just *flies*
From dawn
To dawn

the singer holding his note like Caruso, the rest pumping behind him, until like Gene Vincent pleading for mercy and love from the lip of a stage they are beside themselves with ardor, flinging their words far out ahead of themselves and then, no matter how long it takes, catching them on the run:

Look at that old floorbird, he just
Fly
From dawn
To daaaaawwwwwwwwnnnnnnn
Dig that crazy floorbird, he just
FLY
FROM DAWN
TO DAAAAAWWWWWWWNNNNNNN!
What a floorbird, he just—

They aren't finished, but the people watching laugh and walk off, more spring in their step, all with a single question on their minds: "Floorbirds?"

BACK TO THE WORLD

. . . one of the most fascinating stories in the world [is] that of the secret, or nonofficial, musical life of this country. It would seem that this is all bound up with religious dissent. It includes as much dissent from official America as from official Europe. It is based on the privilege of every man to praise God, as well as to court a damsel, with songs of his own choosing. For two hundred years it has refused institutional mediation in culture, as it has denied the necessity of institutional mediation for salvation. As a result, we have a body of British song that has survived the efforts of churches, of states, and of schools—for all have tried—to kill it.

—Virgil Thomson,
"America's Musical Autonomy," 1944

Few performers have made their way onto the stage of the twentieth century with a greater collection of masks than Bob Dylan. From the balladeer who first presented himself not as the son of a respectable middle-class Jewish family from northern Minnesota but as a vagabond runaway who had no idea if his parents were dead or alive, to the dandy who when controversy over his turn to the pop arena erupted declared that his investment in folk music had been a con from the start, he was, it was sometimes said, a different person every time you saw him. As an artist he was funny, outrageous, prophetic, denunciatory, appalled, unpredictable; inside any of those qualities you could hear wariness, slyness, thinking, a will to stay a step ahead, in control.

But when he set out in the fall of 1965 with the Hawks, and especially when the troupe reached the United Kingdom in the spring of 1966 and their shows became increasingly embattled and defiant, Bob Dylan found himself unmasked by the crowd. Their resistance and engagement forced him to confront his audiences directly. He had to use everything he had to keep up with them, let alone stay ahead. Discourse of whatever kind—the discourse of singing, talking back, playing in a group that at times must have felt as much like a lost patrol as a band—could no longer hide anything: the way he had to fight his way into a song simply to get it started, what he had to do to put the song across, the reach he'd make for the greater sound he knew was there. His Little Tramp naïveté, his aesthete's fey sidelong glance, his righteous preacher's taciturn disapproval—none of this would do. To be heard at all, speech had to be taken to extremes, and so there is no strategy, no calculation, no mask, in the highest moments these performances left behind. There is an uncovered, naked face ready to say whatever must be said to make it to the next song. It's no accident that the most inspired and unhinged of all the performances on this tour, "Just Like Tom Thumb's Blues" as it was played in Liverpool on May 14, 1966, ends with a poker game a poker face can't win, and in an empty room: "There was nobody even there to call my bluff."

Beginning about a year later, the basement tapes are a casually drawn out play about once again going about one's business in a setting of familiarity and trust, properly dressed and comfortably masked. Danger had been seen plain and protection was no longer taken for granted. With Dylan, Robbie Robertson, Garth Hudson, Richard Manuel, Rick Danko, and Levon Helm having disappeared from the face of the pop earth, it once again became clear that sometimes it is only the mask of distance, of vanishing, that lets you speak, that gives you the freedom to say what you mean without immediately having to stake your life on every word. So much of the basement tapes are the purest free speech: simple free speech, ordinary free speech, nonsensical free speech, not heroic free speech. Cryptic free speech, and thus what Raymond Chandler described as "the American voice": "flat, toneless, and tiresome," the tone of "Clothesline Saga" and "Lo and Behold!" a voice that can say almost anything while seeming to say almost nothing, in secret, with music that as it was made presumed no audience but its players and perhaps its ancestors, a secret public.

Finally, though, for an artist who went where his art took him, such speech could only take you so far. A definite tension rises up in the playfulness of the music, and there is an edge in even the most ludicrous of the songs; the mask loosens, and then it begins to fray and tear. The paradox of the old music that is so present in the basement becomes the premise of the new music. It's the paradox evident in the primitive modernism of Clarence Ashley, Furry Lewis, Frank Hutchison, the Memphis Jug Band, Geechie Wiley, Bascom Lamar Lunsford, Rabbit Brown, and Dock Boggs, the paradox of the representative one-of-a-kind democratic artist Bob Dylan is on the basement tapes: the passion in the flatness, stoicism in fear, the remorse in the deadpan. The mask comes to seem like a precondition for any revelation of a true face—a face that neither invites nor can endure a gaze that lasts very long. Those who had left their stages as betrayers of immemorial traditions discovered deeper traditions, and in a room without mirrors refashioned them. The traditional people, still living, were laid to rest and raised up with new faces. The cuckoo turned into a floorbird.

With the basement sessions all but over, Bob Dylan set about making a real album and went back to his career; the Hawks became the Band and went on to theirs. That was thirty years ago—but so much time was loaded into those sessions their results have escaped it. Most of the basement tapes still travel the fugitive path the music took from the first; each performance makes part of a map, which like so many of the songs, and the territory they describe, remains unfinished.

WORKS CITED

Except when the interviewer is mentioned in the text, interview quotations are noted according to each interviewee, in the order in which quotations appear in the text. News stories referred to in the text are noted by headline or tagline.

Bardin, John Franklin. *The Deadly Percheron* (1947). In *The John Franklin Bardin Omnibus*. Harmondsworth, UK and Baltimore, MD: Penguin, 1976.

Bloomfield, Michael. "Dylan Goes Electric." In *The Sixties*, ed. Lynda Obst. New York: Random House/Rolling Stone Press, 1977.

Boyes, Georgina. *The imagined village: Culture, ideology and the English Folk Revival.* Manchester, UK and New York: University of Manchester/St. Martin's, 1993. A tough-minded and revelatory study.

Bronson, Fred. *The Billboard Book of Number One Hits*, 3rd ed. New York: Billboard, 1992. Entry on "Ode to Billie Joe."

Buck-Morss, Susan. "Benjamin's *Passagen-Werk*: Redeeming Mass Culture for the Revolution." *New German Critique* 29 (1983).

Cándida Smith, Richard. *Utopia and Dissent: Art, Poetry, and Politics in California.* Berkeley: University of California Press, 1995. A deep and lucid study of individuals seeking a community of paradox and righteousness.

Cantwell, Robert. *Ethnomimesis: Folklife and the Representation of Culture.* Chapel Hill, NC: University of North Carolina Press, 1993.

———. "Smith's Memory Theater: *The Folkways Anthology of American Folk Music.*" *New England Review* (Spring/Summer 1991). Reading this visionary essay as I began my own work on Smith's *Anthology*, I did my best to forget it, knowing that if I didn't I would never be able to proceed as if my work were my own. How well I may have succeeded—avoided walking precisely in Cantwell's footsteps—is for others to judge, but here as elsewhere I gratefully acknowledge him as pathfinder and guide.

———. "When We Were Good: Class and Culture in the Folk Revival" (1993). In Rosenberg.

———. *When We Were Good: The Folk Revival.* Cambridge, MA: Harvard University Press, 1996.

Claudill, Harry. *Night Comes to the Cumberlands: A Biography of a Depressed Area.* Boston: Atlantic Monthly Press/Little, Brown, 1962, 1963.

Cohen, John. "A Rare Interview with Harry Smith." *Sing Out!* (April/May, June/July 1969). Facsimile reprint (with reproduction of Theodore DeBry etching used as original *Anthology of American Folk Music* cover art) in *American Magus: Harry Smith—A Modern Alchemist*, ed. Paola Igliori. New York: Inanout Press, 1996. Smith quotations not otherwise identified come from this interview.

———. Talk on Harry Smith (St. Mark's Church Poetry Project, November 10, 1995). Recording courtesy Rani Singh/Harry Smith Archives.

Conner, Bruce. To GM, 1991, 1995.

Costello, Elvis. Interview with Philip Watson, "Invisible Jukebox" (blindfold test). *The Wire* (London, March 1994).

Dickinson, Jim. Notes to Howlin' Wolf, *Memphis Days—The Definitive Edition, Vol. 2* (Sun/Bear Family, Germany, 1990). "I heard Sam Phillips say that his discovery of Wolf was more significant than his discovery of Elvis Presley. The only artist to share the surreal darkness of Robert Johnson, Wolf brings out of his band an ensemble counterpoint unlike anything else in the blues. His voice seems to hang in the air, and make the room rumble with echo. His singing is so powerful that between the vocal lines the compressor-limiter through which the mono recordings were made sucks the sound of the drum and the French harp up into the hole in the audio mix. Notes blend together and merge into melody lines that are not being 'played' by any one instrument. Wolf is not bound by the three-chord blues pattern, and often seems to erase the bar lines of western music. He is a Primitive-Modernist, using chants and modal harmonies of the dark ritualist past brought up from Mother Africa and slavery through electric amplifiers."

Dorgan, Howard. *The Old Regular Baptists of Central Appalachia: Brothers and Sisters in Hope.* Knoxville, TN: Tennessee University Press, 1989.

Dylan, Bob. *Tarantula.* New York: Macmillan, 1971.

———. "How Do You Get Your Kicks." Nat Hentoff, "The Playboy Interview." *Playboy* (March 1966). In McGregor.

———. "Dylan Questions the Comparisons." David Fricke, "Dylan's Dilemma." *Rolling Stone* (December 5, 1985).

———. "Were You Surprised." "Bob Dylan: The Rolling Stone Interview" (transcript of press conference, San Francisco, December 2, 1965). *Rolling Stone* (January 20, 1968).

———. "Call It Historical-Traditional." To Robert Shelton, March 1966. In Shelton's *No Direction Home: The Life and Music of Bob Dylan*. New York: Beech Tree/Morrow, 1986.

———. "What Folk Music Is." From press conference, Austin,

Texas, September 24, 1965. Quoted in Ralph J. Gleason, "The Children's Crusade." *Ramparts* (March 1966). In McGregor.

———. "How Do You Know." John Cohen and Happy Traum, "The Sing Out! Interview." *Sing Out!* (October/November 1968). In McGregor.

———. "All the Authorities." Nora Ephron and Susan Edmiston, "Bob Dylan Interview." *New York Post* (September 26, 1965). In McGregor.

———. "I Have to Think." In Hentoff, "The Playboy Interview."

Erickson, Steve. *Amnesiascope.* New York: Henry Holt, 1996.

Gentry, Bobbie. See Bronson.

Guralnick, Peter. *Feel Like Going Home* (1972). New York: HarperCollins, 1994.

Guthrie, Woody. On Sonny Terry. Quoted in Ron Radosh, "Commercialism and the Folksong Movement." *Sing Out!* (1959). Collected in *The American Folk Scene: Dimensions of the Folksong Revival*, ed. David A. DeTurk and A. Poulin, Jr. New York: Dell, 1967. Courtesy Dave Marsh.

Hampton, Howard. "Archives of Oblivion" (review of Clinton Heylin, *The Great White Wonders: A History of Rock Bootlegs*). *LA Weekly* (July 14–20, 1995).

———. "Stillborn Again" (review of Bob Dylan, *Oh Mercy*). *LA Weekly* (October 13–19, 1989).

Hawthorne, Nathaniel. "The Shaker Bridal," from *Twice-Told Tales* (1837).

Hayden, Casey. "The Movement." *Witness* (Summer/Fall 1988).

Heylin, Clinton. *Bob Dylan: The Recording Sessions (1960–1994).* New York and London (as *Behind Closed Doors: Bob Dylan: The Recording Sessions, 1960–1994*). New York and London: Viking, 1995.

"HIGHWAY BEHEADING." *USA Today* (July 24, 1995).

Jefferson, Thomas. Rejected passages from the Declaration of Independence (" 'The Rough Draft' as it probably read when Jefferson first submitted it to Franklin") quoted from Carl L.

Becker, *The Declaration of Independence: A Study in the History of Political Ideas* (1922, 1942). New York: Vintage, 1958.

Johnson, Denis. "Emergency," in *Jesus' Son.* New York: Farrar Straus Giroux, 1992.

Jones, Loyal. *Minstrel of the Appalachians: The Story of Bascom Lamar Lunsford.* Boone, NC: Appalachian Consortium Press, 1984.

Landau, Jon. "*John Wesley Harding.*" *Crawdaddy!* (May 1968). In McGregor.

Lawrence, D. H. *Studies in Classic American Literature* (1923). New York: Viking, 1964.

Lunsford, Bascom Lamar. "Mine Own." *Southern Exposure* (January/February 1986). On Naomi Wise. Courtesy Loyal Jones.

Mailer, Norman. "The White Negro." *Dissent* (1957). In Mailer's *Advertisements for Myself* (1959). Cambridge, MA: Harvard University Press, 1992.

McCrumb, Sharyn. *If Ever I Return, Pretty Peggy-O.* New York: Scribner's, 1990.

———. *She Walks These Hills.* New York: Scribner's, 1994.

McGregor, Craig, ed. *Bob Dylan: A Retrospective.* New York: Morrow, 1972. Reissued as *Bob Dylan: The Early Years—A Retrospective.* New York: Da Capo, 1990.

Mellers, Wilfrid. *A Darker Shade of Pale: A Backdrop to Bob Dylan.* New York and London: Oxford University Press, 1985.

Merlis, Mark. *American Studies.* New York: Houghton Mifflin, 1994.

Miles, Emma Bell. *The Spirit of the Mountains* (1905). Knoxville, TN: University of Tennessee Press, 1975.

Miller, Perry. *Jonathan Edwards* (1949). New York: Meridian, 1963.

———. "Jonathan Edwards and the Great Awakening" (1949, as part of "American Response to Crisis" lecture series, first published 1952). In Miller's *Errand into the Wilderness* (1956). New York: Harper Torchbooks, 1964.

Morton, Brian. *The Dylanist.* New York: HarperCollins, 1991.

Murray, Albert. See Scherman, Tony.

Nelson, Paul. "Newport Folk Festival, 1965." *Sing Out!* (September 1965). In McGregor.

Newman, Randy. To Stephen Holden, "Can a Pop Composer Help Out Broadway?" *New York Times* (September 24, 1995).

Ochs, Phil. Interview in *Broadside* (October 1965). Quoted in Clinton Heylin, *Dylan: Behind the Shades*. New York: Viking, 1991.

Pisaro, Michael. To GM, 1996.

Rexroth, Kenneth. Review of *Letters of Carl Sandburg*. *New York Times Book Review* (September 28, 1965). Quoted in Cantwell, *When We Were Good*. Citation courtesy Robert Cantwell.

Rooney, Jim. On Newport Folk Festival, 1965. Quoted in Nelson.

Rosenberg, Neil V., ed. *Transforming Tradition: Folk Music Revivals Examined*. Urbana, IL: University of Illinois Press, 1993.

Rourke, Constance. *American Humor: A Study of the National Character* (1931). New York: Anchor.

———. *The Roots of American Culture.* New York: Harcourt, Brace & World, 1942.

Savage, Lon. *Thunder in the Mountains: The West Virginia Mine War 1920–21* (1985). Pittsburgh: University of Pittsburgh Press, 1990. Reissued, ironically, because of the critical success of John Sayles's 1987 film *Matewan* (a puerile travesty, despite a fine performance by David Strathairn as Sid Hatfield). The events of the West Virginia Mine War are traditionally distorted and misdated (by years or even decades) in otherwise carefully researched books and essays; Savage's is the only reliable secondary source.

Scherman, Tony. "The Omni-American" (interview with Albert Murray). *American Heritage* (September 1996).

Seeger, Mike. Interviews with Dock Boggs, 1963–1969. Used by permission of Mike Seeger and Smithsonian/Folkways Archives, with the assistance of Jeffrey Place. All rights reserved. See also Discography.

Shelton, Robert. *The Face of Folk Music.* New York: Citadel, 1968. Text to photo essay by David Gahr. Includes Dylan graffiti war. Courtesy Dave Marsh.

Smith, Harry. Handbook to *Anthology of American Folk Music*. See Discography.

———. *Heaven and Earth Magic: Film No. 12* (1957–62). Mystic Fire Video, P.O. Box 1202, Montauk, NY 11954. Courtesy Rani Singh/Harry Smith Archives, as are all Smith interviews noted below.

———. "There's No Subject." Dawn Koliktas, "Film and the Occult: An Interview with Harry Smith." Unpublished (July 1988).

———. "Maybe Every Three or Four Months." Mary Hill, "Harry Smith Interviewed" (1972). *Film Culture* (June 1992).

———. "I Once Discovered." P. Adams Sitney, "Harry Smith Interviewed." *Film Culture* (Summer 1965).

———. "The Universal Hatred." Clint Fraker, "Interview with Harry Smith." *Once and for All Almanac.* Boulder, CO: 1989.

———. "Everywhere Jimmie Rodgers Went." A. J. Melita, interview with Harry Smith. Unpublished (1976).

———. "I Could Really Believe." Paul Nelson to GM.

———. "When I Was Younger." Melita interview with Smith.

Smith, Lee. *The Devil's Dream.* New York: Putnam's, 1992.

Stein, Stephen J. *The Shaker Experience in America.* New Haven, CT: Yale University Press, 1992.

Stekert, Ellen. "Cents and Nonsense in the Urban Folk Revival" (1966). In Rosenberg.

"SUSAN SMITH WAS MOLESTED BY STEPFATHER." Associated Press/*San Francisco Chronicle* (February 21, 1995).

Thomson, Virgil. "America's Musical Autonomy" (1944). In *A Virgil Thomson Reader*, ed. Virgil Thomson and John Rockwell. Boston: Houghton Mifflin, 1981. Courtesy Lang Thompson.

"TOWN STUNNED BY SLAYINGS OF THREE CHILDREN." Associated Press/*San Francisco Chronicle* (February 21, 1995).

U.S. Term Limits v. Thornton. Opinions by Justices John Paul Stevens and Clarence Thomas. *New York Times* (May 23, 1995).

Van der Merwe, Peter. *Origins of the Popular Style: The Antecedents of Twentieth-Century Popular Music.* New York and London: Oxford University Press, 1989.

Van Ronk, Dave. Notes to *Dave Van Ronk: The Folkways Recordings* (Smithsonian/Folkways, 1991).

Von Schmidt, Eric, and Jim Rooney. *Baby Let Me Follow You Down: The Illustrated History of the Cambridge Folk Years* (1979). Hanover, NH: University Press of New England, 1994.

Vowell, Sarah. *Radio On: A Listener's Diary* (entry for January 1, 1995). New York: St. Martin's, 1997.

Whisnant, David E. "Gone Country: *High Lonesome* and the Politics of Writing About Country Music." *Journal of Country Music* (Spring 1995).

Wigglesworth, Michael. "God's Controversy with New-England—Written in the Time of the Great Drought Anno 1662 (God Speaks Against the Languishing State of New-England)." From *The Puritans: A Sourcebook of Their Writings, Volume 2*, ed. Perry Miller and Thomas H. Johnson (1938). New York: Harper Torchbooks, 1963.

Wilson, Edmund. "Frank Keeney's Coal Diggers" (1931). In Wilson's *The American Earthquake.* New York: Farrar Straus Giroux, 1958.

Winthrop, John. "A Modell of Christian Charity." From *The Puritans: A Sourcebook of Their Writings, Volume 1*, ed. Perry Miller and Thomas H. Johnson (1938). New York: Harper Torchbooks, 1963.

Wright, Lawrence. *In the New World.* New York: Knopf, 1987.

"Yahweh Has Placed an Invisible Barrier." From "GRITZ GIVES UP ON FREEMEN." *San Francisco Chronicle* (May 2, 1995).

Yoon, Carol Kaesuck. "Thuggish Cuckoos Use Muscle to Run Egg Protection Racket." *New York Times* (November 14, 1995).

DISCOGRAPHY

All records are cds unless otherwise noted. "Anthology" indicates a collection of recordings by different performers.

BOB DYLAN

1961–1966

"Pretty Polly." Recorded May 1961 in Minneapolis. On *The Minnesota Tapes* (Wanted Man bootleg).

Bob Dylan (Columbia). Released March 22, 1962.

"No More Auction Block." Recorded October 1962 at the Gaslight Cafe, New York City. *the bootleg series volumes 1–3 {rare & unreleased} 1961–1991* (Columbia).

"I Shall Be Free" & "A Hard Rain's A-Gonna Fall." *The Freewheelin' Bob Dylan* (Columbia). Released May 27, 1963.

"Talkin' John Birch Paranoid Blues." Included on mistakenly released version of *The Freewheelin' Bob Dylan* (Columbia). On *The Freewheelin' Outtakes* (Vigatone bootleg).

"The Ballad of Medgar Evers." Included in fragmentary form on *We Shall Overcome* (Folkways lp, 1964), documentary recordings of the August 28, 1963, March on Washington. Complete performance collected as "Only a Pawn in Their Game" on *Bob Dylan: Broadside* (Gunsmoke bootleg).

"With God on Our Side" & "The Times They Are A-Changin'." *The Times They Are A-Changin'* (Columbia). Released January 13, 1964. Also includes "Only a Pawn in Their Game," retitled version of "The Ballad of Medgar Evers."

Bringing It All Back Home (Columbia). Released March 22, 1965.

"Like a Rolling Stone" (Columbia). Released July 20, 1965.

Bob Dylan—Live in Newport 1965 (Document bootleg; label not to be confused with Document, Austria). Recorded July 25, 1965. Bob Dylan: rhythm guitar, harmonica; Michael Bloomfield, lead guitar; Al Kooper, organ; Jerome Arnold, bass; Sam Lay, drums; Barry Goldberg, piano. Stunning footage of "Maggie's Farm" can be seen in *The History of Rock 'n' Roll: Plugging In*, dir. Susan Steinberg (Time-Life Video, 1995).

Forest Hills Concert, August 28, 1965. Bob Dylan: acoustic guitar, harmonica, rhythm guitar, piano; Robbie Robertson, lead guitar; Al Kooper, electric piano; Harvey Brooks, bass; Levon Helm, drums. Poor audience recordings included on *1965 Chronicles* (a bizarre 14-cd bootleg apparently comprising every unofficially recorded Bob Dylan moment of the year).

Highway 61 Revisited (Columbia). Released August 30, 1965.

Long Distance Operator (Wanted Man bootleg). Audience recording, December 4, 1965, Berkeley, California. Bob Dylan, rhythm guitar, harmonica, piano; Robbie Robertson, lead guitar; Richard Manuel, piano; Garth Hudson, organ; Rick Danko, bass; Bobby Gregg, drums. The title song, a Dylan composition here sung by Dylan, appears on Bob Dylan and the Band, *The Basement Tapes* (Columbia), in a version by the Band.

"I Still Miss Someone." Recorded backstage, Cardiff, May 11, 1966. With Johnny Cash. Fragmentary film footage by D. A. Pennebaker in *Eat the Document*, dir. Dylan and Howard Alk; complete breakdown in Pennebaker's unfinished, unreleased

"Something Is Happening." Also recorded in 1969 as a Dylan-Cash duet (on *The Dylan/Cash Sessions*, Spank bootleg).

"Just Like Tom Thumb's Blues." Recorded May 14, 1966, Liverpool. B-side of "I Want You" (Columbia). Released June 1966, reissued on *Masterpieces* (CBS/Sony, Japan, 1978). The ultimate recording from this long tour: the most elegant and the most extreme. Bob Dylan: rhythm guitar, harmonica; Robbie Robertson, lead guitar; Richard Manuel, piano; Garth Hudson, organ; Rick Danko, bass; Mickey Jones, drums (as on all live recordings listed below unless noted to the contrary).

"Mr. Tambourine Man." Audience recording, May 15, 1966. On *Leicester 66* (bootleg). Bob Dylan, acoustic guitar and harmonica. The sound is all clouds, until for these nine minutes the moon comes out.

Blonde on Blonde (Columbia). Released May 16, 1966.

Guitars Kissing & the Contemporary Fix (bootleg). Recorded May 17, 1966, Manchester. A double cd, with both acoustic and electric sections of a Dylan/Hawks performance complete. The "Judas!" concert, bootlegged since 1969 as "Royal Albert Hall," "In 1966 There Was," etc. This edition based on tapes remixed and remastered through Dylan's agency for scheduled and then canceled 1995 official release. History as theater, and vice versa. Frightening.

A Week in the Life (bootleg). Performances drawn from Birmingham, May 12, to Manchester.

Bob Dylan and the Hawks Play Fucking Loud! (bootleg). As in *A Week in the Life*, with better selection and better sound. Shocking.

Before the Crash Vol. 2 (Music with Love bootleg). Includes recordings from May 26, 1966, Royal Albert Hall, London.

Sings the Body Electric (Parrot bootleg). Includes recordings from May 20, 1966, Edinburgh ("Like a Rolling Stone") and May 26 & 27, Royal Albert Hall.

"Like a Rolling Stone." May 27, 1966. Royal Albert Hall,

London. The last performance on the last night, with an introduction of the band ("They're all poets"). On *The Genuine Bootleg Series, Take 2* (bootleg).

THE BASEMENT TAPES

Bob Dylan, acoustic guitar, rhythm guitar, piano, harmonica, autoharp; Rick Danko, bass, fiddle, acoustic guitar, trombone; Garth Hudson (engineer/producer), organ, piano, clavinette, trombone, saxophone, euphonium; Richard Manuel, piano, organ, drums, lap Hawaiian guitar; Robbie Robertson, lead guitar, acoustic guitar, drums, autoharp; Levon Helm (later recordings), drums, harmonica.*

Following is a log of the known recordings that travel under the name "The Basement Tapes," from "The All American Boy" to "You Win Again." There is no common memory, let alone documentation, to provide the exact dates when Bob Dylan and the former Hawks began meeting to try their hand at old songs, or when old songs gave way to a long burst of mockery and novelty ("Bob would be running through an old song," Robbie Robertson says, "and he'd say, 'Maybe there's a *new* song to be had here' "). Certainly they began playing, and occasionally taping the results, in the Red Room in Dylan's house in Woodstock. Most of the commonplace or covered material, the least finished and sure, from Ian and Sylvia hits to "Johnny Todd," from Johnny Cash classics to "Cool Water," comes from there, beginning in the early summer of 1967. The basement of Big Pink, the house Rick Danko, Garth Hudson, and Richard Manuel were renting in West Saugerties, was more of a hideaway, or a hideout. Sessions there

*Rick Danko: "There was also a pedal steel guitar in the basement that Bob had been given. Everybody played that once in a while." Robbie Robertson: "Everybody *tried* to."

went on through the summer, then off and on through the rest of the year and into the next. The first few months produced most of the best-known basement originals, and the series of parodies and breakdowns that stretches from "Tupelo" through "I'm in the Mood" into "See You Later, Allen Ginsberg." Likely later (though possibly much earlier) are the unfinished, visionary songs that take such disarming titles as "I'm a Fool for You" or "Baby, Won't You Be My Baby?" and perhaps the excursions that throw off all attempts to fold them together: such performances as "The King of France" and "Hills of Mexico." There is no consensus on the site of the last cycle of recordings, those made with Levon Helm as part of the ensemble: "Gimme Another Bourbon Street," "Wildwood Flower," "Confidential," "Coming Round the Mountain," "Flight of the Bumblebee," "See that My Grave Is Kept Clean," and "All You Have to Do Is Dream." Hudson and Danko remember them as recorded in the house they moved to after leaving Big Pink, a place on Hale Mountain, in Woodstock, built by the beloved local artist Clarence Schmidt; to Robertson they definitely have the feel of the basement. In either case they have the feel of a rightful conclusion, of people shaking hands, ready to go their own ways. "It's interesting what nobody remembers," Robertson says. "Facts aren't always the most interesting."

The basement tapes have appeared in a number of forms: as the original "Basement Tape," the fourteen-song acetate of Dwarf Music publishing demos sent to various performers in 1968; on the official Columbia release of Bob Dylan and the Band's *The Basement Tapes* in 1975 (then a double lp, now a double cd, and both in false mono with a number of after-the-fact overdubs); in the case of three songs so far, on official Dylan retrospectives on Columbia; and, after nearly thirty years of scattershot bootlegging, on the five-cd bootleg set titled "The Genuine Basement Tapes" (mostly in the separated stereo of the original tapes, but without approaching the fullness and density of their sound), which with two exceptions collects Dylan's extant basement pieces. ("They've got it all," Garth Hudson said after looking over the discs; what they didn't have were more than muddy fragments of "Even If It's a Pig Part I" or anything at all of "Part II.")

The entries here note where each recording has appeared, with material from the five-disc set cited simply by volume number and track number, plus the time of each recording, authorship* or origin, and other details that seem relevant. Songs not otherwise credited are by Bob Dylan; performances without comment play a part in the main text.

"All American Boy" ("Bill Parsons" & Orville Lunsford). V.4, 3. 3.54. In a series of happily blasted basement numbers that may come from the same session, only "I Am a Teenage Prayer" and "Tupelo" top this Vietnam-era version of Bobby Bare's burlesque on the rise of Elvis Presley. (As Joe Sasfy writes in the notes to the anthology *1959: The Rock 'n' Roll Era*, Time-Life Music, where the original can be found, Bare recorded "The All American Boy" as "a demo for his friend Bill Parsons to use as a B side should Parsons land a record deal . . . Fraternity Records released the song, mistakenly attributing it to Parsons, and it soared to No. 2.") Bare essayed a hilariously deadpan, first-person, I-am-Elvis account of the capture of the Memphis Flash by manager Col. Parker and the Army; Dylan, even more deadpan, riffing off gurgling asides from Richard Manuel, weaves around Bare's story line ("Rippin' up draft cards," Manuel offers helpfully when the Uncle-Sam-needs-you part of the tale comes due, not that Dylan picks up the cue) while pulling new verses out of the air. "Makin' the girls *giggle*," Manuel says of the task of the pop star. "Yes," Dylan replies, veteran rock 'n' roll hero now offering sage advice to whoever might come after him, "you'll be making the little

*For parodies, the name of the original author is given, even if (as with Parsons and Lunsford for "The All American Boy") only the structure of the original song remains.

girlies giggle"—but the business that appears to interest him most comes when the manager arrives in the song. Here that seems to involve a character who will take the young singer home to meet his wife, where the innocent will have to have sex with both of them.

"All You Have to Do Is Dream" 1. V.1, 1. 3.44. With Levon Helm on drums, a languid run-through, with hints of Bing Crosby.

"All You Have to Do Is Dream" 2. V.1, 19. 3.45. The pace quickens even if the tempo doesn't, and the floorbirds lift off into the sky.

"Apple Suckling Tree" 1. V.2, 6. 2.37. Robbie Robertson on drums but not on the beat. Still, with Garth Hudson's organ sweeping up the melody—the melody of "Froggy Went A-Courtin'," the ancient children's ditty Dylan sang with such a plain, mysterious tone on his 1992 *Good as I Been to You*—this may be the freest sound on the basement tapes.

"Apple Suckling Tree" 2. *The Basement Tapes;* V.2, 7. 2.47. Robertson gets the beat and swings it, the piano sounds it, the organ quiets, and the vocal is cooler, then infinitely harder, the feeling changing from the uproarious to the ominous in the blink of an eye. "It all felt natural," Rick Danko says. "We didn't rehearse. One or two takes, from conception, on paper, to the finish. We all knew it would never happen twice."

"Baby Ain't that Fine" (Dallas Frazier). V.1, 6. 2.00. A 1966 country hit for rock 'n' roll angst maestro Gene Pitney and country fiddler and guitarist Melba Montgomery. In the original—or as recorded by Frazier himself, a writer whose hipster sensibility produced such sui generis discs as the Hollywood Argyles' 1960 "Alley-Oop," Charlie Rich's 1965 "Mohair Sam," and Billy "Crash" Craddock's 1972 "Ain't Nothing Shakin' (But the Leaves on the Trees)"—this was a tune in the measured, reflective style of soul singer Joe Tex, who was rarely far from country himself. (See Pitney's *The Great Recordings*, Tomato.) As taken up by Dylan and the band only a year later, with Robertson's guitar chiming softly and Hudson's organ sneaking behind the singing, the song has become a satisfied reverie—something old and weathered, as if it were a tune known not for months but for decades, remembered as something Clarence Ashley and the Carolina Tar Heels cut in 1929, or forgot to.

"Baby, Won't You Be My Baby?" V.1, 17. 2.47.

"Be Careful of Stones that You Throw" (Bonnie Dodd). V.1, 9 (as "Stones that You Throw"). 3.15. First cut in 1949 by country singer Little Jimmie Dickens and again in 1952 by Hank Williams, who released it under his "Luke the Drifter" alias, this was one of two Williams recordings covered on the basement tapes. (The other, "You Win Again," was recorded at the same '52 session; for both, see Williams's *I Won't Be Home No More: June 1952–September 1952*, Polydor.) After a false start with the basement combo, Dylan eases into the spoken piece, half sly over the lesson he's going to preach, half bored with its obviousness, with the way some people never learn. The rest strain with him as they sing the title line, or mutter behind him as if they too have seen this all before, too many times: the small-town gossip that made the neighbor who kept to herself into a drunkard, a whore, a witch, even though it turns out she had the purest heart of all, and you only found out—too late.

"Belshazar" 1 & 2 (Johnny Cash). V.4, 17. 3.19. Originally recorded in 1957; see *Johnny Cash & the Tennessee Two: 1955 to 1958 Recordings* (Sun/Charly). "No one around could understand / What was written by this mystic hand."

"The Bells of Rhymney" (Idris Davies-Pete Seeger). V.5, 10. 3.09. Originally recorded by Pete Seeger in 1965 (see *The Essential Pete*

Seeger, Vanguard) but most memorably that same year by the Byrds on their Dylan-drenched debut album (see *Mr. Tambourine Man*, Columbia Legacy). "With the covers," Robertson says, "Bob was educating us a little. The whole folkie thing was still very questionable to us—it wasn't the train we came in on. He'd be doing this Pete Seeger stuff and I'd be saying, 'Oh, *God* . . .' And then, it might be music you knew you didn't like, he'd come up with something like 'Royal Canal,' and you'd say, 'This is so beautiful! The expression!' He wasn't obvious about it. But he remembered too much, remembered too many songs too well. He'd come over to Big Pink, or wherever we were, and pull out some old song—and he'd prepped for this. He'd practiced this, and then come out here, to show us.

"But 'Bells of Rhymney,' '900 Miles,' Pete Seeger—it always seemed so nerdy to me. It was so fucking *white*. It was corny. It was collegiate. We used to play a lot of colleges, with Ronnie Hawkins—but only in the South. Places where people got wild, got seriously fucked up. It seemed like whenever we got to one of those places Hank Ballard and the Midnighters had just left. We had to follow them, and they had a routine where for an extra thousand dollars they'd play naked. Maybe with little gold jockstraps. We had to follow that. That's what we did at colleges—but when Bob would do this stuff, when he'd pull out 'Bells of Rhymney,' it didn't seem corny. I didn't think that anymore."

"Big Dog Won't You Please Come Home." V.4, between 13 and 14 as an untitled fragment. .21. A growl toward a comic blues with the band full of bark: "BIG DOG BIG DOG! WHERE YOU GO WHERE YOU GO?"

"Big River" 1 & 2 (Johnny Cash). V.5, 8. 3.10. Originally recorded by Cash in 1958 for Sun but as a basement number probably worked up from "his great album *I Walk the Line*" (Danko). Cash's first for Columbia, in 1964, the lp also included the basement covers "Folsom Prison Blues" and "Still in Town":

"Our tribute to Johnny Cash, that summer" (Danko). Here the group gets nearly a minute into the tune before letting it go; a second try seals it. Also recorded in 1969 as a Dylan-Cash duet (on *The Dylan/Cash Sessions*, Spank bootleg).

"Bonnie Ship the Diamond" (traditional). V.1, 4. 3.20. A sea shanty commonplace during the folk revival—performed by Ewan MacColl and Peggy Seeger, Judy Collins, the Kingston Trio, and scores more—here the story takes place before your eyes. Dylan sets the theme on his acoustic guitar and the ship's ropes strain against the dock, as if the ship wants to leave of its own accord; when Robertson's guitar comes in the ropes are loosed, but it's impossible to imagine the ship returning. The melody weights every word of the chorus with fatal prophecy: "So it's rise up, my lads / Let your hearts / Never fail / Let Bonnie Ship the Diamond / Go fishing for the whale."

"Bring It on Home." V.4, 18. 2.55. Coming out of a breakdown on the Rays' "Silhouettes," a hard blues beat with Dylan commanding "Richard, take a verse." "What's the song?" "Just take a verse!" It was supposed to be Bo Diddley's "Bring It to Jerome" (from 1958, on Diddley's first album, *Bo Diddley*, Chess/Vogue)—that is, Diddley's tribute to his maracas player ("He used to put bee-bees in them," Robertson remembers fondly). But as soon as the word "home" comes in everyone is off and cackling and the beat is an end in itself.

"Clothesline Saga" (Answer to 'Ode'). *The Basement Tapes.* V.2, 5. 3.20. Bobbie Gentry's "Ode to Billie Joe" is best heard on *Best of Tragedy* (DCC), a collection that links Appalachian murder ballads to the teen death songs so much in vogue in the early '60s—here, the likes of Mark Dinning's 1960 "Teen Angel" (a highlight of the Rock Bottom Remainders' repertoire in the early 1990s, with lead vocals by Stephen King and with Dave Marsh, in bloodied prom dress, as the dead girlfriend), J. Frank Wilson and the

Cavaliers' 1964 "Last Kiss," and Ray Peterson's unspeakable 1960 "Tell Laura I Love Her." In the context of this set, the 1967 "Ode to Billie Joe" is plainly as close to the Kingston Trio's 1958 "Tom Dooley" as to the Shangri-las' 1964 "Leader of the Pack," even if "Clothesline Saga" is closer to Frank Hutchison's "Cannon Ball Blues" than to either.

"Come All Ye Fair and Tender Ladies" (traditional). 2.04. Again a folk revival standard: a warning against faithless men, but less threatening than most (nobody dies). The keening vocal begins in a faraway place and stays there.

"Coming Round the Mountain" (traditional). V.4, 6. 1.37. An old western railroad song (copyrighted in 1923 by Spencer Williams) that by the 1950s had turned into a summer-camp singalong. With Helm on harmonica and Robertson on autoharp, this perhaps draws on Ernest Stoneman's "She'll Be Coming Round the Mountain" (on *Mountain Music Played on the Autoharp*, Folkways lp, 1965, recorded by Mike Seeger), though Uncle Dave Macon and any number of movie and TV cowboys could be in here, too. The performance is relaxed, the sound of people used to waiting or who don't care if the train comes off the mountain or not. As in "See that My Grave Is Kept Clean," there are white horses in the song; whether they're the same ones is another question.

"Confidential" (Dorinda Morgan). V.4, 8. 1.32. An uncertain reading of the 1956 hit by Sonny Knight, a rock 'n' roll singer from Los Angeles now better known—under his real name, Joseph C. Smith—as the author of *The Day the Music Died* (New York: Grove, 1981), a coruscating novel about racism and the beginning of rock (see Knight's *"Confidential,"* Mr R&B lp, Sweden).

"Cool Water" (Bob Nolan). V.5, 20. 2.57. A cowboy tune done by everyone from Burl Ives to Walter Brennan to the Sons of the Pioneers, and probably best by Marty Robbins on his *Gunfighter*

Ballads and Trail Songs (Columbia, 1959)—straight out of a Hollywood western, nothing like this seeking, reflective version, a performance that lights its own campfire.

"Crash on the Levee (Down in the Flood)" 1. V.3, 6. 2.06. Strident and off-kilter—not the panic a disaster might call up, just the first time through the number.

"Crash on the Levee (Down in the Flood)" 2. Acetate; *The Basement Tapes;* V.3, 7. 2.02. The organ comes up, and the singer is absolutely sure of himself: sure that along with houses, trees, cars, and people, any flood carries home truths. Jaunty here—"Ooooo, *mama*" seems like the key line—and nothing like the stunningly rangy, fierce ride Dylan gave it on stage in 1995, when the flood seemed to be less set in any American place than in Genesis 6–7. Rerecorded by Dylan in 1971, with Happy Traum accompanying, for *Bob Dylan's Greatest Hits, Vol. II* (Columbia).

"Don't Ya Tell Henry." V.2, 21. 2.23. Great as the Band performs it alone on *The Basement Tapes*, and great with Dylan leading, shouting encouragement through a stuttering horn break, the singing wild ("I was outasight!") and then cool, distant: what other tone do you take when you're looking for your girlfriend in a whorehouse? "I always thought of these things as pieces," Danko says. "I thought we'd get back to them, and Bob would finish the ones he wanted to finish."

"Don't You Try Me Now." V.1, 18. 3.08. A harsh, accusatory blues, all vehemence, except at the start, when the singer is straining toward the song, not catching it. In the middle eight everything explodes: "Well, try me on a table, I scream like a dog / Try to leave me, you know I quit like a hollow log"—and if you can feel that scream, you can't believe anyone would leave the singer, for fear of what she might find if she came back.

"Down on Me" (traditional). V.1, 3. .35. Long enough.

"Flight of the Bumble Bee" (Rimsky-Korsakov). V.4, 7. 2.17. Yo Yo Ma did it with Bobby McFerrin, the Ventures did it in Japan, countless music students have done it—but not likely as it's done here, with such philosophical wistfulness, as if it's poetry night in a 1956 San Francisco jazz club.

"Folsom Prison Blues" (Johnny Cash). V.5, 9. 2.41. Taken fast, Dylan's fuck-it-all singing for the verses rising high on the choruses with the group's help, as if for a second he could actually make it over the wall. First recorded by Cash in 1956 for Sun Records and entering into legend a year after the basement version was cut on *Johnny Cash at Folsom Prison* (Columbia).

"Four Strong Winds" (Ian Tyson). V.5, 1. 3.36. With lumpy drums, a groaning version of the Ian and Sylvia warhorse (on their *Greatest Hits!*, Vanguard, along with their other numbers covered on the basement tapes, plus versions of "This Wheel's on Fire" and "Quinn the Eskimo"). They were bland, they were smooth, and as much as Dylan might love the Canadian duo's songs, there's nothing in them for him to sing—it's like grabbing air. "Ian and Sylvia was part of Bob's background," Robertson says—they and Dylan shared the same manager, and they always said it was Dylan who inspired them to write their own songs. "But we didn't know anything about Ian and Sylvia. Oh, you knew 'Four Strong Winds,' everyone knew that, it was Canada, but 'Spanish Is the Loving Tongue'—that was one of those 'where did *that* come from?' moments. Ian and Sylvia—it was a different side of the tracks for us. Ian and Sylvia, Joni Mitchell, Neil Young: the Yorkville people" (that is, the coffeehouse people). "We didn't get over to Yorkville until after hours, and by then they were gone. And when we got to Yorkville, we weren't looking for music. At one time, though, we had a house there—we were all living with my mother in Toronto, but it got too wild, and the guys were embarrassed in front of her. So Rick and Richard and Levon got a house in Yorkville—the wide-open part of Toronto. It made me nervous. Shady characters, people just walking in off the streets into the house. Gangsters, after hours, drug lords. Supposedly jazz musicians who played just enough to get the money to go to London and become full-out heroin addicts."

"The French Girl" (Ian Tyson). V.5, 2. 5.32. Ian and Sylvia's 1966 recording makes the strangled, two-part basement rendition sound decent; full of itself, drowning in strings, the original is pure Rod McKuen or, for a more present-day analogue, Michael Bolton. The basement rendition still sounds phony, unless you believe self-pity defines the depths of the soul.

"Get Your Rocks Off." V.2, 4. 3.42. Beginning with the hoary folk-lyric lines "There was two old maids, lyin' in the bed," then meandering lazily down all the back roads of all the songs those lines call up, until the title phrase can serve as the answer to any question: half obscenity, half "Don't tread on me."

"Gimme Another Bourbon Street." V.4, 2 (as "Bourbon Street"). 2.24. With Danko leading on trombone, a gaggle of New Orleans street musicians stagger down Bourbon Street at 4 A.M., hugging strip-club pitchmen, lampposts, or fellow drunks with equal ardor. No more coins for the boys this night: they've bypassed oblivion for a perfect state of obliviousness.

"Going Down the Road" (traditional). V.5, 12 (as "No Shoes on My Feet"). 3.14. At first a crying, broken account of a long walk to nowhere: this road really does lead to oblivion, but the thudding beat lifts the singers' feet, and in an instant they're indomitable, a tramp army with a nation trailing behind it. That was not the spirit of the song when it was first recorded, in 1923, when Henry Whittier of Virginia took up an old black lament and remade it as "Lonesome Road Blues," one of the earliest commercial country records, but that was the spirit during the Depression, when dispossessed Okies and Arkies made the song their own. By 1940 it was playing in John Ford's film of John

Steinbeck's *The Grapes of Wrath*, and Woody Guthrie cut his first version of the tune, as "Blowin' Down this Road," later recording it for Folkways with Cisco Houston as "Goin' Down the Road." (See the anthology *The Music Never Stopped: The Roots of the Grateful Dead*, Shanachie.) The song had been in Dylan's repertoire from his earliest folk days, but never like this: with a hurdy-gurdy piano and Hudson's carnival organ. "I ain't gonna be treated this-a-way," the singers shout, but in the moment there's no better road in the land.

"Goin' to Acapulco." *The Basement Tapes*. V.2, 8. 5.28. Is this where the road leads, to luxury and the deepest oblivion? The number is part of the series of late-summer, early-fall basement tunes where the vocals are desperate and the accompaniment delicate, each note a separate choice. Here the feeling is as bereft as it is in "Tears of Rage," the music as restrained and as hard; as the singer rises to the chorus, the words "going to have some fun" translate as "crawl into a hole and die."

"Gonna Get You Now." V.2, 9. 1.26. The blues and the backwoods come together as a man shouts at the sun, the freedom of the folk-lyric form letting language play its tricks: "I was daydreamin' on a Sunday / Monday came both ways."

"Hills of Mexico" (traditional). V.1, 10. 2.51. " 'Twas in the town of Griffin / In the year of '65 . . ." Leading on acoustic guitar, with Manuel's drums quietly building pressure and Robertson's guitar tensing it, Dylan sang this cowboy ballad as he had in a friend's living room in New Jersey in 1961: all foreboding, though by 1991, on stage in Madison, Wisconsin, he was all suspicion. Collected by John Lomax and Carl Sandburg, the song was a staple for Woody Guthrie and Pete Seeger under the more common title "Buffalo Skinners" (for Guthrie's version see *Early Masters*, Tradition/Rykodisc, or *Struggle*, Smithsonian/Folkways); if it suggests any western, it's John Huston's 1948 *The Treasure of the Sierra Madre*, right at that point where everyone starts sleeping with a gun. A stunning performance very close to Dylan's is Roscoe Holcomb's "Hills of Mexico," taped by John Cohen in 1959, though his recording was not released until 1996 (see the anthology *Mountain Music of Kentucky*, Smithsonian/Folkways). Almost as close, musically anyway, is Beck's "Mexico" (on the 1994 anthology *Rare on Air: Live Performances, Vol. 1*, Mammoth), wherein the singer gets fired from McDonald's after it's robbed, pulls together some friends for a trip to Tijuana, robs his old McDonald's to finance it, and ends up working for McDonald's in Mexico, all without cracking a smile. Hank Williams's "Alone and Forsaken," recorded with just acoustic guitar in 1949, released only posthumously, is all over Dylan's performance, which in its bitter way matches anything in the basement sessions. "You don't have to take this down, Garth," Dylan says as he breaks off the music about a third of the way into the song. "Just wasting tape." He knew how the song comes out.

"I Am a Teenage Prayer." V.4, 15. 3.46.

"I Can't Come in with a Broken Heart." V.5, 15. 2.19. A noisy, rough groove, but just a sketch.

"I Can't Make It Alone." V.1, 2. 3.25. Another sketch—from a long way off, well before collaboration is second nature—perhaps a sketch of "This Wheel's on Fire."

"I Don't Hurt Anymore" (Don Robertson-Jack Rollins). V.1, 15. 2.25. A terrific cover of Hank Snow's 1954 number one country hit (see *Snow Country*, Pair/RCA), but if Snow's lovely original, with slow fiddles, is easy self-knowledge—he really doesn't hurt anymore—Dylan's has a bit of Timi Yuro's fabulously vengeful 1962 "What's a Matter Baby (Is it Hurting You)" in it, especially at the roaring close. "The only way this could have come up," Robertson says, "is because I suggested it. My cousin Herb Myke used to sing it—he was the first person who ever showed me anything on guitar. People were always asking him to sing 'I Don't Hurt Anymore,' and he hated to sing it—it made him too sad. 'You have to be kind of lonely to play the guitar well,' he said. 'It's sadness. Sadness medicine.' "

"I Forgot to Remember to Forget" (Stan Kesler-Charlie Feathers). V.5, 4. 3.15. This is nothing like Elvis Presley's original, made for Sun in 1955 (see his *The Complete Sun Sessions*, RCA), but soft, reflective, a long look back—very country, full of musing, with hints of the what-does-it-all-mean voices in "Sign on the Cross." "I used to be disgusted, now I try to be amused," as Elvis Costello would put it. Also recorded by Dylan in 1970, during the sessions for his *New Morning*.

"I'm a Fool for You." V.4, 9. 3.53.

"I'm Alright." V.1, 11 (as "It's Alright"). .54. A riff.

"I'm Guilty of Loving You." V.5, 18. 1.05. A fragment, with the tape cut, and too bad—it's fine. Dylan is all the way into the song—perhaps loosely based on Jim Reeves's 1963 "Guilty"—from the first notes, pained and trapped; Robertson slashes down with Curtis Mayfield–styled guitar.

"I'm in the Mood" (John Lee Hooker). V.4, 16. 1.51. Dylan draws out the words as far as he can—"I'm in the *moooood* for love"—which gives the rest the chance to pump him up: "He's in the mood!" "Yes, he is!" "He's in the mood, he's in the mood!" (Do they get to watch?) The 1951 original is on *The Best of John Lee Hooker* (MCA); Danko and Robertson also recorded the number with John Hammond, Jr., on his 1965 *I Can Tell* (Atlantic).

"I'm Not There (1956)" (I'm Not There, I'm Gone). V.2, 20 (and in perfect sound reproduction on *The Genuine Bootleg Series, Take 2*). 5.04. Michael Pisaro: "What's truly galling about this performance is his composure. Here he is, improvising (?) lyrics, modifying the lengths and not making any real sense, stretching it out over five verses and choruses without a crack in his tone. He's not just serious, he's oblivious to the idea that things could be any different from the way he's telling them." Danko plays as if he knows that all his life this song has been waiting for him to complete it, and that he will be given only one chance; Hudson and Manuel play as if they arrived late, but with the confidence that the funeral wouldn't really start without them. No covers, but one tribute: the Mekons' "I'm Not Here (1967)," from their *So Good it Hurts* (TwinTone, 1988). "We had played together for years; we could almost predict what we were going to do next," Danko says of the Band. "We reached that stage with Bob." "I thought, this needs to be *finished*," Robertson says. "This is a *great idea*. It popped up again on *Planet Waves*: 'Going, Going, Gone.' " And perhaps cast back to Warren Smith's 1957 "So Long I'm Gone."

"I Shall Be Released." Acetate; on Dylan's *the bootleg series volumes 1–3 {rare & unreleased} 1961–1991* (Columbia); V.3, 14. 3.42. The most famous basement number and by far the most widely covered, usually with unbearable piety (as at the Last Waltz, the Band's 1976 farewell concert, with Dylan and Manuel leading a mass choir of Neil Young, Joni Mitchell, Ronnie Hawkins, Neil Diamond, Van Morrison, Bobby Charles—stage name of Robert Guidry, who wrote "See You Later, Alligator"—Eric Clapton . . . see *The Last Waltz*, Warner Bros.). The original remains a thing apart, but no one spoke the language of the song more clearly than Elvis Presley—for less than a minute, merely singing his way through the chorus one day in the studio in 1971. "*Dylan*," he says with finality just as his band begins to come in behind him; for a moment his life has shone as brightly as the song promised it would (see *Elvis: Walk a Mile in My Shoes—The Essential 70's Masters*, RCA). Rerecorded by Dylan in 1971, with Happy Traum, for his *Greatest Hits, Vol. II*.

"Johnny Todd" (traditional). V.5, 19. 1.59. A happy sea shanty, perhaps best known during the folk revival from the early 1950s version by Bob Roberts. (See the anthology *Sea Songs and Shanties—from the last days of sail*, Saydisc.)

"Joshua Gone Barbados" (Eric von Schmidt). V.5, 3. 2.42. An extremely detailed protest song as von Schmidt recorded it in 1963 (see the anthology *The Prestige/Folklore Years: Vol. 1*, Prestige/Folklore), but as Dylan sings it, it's a legend. "Joshua was his *last* name," Schmidt explained. "When I arrived with my wife and daughter, Giles Joshua had just been elected Prime Minister of the tiny island of St. Vincent. The events described in the song, as seen through the eyes of the cane-cutters and their families, sadly mirrored our own. It is a ballad of brief hope, crushing disappointment, and the task of picking up the pieces . . ." Or, as Dylan puts it, calling a halt: "That's enough. It's a very long song."

"The King of France." V.4, 19. 3.20. A strange song (Robertson: "I'm not sure it *is* a song") with tremendous momentum and verve, plus dim echoes of the Duke and Dauphin from *Adventures of Huckleberry Finn* and even Child Ballad 164, "King Henry V's Conquest of France" (regarding Charles VI's overdue tribute payment: he sent tennis balls instead of gold). But now the King of France, dressed all in green, is coming to the U.S.A., because "he knows what it's all about"—because "he really has something to say." What it is one never finds out, but the basement five sound as if they'll be waiting at the dock.

"Lo and Behold!" 1. V.3, 8. 2.47.

"Lo and Behold!" 2. Acetate; *The Basement Tapes;* V.3, 9. 2.43.

"Lock Your Door." V.1, 17. .19. A fragment; shouts.

"The Mighty Quinn (Quinn the Eskimo)" 1. Acetate; V.2, 13 (as "Quinn the Eskimo"). 1.52. With Hudson's famous fanfare, a famous song about deliverance from nothingness, about a hero's conquest of boredom. Recorded by all sorts of people—Ramsey Lewis, the 1910 Fruitgum Company—and before that a #10 hit for Manfred Mann in 1968, one of the first basement tunes to go public. Included on Dylan's 1970 *Self Portrait* (Columbia) in a performance recorded with the Band at the 1969 Isle of Wight Festival, which also appears on *Bob Dylan's Greatest Hits, Vol. II* (Columbia).

"The Mighty Quinn (Quinn the Eskimo)" 2. On Dylan's *Biograph* (Columbia, 1985); V.2, 14. 2.11. A straighter performance of a song that now sounds dull. It has a history, though. Dylan fans long ago concluded that the inspiration was the Eskimo Anthony Quinn plays in the 1960 Nicholas Ray film *The Savage Innocents* (Quinn leads the fight for "simple ways of Eskimo people" vs. "civilization," in Leonard Maltin's words), but it was the song that titled Carl Schenkel's 1989 *The Mighty Quinn*, a Denzel Washington vehicle about a dogged Caribbean police chief. The soundtrack (on A&M) featured a version of the title tune by Sheryl Lee Ralph with Cedella Marley and Sharon Marley Prendergast: a big pop reggae treatment with all new verses. "Sunshine is for everyone," they sing, and who could argue with that?

"Million Dollar Bash" 1. V.3, 1. 2.32 (with a .20 bassman's coda). Dylan leading off on harmonica, and all foolery.

"Million Dollar Bash" 2. Acetate; *The Basement Tapes*; V.3, 3. 2.29. Completely different; in a way, you can tell the singer has already been to the party, he's already lived through the day, it holds no surprises, and yet a day this good—who wouldn't want to live it twice?

"Next Time on the Highway." V.4, 10. 2.15. A marvelously syncopated folk-lyric stomp, with Dylan ragging Manuel obscenely under the instrumental break. "Next time on the highway it was / 19 and 10 / They were treating the women just like they was / Treating the men," go lines taken from any number of old chain-gang songs, but here everything feels right.

"900 Miles" (traditional). V.5, 11. .42. Dylan first recorded this Woody Guthrie standard in a St. Paul living room in 1960, and across the river in Minneapolis a year later he recast it as "I Was Young When I Left Home," but neither sorrowful confession is any preparation for the ragged, searing intensity of these few seconds. The oldest recording seems to be Fiddlin' John Carson's 1924 "I'm 900 Miles from Home," perhaps derived from the much older tune "Reuben, Oh Reuben"; Guthrie and Pete Seeger were working on arrangements in 1940, and in 1944 Guthrie cut both instrumental (Guthrie on fiddle, Cisco Houston and Bess Lomax on guitar: see the anthology *Folksongs: Old Time Country Music/USA/1926–1944*, Frémeaux & Associés, France) and vocal versions; Cisco Houston recorded a straight, not to say square, treatment, from the harps-and-long-dresses school of folk music, for Folkways in 1953. But again, none of this has anything to do with 1967, or for that matter 1823, somewhere up the Yellowstone, on Mike Fink's last ride, which is what this basement moment feels like.

"Nothing Was Delivered" 1. V.2, 3. .30. A fragment; quick pace and heavy drums. As an arrangement, a mistake.

"Nothing Was Delivered" 2. Acetate; *The Basement Tapes;* V.2, 18. 4.15. I've never heard more than one story in this number: a few honest customers holding a dealer who took their money and failed to come up with the goods. With its slow, deliberate tempo, Dylan's cool cowboy vocal, and the lift of the piano, it's also the best rewrite of Fats Domino's "Blueberry Hill" anybody's ever heard.

"Nothing Was Delivered" 3. V.2, 19. 3.36. With an off-kilter beat, terrible drumming, and a confused vocal, this is quite painful—save for Dylan's wild speechifying halfway in, as if the real challenge here is not to get payback but to get away from the drummer: "You must do that! Yes you must!" "The Band had been in a rut," Danko says, referring to their days as the Hawks. "Six, seven days a week in nightclubs, it was all we could afford to do. With Bob, we broke that. We had time to do nothing. To think about what a career might be. We had a long sabbatical. Then we were together every day—six or even seven days a week, for seven months, from twelve to four or five in the afternoon—and it felt good. A lot of laughs. A *clubhouse*. It was wonderful."

"(Now and Then There's) A Fool Such as I" (Bill Trader). V.1, 8 (as "A Fool Such as I"). 2.42. A country hit for Hank Snow in 1953, a #2 pop hit for Elvis Presley in 1959: the basement version combines Snow's relaxed approach with Elvis's spoken interlude, but neither remotely anticipates the sly character who shows up here. He could be testifying in church or coming on to you in a bar, but as in "Sign on the Cross" perfect timing transcends all uncertainty: by the time this man is finished with you, it's you who'll be the fool. This is unforgettable; a 1969 version ended up on the 1973 garbage release *Dylan*. (Dylan had temporarily jumped to Asylum and Columbia punished him by combing their vaults for the worst stuff they could find.)

"Odds and Ends" 1. V.2, 1. 1.46. Rockabilly.

"Odds and Ends" 2. *The Basement Tapes;* V.2, 3. 1.45. Better rockabilly.

"Ol' Roisin the Beau" (traditional). V.5, 17. 4.47. With Dylan on harmonica, Hudson on clavinette, and the rest of the ensemble chiming in behind them, they float on the melody of this folk revival standard—a melody that all through the nineteenth century was adapted for other songs, many of them political singalongs. Swaying back and forth, remembering a dead alcoholic friend, there's really nothing to say, nothing you need words for, anyway, so a Robertson guitar solo at the end says it all. The tune was used by Van Dyke Parks, down to its real depths, as the running theme of his soundtrack to Walter Hill's 1995 *Wild Bill*, where Roisin the Beau was played by James Butler Hickok, if not vice versa.

"On a Rainy Afternoon." V.5, 14. 2.46. And just as dull.

"One for My Baby (And One More for the Road)." V.1, 14 (as "One for the Road"). 4.41. Inspired by the Johnny Mercer–Harold Arlen classic—take Frank Sinatra's version, take Fred Astaire's—but no more than that. From the first bars this is much closer to a desperate blues, nothing but a cry—this guy is not looking forward to anything. There's a big piano, subtle guitar, and the piece never presses, it merely develops, as if for once the group is working out the arrangement, not dowsing for it.

"One Man's Loss (Always Is Another Man's Gain)." V.1, 5. 3.36. The crying vocal is all but lost under guitar, drums, and likely Dylan's own piano; as with so many of the basement numbers, what the song really seems to be about is a refusal to be rushed. If what you're telling is the truth, there's no need to get it over with. Probably loosely based on Dick Thomas's 1950 Hank Williams–styled "One Man's Loss Is Another Man's Gain."

"One Single River" (Ian Tyson-Sylvia Fricker). V.1, 12. 4.05. Could be by Stephen Foster, as it's done here.

"Open the Door, Homer" 1. Acetate; *The Basement Tapes;* V.2, 15. 2.41. A light and bouncy take on an interesting song that seems to be about how hard it is to maintain friendships. It goes right back to the 1947 hit "Open the Door, Richard," which is the first line of this song's chorus (Danko: "Bob changed the title; given that Richard was *there*, it was a little obvious"), but not for what might be the most playfully teasing basement couplet: ". . . everyone must always flush out his house / If he don't expect to be housing flushes."

"Open the Door, Homer" 2. V.2, 16. .54. Very country, very mournful, spoken in the voice of an old card, with high, sad chorus singing—too bad it breaks off. If it had gone on all the lessons might have changed.

"Open the Door, Homer" 3. V.2, 17. 3.12. Too slow—they push it, and by the time the chorus arrives it's weighted with something of its own complaint. " 'Open the door, Richard,' I've heard it said before," Dylan sings with easy pleasure. "But I ain't gonna hear it said no more." *He* was old enough to remember 1947, when the broken-beat novelty item, the "How Much Is that Doggie in the Window?" of its time, was number one on the oppression charts—and, on the pop charts, number one for Count Basie, number 1 for the nightclub trio Three Flames, #3 for vaudevillian "Dusty" Fletcher, #3 for former Lionel Hampton saxophonist Jack McVea, #6 for the vocal group the Charioteers, #6 for jump blues combo Louis Jordan and his Tympani Five, #8 for the Pied Pipers, with Jo Stafford in the lead—you couldn't get away from it, you couldn't get it out of your head.

"People Get Ready" (Curtis Mayfield). V.1, 16. 3.18. A groaning version of the Impressions' 1965 nightclub-gospel hit (see the Impressions' *Definitive*, Kent). Also recorded by Dylan for his film *Renaldo & Clara* (see the 1978 CBS promotional disc *4 Songs from Renaldo & Clara*) and for the soundtrack of the 1990 *Flashback*, in which Dennis Hopper plays a recently captured '60s political fugitive who has spent two decades underground for the crime of disrupting a Spiro Agnew rally.

"Please Mrs. Henry." Acetate; *The Basement Tapes;* V.3, 5. 2.30. Over a light cakewalk on the piano, a detailed explanation, addressed to a landlady or a madam, of just what it means to be too drunk to move, if not complain. One of the most covered basement tunes; during the *Let It Be* sessions in 1969, Paul McCartney tried to get the Beatles to do it.

"Po' Lazarus" (traditional). V.5, 22. .56. Although cut off almost before it begins, this is a fully realized arrangement of a song

Dylan often sang in 1961: a song about a black man who's murdered for refusing to back down. Here the feeling is immediately dramatic, even glamorous, the backing vocals strong, and the sense of tragedy overwhelming. The whole thrust of the piece—a work song, a chain-gang song—is summed up in an exchange between bluesmen Big Bill Broonzy and Memphis Slim, as recorded in 1947 by folklorist Alan Lomax:

Broonzy: ". . . the Negro that will fight the white man, they call him crazy, they don't call him bad, see, because, fact of the business, they say he's gone nuts. The white man will call a Negro a bad seed among . . . just like you plant a seed . . ."

Memphis Slim: "Oh yeah. He'd ruin the rest of the Negroes . . . you understand the point that I mean now. Well, he would open the eyes of a lot of Negroes, tell 'em things that, uh, that they, you know, they didn't know. Otherwise he was a smart Negro." (From the invaluable *Blues in the Mississippi Night*, Rykodisc.)

"Rock Salt and Nails" (Bruce "U. Utah" Phillips). V.1, 7. 4.17. A contemplative, devastating reading of what feels like a very old ballad—any song that quietly opens "On the banks of a river," where, in the American ballad, promises are made, lies are told, love is consummated, and the pregnant girl's body is dumped, brings countless other songs to bear upon itself—and also feels like a number Dylan himself must have written. First recorded in 1965 by Rosalie Sorrells, rather uncomfortably (no surprise, given the last lines about women as squirrels), on *Rosalie's Songbag* (Prestige International lp) but popularized that same year by the veteran bluegrass duo Flatt and Scruggs (on *The Versatile Flatt and Scruggs*, Columbia lp).

"The Royal Canal" (Brendan Behan). V.5, 21. 5.41. This prisoner's song of utter longing and despair opens Behan's first play, *The Quare Fellow,* and frames it thereafter; sung off-stage (originally, when the play was first produced, in Dublin in 1954, by Behan himself), it comes as if from a lockdown cell. The play is about "judicial hanging"—capital punishment—and based on Behan's imprisonment from 1942 to 1946 in Mountjoy Gaol for republican activities; the song is about routine, every day being the same, about the way prison destroys time and, with it, any sense of history. There seems to be no bottom to Dylan's tone here, and no desire in it either. "Jingle, jangle," goes the triangle that rouses the prisoners each morning (Hudson gets the sound out of his clavinette)—"The Old Triangle," as the song is sometimes called, as if the singer admits the hated instrument was here before he was, that it will be here when he's gone. With the band picking up the theme, never pressing it, but slowly filling it out, they seem almost to lose themselves in the song, in its miasma—but with each day's details repeating, with never a new thought, no spark of passion, this is "I Shall Be Released" without any hope for freedom. A Greenwich Village commonplace in the early 1960s and never done better than by Liam Clancy. (See *Liam Clancy*, Vanguard, 1965).

"Santa Fe." On Dylan's *the bootleg series volumes 1–3 {rare & unreleased} 1961–1991* (Columbia); V.3, 17. 2.01. A riff.

"See that My Grave Is Kept Clean" (traditional/Blind Lemon Jefferson). V.4, 5. 3.36. It seemed impossible that a twenty-year-old folkie could find his way through this profound song, learned from the 1928 Jefferson recording collected on the *Anthology of American Folk Music*, but on his self-titled first album (Columbia, 1962) Dylan pulled it off. He did more than that: the intensity he brought to the piece all but broke it down, until Jefferson's challenge to Death became a kind of invitation, an almost hysterical dare.

The song went back a long way, to the years just after the Civil War, when it emerged as a composed piece meant to comfort a land now covered with hundreds of thousands of new graves—mass graves, unmarked graves. Then the song was called "See that My Grave Is Kept Green," and it was sentimental, a singalong, a reach to heaven for the blessing of dignity in death. As recorded in 1927 by Bela Lam and His Greene County Singers, led by banjoist Zandervon Obeliah Lam, the plea remained as it had been generations before: abstract, impersonal, a joyous prayer for all, and the singers know it will be answered. If somehow your loved ones cannot water the grass around your place of rest, god will send the rain. (See *Rural String Bands of Virginia*, County.)

When the song migrated into the repertoires of itinerant black singers, it was not only new words and new imagery that changed it (the six white horses, the tolling bell) but a new tone. It turned harsh and cold, and the community was no longer present in the music. Now it was a solitary's protest against death, which is to say against life. There is no polite request for a sylvan grave: just keep it clean, Jefferson says. Death has taken god's place in the song; Jefferson might be giving over his body as long as Death is willing to sweep up. Death apparently agrees; not halfway through Jefferson's performance, you can feel that it is Death, not Jefferson, that is singing. The voice is that sure. (See Jefferson's *King of the Country Blues*, Yazoo, or his *Complete Recorded Works in Chronological Order, Vol. 3, 1928*, Document, Austria.)

The extraordinary performance set down in late 1967 or early 1968, at the end of the basement sessions, seems to draw as deeply from both traditions. The words are Jefferson's, and they still tingle the skin, but the feeling of fatalism in the music is a feeling of acceptance, a kind of pleasure. Dylan's singing comes from a distance, the distance of age, of experience; this man is not satisfied, but he knows he will never be more satisfied than he is now. With Helm playing a swaying blues harmonica, Danko's bass adding muscle everywhere, and Robertson's autoharp putting everything on a level plane, the singer seems to have found perfect company, until after he finishes the rest take the song elsewhere, into a complex excursion full of refusal and violence, every note defined and hard, the last strum hanging in the air until, you can imagine, Hudson just got tired of waiting for it to die and turned off the tape recorder.

"See You Later, Allen Ginsberg" (Robert Guidry). V.4, 13. 3.32. Well, they start with the original, anyway, with Dylan wrestling "crocodile" into "croc-a-gator," but it's a voice from the side that coins the title phrase and cracks Dylan up; the song stops, then a second take begins right where the first one left off, as if this was all written out. A longtime hit in Ginsberg's office.

"Sign on the Cross." V.3, 20. 7.18. The longest basement recording, and so strange: a pilgrim's quest; a sermon you can't gainsay; the taunts of an unbeliever, until finally all are one and it seems as if the fool in the Rolling Stones' "Far Away Eyes," sending in his money to a radio preacher so he can hear his prayer on the air, is turning into Luke the Drifter.

"Silent Weekend." V.3, 18. 2.56. More frustrated than lonely (she won't be back till Monday). A rockabilly feel on the title phrase, otherwise like a very fine 1962 Dylan publishing demo (Dion would have been the perfect choice); for these sessions, unusually direct and shapely.

"Silhouettes" (Frank C. Slay, Jr.-Bob Crewe). .22. Just enough to catch the delight of the Rays' #3 1957 doo-wop classic, about the new suburbias where all the houses look alike: the singer comes home from work, sees silhouettes of kissing lovers on the shade, realizes that his wife's cheating on him—and then that he's "on the wrong block." What the boys do with doo-wop like this is what people have always done with it—they use it to crack each other up, even if Hudson had to be remembering his own '50s rock 'n' roll combo, up in Ontario: the Silhouettes.

"Spanish Is the Loving Tongue" (Charles Badger Clark-J. Williams). V.5, 13. 3.52. Another Ian and Sylvia favorite, and more awful than a few years later, when Dylan cut versions of it that showed up as the flip of his 1971 single "Watching the River Flow" (Columbia) and on the 1973 *Dylan* embarrassment. Still, Dylan was always looking for something when he took up this song: some bordertown detective story, maybe.

"The Spanish Song" 1 & 2. V.4, 14. 2.55, 2.06. This travels under different names—"Amelita," "Luisa," "Carmelita"—but that hardly matters. What does is that these late recordings seem to be what the maddest of the basement adventures were pointing to all along: complete dementia, with the spirit of Sam Peckinpah present to crack the whip. Remember the insane cackling the he-men in *The Wild Bunch* break into just before a shootout? This is the lunatic version, and they skip the shootout. "You want to tape this one?" Dylan asks Hudson between takes. "All right." "O.K." Dylan says, barely able to contain himself, "we'll play it just like that. But it goes very easy during the verses. O.K., ready?" And they go right off a cliff.

"Still in Town" (H. Cochran-H. Howard). V.5, 6. 2.59. Again taken from Johnny Cash's *I Walk the Line*. Cash's delivery of this tale of an abandoned lover is flat, Dylan's so delicate you can feel the man's hands shaking. The bridge the man turns back from might be an invitation to suicide in Cash's version; here there's nothing else it could be.

"Tears of Rage" (Dylan/Manuel) 1. V.2, 10. 3.55. "Listen!" Dylan says; with the lightest guitar figures, Robertson leads him into the song.

"Tears of Rage" (Dylan/Manuel) 2. V.2, 11. 2.28. A botch, and broken off. "Has to be in rock tempo," someone says.

"Tears of Rage" (Dylan/Manuel) 3. Acetate; *The Basement Tapes;* V.2, 12. 4.09. An unsure beginning and the deepest ending.

"This Wheel's on Fire" (Dylan/Danko). Acetate; *The Basement*

Tapes; V.3, 12. 3.37. Unspeakably dramatic, and the most immediately striking of the basement performances, again and again reaching a pitch of nearly unbearable intensity. Covered often, and never memorably, except perhaps in a scene in the early 1990s BBC sitcom "Absolutely Fabulous," which followed the misadventures of Edina and Patsy, two middle-aged sixties people whose lives are a riot of self-indulgence within an alcoholic haze of self-righteousness: "I was *there*, man," they seem to say every other minute to Edina's terrified teenage daughter Saffron. After Edina's disastrous fortieth birthday party, the two old pals, drunk out of their minds, climb a table and sing '60s chestnuts karaoke-style; "This Wheel's on Fire" is right up there in the pantheon with "Satisfaction."

"Tiny Montgomery." Acetate; *The Basement Tapes*, V.3, 11. 2.50. Once rumored to be named for a stock-car racer: a man blows into town, leaves behind a greeting for everyone, and what sounds like the town as one answers right back, with the best "Hello" you'll ever hear. "We played some of the basement songs for friends," Danko says. "I remember we played 'Tiny Montgomery.' People laughed at us."

"Too Much of Nothing" 1. *The Basement Tapes;* V.3, 19. 2.40. "On the waters of oblivion," Dylan sings in a crying voice, but the song never gets there. This first take is melodrama without rhythm, a fatal combination.

"Too Much of Nothing" 2. Acetate; V.2, 22. 2.43. Smoother and intriguing. A Top 40 hit in late 1967 for Peter, Paul & Mary: the first basement tune to be commercially recorded (only fair, since the originals were recorded on P P & M's equipment), and with a fine touch.

"Try Me." V.1, 13. 1.30. An exuberant rehearsal in falsetto.

"Tupelo" (John Lee Hooker). V.4, 11 (as "The Big Flood"). 2.16.

First recorded by Hooker in 1959 (see *The Best of John Lee Hooker*, GNP Crescendo).

"Under Control." V.5, 16. 2.47.

"Waltzing with Sin" (Hayes-Burns) 1 & 2. V.5, 7. 1.58 & 1.16. An obscure country ballad first recorded by Red Sovine in 1963 and only slightly more prominent as a posthumous Cowboy Copas release in 1965. (He went down in the same 1963 plane crash that killed Patsy Cline.) The group follows the Copas version; after a false start, the plumminess in Dylan's vocal fades into a dreamy mood where the clichés of the evil-woman lyrics ("You're satan made over / In perfect disguise") create a discomfort, a weariness, almost as finished as that in "The Royal Canal." The sin the singer is waltzing with, at first personified by the woman who betrayed him, is soon disembodied; you picture the singer twostepping through a bar filled with dancing couples, making his turns, his arms holding nothing but smoke.

"Wildwood Flower" (A. P. Carter). V.4, 4. 2.17. "It's the most popular song we ever recorded," Maybelle Carter of the Carter Family said. "My mother sang it and her mother sang it. It has been handed down for years and years." As a parlor tune the piece went back at least to 1859, as Maud Irving's "I'll Twine Midst the Ringlets"; music historian Charles Wolfe hears "The Pale Amaryllis" entangled in it as well. Autoharpist Sara Carter sang lead when the Carter Family made "Wildwood Flower" the #3 hit in the nation in 1928 (see their *Anchored in Love: Their Complete Victor Recordings*, 1927-1928, Rounder); on the same instrument, with Helm on harmonica alongside him, Robertson sets a mood that rocks the tune just to that point where a slow, shuffling buck dance might be the best response. It's a sun-going-down song here, with Dylan's relaxed but determined vocal taking in the full continuity of the song, its promise that within the confines of family and community gentility will be just another word for justice, that the landscape will open like your own front door.

"Yea! Heavy and a Bottle of Bread" 1. V.3, 2. 2.04. A song full of riddles, all coming from the pull of Dylan's serious, bitter demeanor against the apparent nonsense of his words—that and the great, subterranean pull of Hudson's organ, insisting that something vast is at stake. Here the balance is just a bit off.

"Yea! Heavy and a Bottle of Bread" 2. Acetate; *The Basement Tapes;* V. 3, 4. 2.11. In its way, the ultimate basement performance: an irreducible little throwaway that could have come from nowhere else.

"You Ain't Goin' Nowhere" 1. V.4, 1. 2.41. Given that the verses here are a shambling improvisation on the necessity of finding someone to feed the cat—the aching choruses, perhaps the most appealing air of the basement compositions, are the same as in the finished version of the song—it's hard to see how the number ever *got* finished. Unless it was already finished, merely not yet recorded, and the cat was making a nuisance of itself.

"You Ain't Goin' Nowhere" 2. Acetate; *The Basement Tapes;* V.3, 13. 2.29. It's so sweet, this melody; when Dylan sings, "Ooo-wee, ride me high," he might be singing to his own music. None of the many who have covered this number has ever come close to recapturing its glorious sense of anticipation, its promise that you must learn life's most valuable lessons before you can expect your life to change—not even Dylan himself, redoing the piece with Happy Traum in 1971, for his *Greatest Hits, Vol. II*.

"You Gotta Quit Kickin' My Dog Around" (Webb M. Oungst-Cy Perkins). V.4, 12 (as "Don't Know Why They Kick My Dog"). 2.40. The theme song for the nearly successful campaign by House Speaker Champ Clark of Missouri for the Democratic presidential nomination in 1912, recorded in 1916 by Byron J. Harlan and the American Quartet as "They Gotta Quit Kickin' My Dog Around" (Victor), and a hit on Columbia in 1926 for Gid

Tanner and His Skillet Lickers, featuring the wildest of Tanner's wild Georgia fiddling. (See Tanner's *The Kickapoo Medicine Show*, Rounder lp.)

"Young But Daily Growing" (traditional). V.1, 21 (numbered as 20). 5.30. Also known as "Lang A-Growin' " or "Father Oh Father," this ancient song (often described as "one of the only Child ballads Francis Child missed") is told in the voice of a young woman who discovers that her father has married her to a rich man's son: a child. There's an oddness that can barely be spoken when she hears schoolboys playing—among them her husband. And yet what she never wanted she soon can hardly bear to live without: "At the age of sixteen years, he was a / Married man / At the age of seventeen / He was the father, of a son / At the age of eighteen years / Round his grave the grass grew long." As the song ends, the woman walks through the fields, savoring the springtime, thinking of summer and her young son; it's unsurpassably sentimental, and you can feel sunlight bursting over yourself as you listen.

That's how it is when Dylan sings the song. Whenever he sang it—in May 1961; in November that same year at his first concert; in New York at the Carnegie Recital Hall; in Minneapolis, taping the tune in a friend's apartment (along with, that same night, "Pretty Polly," Rabbit Brown's "James Alley Blues," and Henry Thomas's "Fishing Blues"); or on the basement tapes—he brought everything he had to the story. His approach never changed. Alone, as in 1961, or surrounded by Danko's deep bass, Manuel's lap Hawaiian guitar, with his own acoustic guitar barely leading the music—it's so slow, it barely can be led; the melody pulls back against the singer—he gives himself up to the song, disappears into it, becoming all of its actors, with as much sympathy for the father as for the daughter as for the husband as for the son.

"You Win Again" (Hank Williams). V.5, 5. 2.36. Based not on Williams's 1952 original, but on Jerry Lee Lewis's B-side to "Great Balls of Fire": a #2 country hit in late 1957, just after the

A-side was number one. Dylan's version is more believable. In its way, "You Win Again" is a blues, and whatever else he has been, Lewis was never a blues singer. Williams was, among other things, and Dylan is, among other things.

1968

John Wesley Harding (Columbia). Released December 27, 1967, but heard—experienced—as the first, doomed sound of 1968, and recorded in Nashville the previous October and November during basement hiatus. ("*This* was the voice of the dead," a friend said of my basement metaphors and of how this record sounded in its year, when nothing had been heard from Bob Dylan for almost a year and a half, an unimaginable disappearance in the pop calculus of the time.) Featuring a lot of the Bible and no choruses, it remains an altogether austere, suspicious, ironic version of the whole basement project, a black-and-white movie to the basement tapes' sepias and washed-out Technicolor: the basement's second mind.

1992–1993

Good as I Been to You (Columbia). Released November 3, 1992. A collection of old folk songs ("Jim Jones," "Blackjack Davey," "Canadee-i-o") and commonplaces (Stephen Foster's "Hard Times"), performed solo; at first mainly a simple pleasure, after a bit the music took a harder shape. Linked by the tested character of the voice and the fatalism of the melodies found on the guitar, the songs resolved themselves into a single story: variations on the tale of innocents setting out for long journeys into the unknown and the terrible betrayals they find when they reach their destinations. How was it, though, that at precisely this moment in time a certain singer was offering *this* story as a version of American legacy, a gesture of doubt in a season that was all about the future? November 3, 1992, was Election Day, the day Bill Clinton was elected to the presidency. Bob Dylan would play at the Inaugural, with Clinton sitting only a few feet away, grinning as if he knew what it meant to have this man even unspokenly dedicate a song to him, but if it was any song, it was none of these.

World Gone Wrong (Columbia). Released October 26, 1993. Again old folk songs—"Two Soldiers," "Jack-a-Roe," "Lone Pilgrim"—performed solo, and old blues, twisted and snapped by an adept's guitar playing—"World Gone Wrong," "Blood in My Eyes," "Delia." In fact the songs were raceless, Smithville songs, again a remapping of a lost world always secretly present, biding its time, having long ago issued its warnings, always containing knowledge of how things were certain to turn out. The music was about lust and defeat; here if you never know when the former will appear, you know the latter will never disappear. "Dylan revels in the blind fatalism of the music, its endless capacity for renewal in the face of catastrophe and despair," Howard Hampton wrote in the December 7, 1993, issue of the *Village Voice*. "These performances invert the conventions of careerist wisdom: they make his output of the last 10–20 years sound like a desperately nostalgic play for acceptance instead of the other way around. The affectations that have hobbled his voice and blunted his instincts are set aside, in their stead is gravity, pitch-black humor, distended common sense." On the previous record there had not been a word about what the songs were or where they came from; here Dylan wrote long and tangled essays on each, full of acknowledgment and leaping with interpretations no one else would have had the nerve to make, and the challenge was to hear in the songs even a fraction of what the singer heard. In almost every case, Dylan hurried the past of the songs forward as a critique of the present—a present that, its poverty exposed by the past Dylan carried, was also presented as an open question, which is to say unjudged. As Bob Dylan had said nearly thirty years before, all his songs really ended with "Good luck."

ANTHOLOGY TO WILEY

Anthology of American Folk Music (Folkways, 1952).* Compiled by Harry Smith. Reissued in 1997 on Smithsonian/Folkways as a six-cd set, with original cover art.

Clarence Ashley. Ashley's recordings from the 1920s and '30s have never been collected in one place. His "The Coo Coo Bird" (1929) can be found on the anthology *Folksongs: Old Time Country Music/USA/1926–1944* (Frémeaux & Associés, France), which also includes Buell Kazee's "East Virginia" and "The Wagoner's Lad," Bascom Lamar Lunsford's "I Wish I Was a Mole in the Ground," Dock Boggs's "Pretty Polly" and "Down South Blues," Dick Justice's "Henry Lee," and Frank Hutchison's "Stackalee." His 1929 "Dark Hollow Blues" (a version of "East Virginia") is on the anthology *Old-Time Mountain Ballads* (County), which also includes "Charles Giteau" by Kelly Harrell and Uncle Dave Macon's "John Henry"; his 1930 "House Carpenter," included on Smith's *Anthology*, is on the anthology *Country: Nashville—Dallas—Hollywood* (Frémeaux & Associés, France); his 1931 "Haunted Road Blues" is on the anthology *A Whiter Shade of Blues: White Country Blues 1926–1936* (Columbia Legacy), which also includes numbers by Frank Hutchison (see below). Ashley's 1960s recordings include "House Carpenter," "Little Sadie," and "The Coo Coo Bird" on the anthology *Old-Time Music at Newport* (Vanguard lp, 1963), which also includes three performances by Dock Boggs (see below), and the essential *Doc Watson and Clarence Ashley: The Original Folkways Recordings, 1960–1962* (Smithsonian/Folkways). The video anthology *Legends of Old Time*

*Though most of the nearly 2200 lps originally issued by Folkways between 1947 and 1987 have not been reissued on cd, all are available as specially boxed cassettes, with photocopies of original cover art and liner notes, from Smithsonian/Folkways, Center for Folklife Programs, 955 L'Enfant Plaza S.W., 2600, Smithsonian Institution, Washington, D.C. 20560, tel. 202/287-3262.

Music (Vestapol/Rounder) includes an unforgettable Ashley performance of "The Cuckoo," with accompaniment by fiddler Fred Price and guitarists Clint Howard and Tex Isley, alongside an interview with folklorist D. K. Wilgus. Ashley describes "The Coo Coo Bird" as a "lassy-makin' song"—the kind of song you sing when you're making molasses—and the kind of song New York record men demanded when he first recorded it. Wilgus: "When you were making records, how much did the people who were making the records know about this music?" Ashley: "How much did they know about it?" "That's right." "Not anything." "Well, how did they know what to record?" "Well, they was just looking for something and hoping they'd find it. In other words, they wasn't musicians; they didn't have the talent, and they didn't have the *feeling*—and they wouldn't know whether you was in tune or out of tune." Or, as Emma Bell Miles put it in "Some Real American Music," in her *The Spirit of the Mountains* (1905):

> . . . the mother is crooning over her work, some old ballad of an eerie sadness and the indefinable charm of unlooked-for minor endings, something she learned as a child from a grandmother whose grandmother again brought it from Ireland or Scotland. As she bends above the loom, sending the shuttle back and forth, her voice goes on softly, interrupted by the thump of the batten:
>
> The cuckoo's a pretty bird, she sings as she flies . . .
>
> The loom stands in the porch, shaded by hops and honeysuckle, making with the woman's figure a cool silhouette against the sunshine. Thump—thump—thump! What does she know of lords and ladies, of cuckoo and nightingale? These are mere words to the mountain people; they will often stop to apologize, when asked to sing to a stranger, for the lack of "sense" in the lines; but they dare not alter a syllable; the song is too anciently received.

Sister Mildred Barker with Sister Ethel Peacock, Elsie McCool, Della Haskell, Marie Burgess, Frances Carr, and other Members of the United Society of Shakers, Sabbathday Lake, Maine. "Come Life, Shaker Life," composed 1835 by Elder Issachar Bates. On *Early Shaker Spirituals*, recorded 1963 (Rounder). With extensive notes by Daniel W. Patterson.

Dock Boggs. Bogg's original discs, plus Lonesome Ace outtakes, are collected on *Country Blues: Complete Early Recordings 1927–1929* (Revenant). Later recordings, all produced by Mike Seeger, are *Dock Boggs—Legendary Banjo Player and Singer* (Folkways lp, 1963), which includes Boggs's first recording of "Oh Death"; *Excerpts from Interviews with Dock Boggs*, recorded by Seeger in 1963 (Folkways lp, 1964); *Dock Boggs Vol. 2* (Folkways lp, 1965); and *Dock Boggs, Vol. 3* (Folkways lp, 1970). The anthology *Old-Time Music at Newport* (Vanguard lp, 1963) includes Boggs's performances of "Oh Death," "Drunkard's Lone Child," and "Sugar Baby" (with John Cohen). *New Lost City Ramblers and Friends* (Vanguard) includes a different Boggs Newport performance of "Oh Death" (accompaniment by Mike Seeger); *Georgia Sea Island Singers* (New World) features a powerful a cappella gospel version of the song by Bessie Jones, recorded in 1960 by Alan Lomax. The video anthology *Shady Grove: Old Time Music from North Carolina, Virginia, and Kentucky* (Vestapol/Rounder) includes 1966 footage of Boggs performing "Pretty Polly," "Country Blues," and the parlor tune "I Hope I Live a Few More Days." For first versions of Boggs's work, see, for Rosa Henderson's "Down South Blues," her *Complete Recorded Works in Chronological Order, Vol. 1: 1923* (Document, Austria); and for Sara Martin's "Sugar Blues," her *Complete Recorded Works in Chronological Order, Vol. 1: 1922–23* (Document, Austria).

Richard "Rabbit" Brown. For his "James Alley Blues" plus "Never Let the Same Bee Sting You Twice," "I'm Not Jealous," "Mystery of the Dunbar Child," and "Sinking of the Titanic" (all 1927), see the anthology *The Greatest Songsters: Complete Recorded Works: 1927–1929* (Document, Austria).

William Burroughs. For "Bradley the Buyer" from *Naked Lunch*, see *Call Me Burroughs* (Rhino Word Beat), a 1995 reissue of the album first released by the English Bookshop, Paris, 1965, and first issued in the U.S. by ESP-Disk in 1966.

Reverend J. M. Gates. "Oh! Death Where Is Thy Sting?" and "Must Be Born Again" are collected on Gates's *Complete Recorded Works in Chronological Order, Vol.1: 1926* (Document, Austria). Eight cds follow.

Bobbie Gentry. See entry on "Clothesline Saga" in "The Basement Tapes" section of Discography.

Frank Hutchison. All of Hutchison's work is collected on his *Complete Recorded Works in Chronological Order, Volume 1: 1926–1929* and on *Old-Time Music from West Virginia—Williamson Brothers and Curry: 1927, Dick Justice: 1929, Frank Hutchison: 1929, Complete Recorded Works in Chronological Order* (both Document, Austria). Recordings never previously reissued include the ineffably Sisyphusian original version of "Worried Blues," various instrumentals including "Stackerlee," plus "Cumberland Gap," "The Deal," "The Boston Burglar," and numerous others.

Martin Luther King, Jr. Address to the March on Washington, August 28, 1963 (misdated to August 18), on *MLK: The Martin Luther King Jr. Tapes* (Jerden). The great speech in fact begins poorly, with strained metaphors and contrived laugh lines, the speech of a conventional politician, written by a committee. It's only near the end that King's words turn to music and he speaks as a prophet. (See Taylor Branch, *Parting the Waters: America in the King Years 1954–63,* New York: Simon and Schuster, 1988).

The Kingston Trio. "Tom Dooley" (1958) is best heard on their fascinating *The Capitol Years* (Capitol four-cd box) or on the anthology *Best of Tragedy* (DCC).

Bascom Lamar Lunsford. "I Wish I Was a Mole in the Ground" and four other 1928 commercial recordings, plus fourteen 1949 archival recordings, are collected on Lunsford's *Ballads, Banjo Tunes, and Sacred Songs of Western North Carolina* (Smithsonian/Folkways). See also David Hoffman's 1966 documentary *Music Makers of the Blue Ridge* (NET/Varied Directions).

Ken Maynard. "Lone Star Trail" (Harry Smith: "This passionate description of life"—that was as fulsome as Smith ever got about anybody) and "Home on the Range," both 1930, are collected on the anthology *Western: Cowboy Ballads and Songs 1925–1939* (Frémeaux & Associés, France).

Ninnie (Cindy Norton). "Pretty Polly," on *Cotton Candy Country* (Ninnie, 1467 S. Michigan Ave., 3rd Fl., Chicago, IL 60605, 1995). Courtesy Sarah Vowell.

Elvis Presley. Previously unreleased (but here still censored) 1970 rehearsal version of "Stranger in My Own Home Town," on *Elvis: Walk a Mile in My Shoes—The Essential 70's Masters* (RCA). Complete take courtesy Dave Marsh.

Shakers. See Sister Mildred Barker.

Rosetta Tharpe. "Strange Things Happening Every Day," on *Sister Rosetta Tharpe: Complete Recorded Works in Chronological Order, Vol. 2: 1942–1944* (Document, Austria). Recorded September 22, 1944; a number one R&B hit on April 30, 1945.

Henry Thomas. For "Fishing Blues," just one stop on the map of the South that was Thomas's long life, see his *Texas Worried Blues* (Yazoo).

The Wailers. "Rolling Stone" (1967), on Bob Marley and the Wailers' *One Love at Studio One* (Heartbeat). Lead vocal by Bunny Wailer, who later redid the tune as "Ballroom Floor."

Geechie Wiley. The anthology *Mississippi Blues: Complete Recorded Works in Chronological Order, Vol. 1: 1928–1937* (Document, Austria) includes "Last Kind Words Blues" and "Skinny Leg Blues" (both 1930) plus Wiley's "Pick Poor Robin Clean," with vocal accompaniment by Elvie Thomas, their duet on

"Over to My House," and Wiley's guitar accompaniment to Thomas's "Motherless Child Blues" and "Eagles on a Half" (all 1931). "Last Kind Words Blues" can also be found on the anthology *Before the Blues, Vol. 2* (Yazoo) and on the soundtrack to *Crumb* (Rykodisc), Terry Zwigoff's 1995 film about the misanthropic comix artist Robert Crumb. Crumb is shown in a room lined with shelves of 78s; he picks one, cues it up on the phonograph, and lies back on a daybed to let Wiley wash right over him. "When I listen to old music," Crumb says in voice-over as Wiley plays, "it's one of the few times I actually have a, kind of, a *love* for humanity. You hear the best part of a soul of a common people, their, you know, their way of expressing the connection to eternity, or whatever you want to call it." Michael Pisaro: "What did they send out on that space capsule from Earth? Beethoven? Chuck Berry? Billie Holiday? This is what we got back."

ACKNOWLEDGMENTS

My first debt is to Pete Ciccone, who some years ago sent me the series of bootleg cds that sparked this project. Without his thoughtfulness and generosity this book wouldn't exist.

Many people helped me in many ways, by providing information, tapes of records now impossible to find, forums where I first experimented with the themes the basement tapes revealed, inspiration, friendship and hospitality, good advice, good editing, gossip, and enthusiasm, and for that and more I thank the staff of Amoeba Records in Berkeley, Jack Bankowsky and David Frankel at *Artforum*, Nick Amster, Graham Ashton, the late John Bauldie of *The Telegraph* and *Wanted Man*, Marlon Blackwell of the University of Arkansas at Fayetteville, faithful Dylanist friend and correspondent Betsy Bowden, Bart Bull, Paul Cantor, John Cohen, Michael Conen, Bruce Conner, Elvis Costello, Erika Doss, Sue D'Alonzo, Jim Dickinson, the staff of Down Home Music in El Cerrito, Steve Erickson, David Gans, Tony Glover, Joe Goldmark, Michael Goodwin, Peter Guralnick, Loyal Jones, Ed Kahn, Scott Kempner, Paul Kingsbury and Ronnie Pugh of the Country Music Foundation, Al Kooper, Jon Landau, Elliott

Landy, Jon Langford, Eleanor R. Long-Wilgus, Eric Lott and Jerome McGann of the University of Virginia, Tom Luddy, Bill and Bobbie Malone, Bill Marcus, Steve Marcus, Dave Marsh, Elliot Mazur, Craig McCoy, Sharyn McCrumb, Toru Mitsui, John Morthland, Paul Nelson, Stephen Peeples of Rhino Records, Michael Pisaro, Kit Rachlis, Jeff Rice of Great Expectations in Evanston, John Rockwell, Cynthia Rose, Jon Savage, Tony Scherman, Fritz Schneider, Joel Selvin, Ingrid Sischy and Graham Fuller at *Interview*, Alexia Smith, Lee Smith, Bruce Springsteen, Jim Storey, Chris Strachwitz, Elizabeth Sussman, Connie Wolf, and Anita Duquette of the Whitney Museum of American Art, Lang Thompson, Nick Tosches, Michael Trossman, Gerard van der Leun, Sarah Vowell, Anne Wagner, Ed Ward, Tom Ward and Rudy Walz of Berkeley Typewriter, Lindsay Waters, Robert and Virginia Weil, Holger Wimmer, Wendy Wolf, and M. Richard Zinman of Michigan State University.

Pauline Kael was the first to make it through the manuscript of this book, and I owe her special thanks, and as much to careful readers Jenny Marcus and T. J. Clark. Longtime correspondent Howard Hampton was an unfailing source of bleak inspiration, as were two new friends this book brought me, Barry O'Connell and Robert Cantwell, who I never read without feeling utterly disarmed. I could not have worked without the unfailing assistance and encouragement of Clinton Heylin, Joel Bernstein, Glenn Howard of the Musicians Reference Library in Santa Cruz, Jeff Place, Amy Horowitz, and Andras Goldinger of Smithsonian Folkways in Washington, D.C., and, especially, Mike Seeger, for Dock Boggs, and Rani Singh, of the Harry Smith Archives, for Harry Smith. Someday I hope to be able to return a fraction of the good she has done me. I was lucky to find editors willing to let me develop parts of this work in public, and for that I thank John Lanchester and Sally Singer at the *London Review of Books*, Paul du Noyer and Mat Snow of *Mojo*, Jeff Perl and Robert Nelsen of *Common Knowledge*, and, thirty-two years after he first graded my papers, Michael Rogin of *Representations*. Jeff Rosen of Dwarf Music was always responsive, always ready with an old story or a tape of music I'd not only not heard but never heard of, and always professional. Garth and Maud Hudson welcomed me to their house near Woodstock, and for the next three years put up with my countless phone calls, questions, clarifications, and cross-examinations without betraying a hint of impatience. Rick and Elizabeth Danko offered me more simply by the friendliness with which they answered my calls than I can tell them. As for more than twenty years now, Robbie Robertson was never short of an invaluable tale, or a phrase or a metaphor capable of instantly reshaping whatever I was writing. Again and again, I found myself framing questions for Richard Manuel, almost forgetting that he could not answer them.

As in the past I relied on Wendy Weil and Claire Needell of the Wendy Weil Agency and Anthony Goff of the David Higham Agency in London; no call goes unreturned, no question unanswered, and, as time has gone on, their commitment more and more becomes something I couldn't do without. It is the same with Jon Riley of Picador, who I first worked with at Penguin in 1990; the depth of his responsiveness made this book possible. At Picador I owe thanks as well to designers Josine Meijer and Suzanne Dean and publicist Rosie Glaisher. At Henry Holt, I was lucky to work with Lucy Albanese, John Candell, Ruth Weiner, Jeanne Tift, Marion Brown, and Bill Strachan. Bill and I first worked together at Anchor Books in 1973 and 1974, on my book *Mystery Train*; in some ways this book is a sentence or a paragraph of that one, blown up, and I am lucky that if the lines that book traced can be extended, we could take them up together, rekindling a partnership and a friendship too long in abeyance.

Emily and Cecily—hope you like it. Hope it stays with you.

Grateful acknowledgment is made to Dwarf Music for granting permission to quote from the following songs: "Leopard-skin Pill-Box Hat"—copyright © 1966 by Dwarf Music, renewed 1994 by Dwarf Music; "Lo and Behold!"—copyright © 1967, 1975 by Dwarf Music, renewed 1995 by Dwarf Music; "Million Dollar Bash"—copyright © 1967, 1975 by Dwarf Music, renewed 1995 by Dwarf Music; "Apple Suckling Tree"—copyright © 1969, 1975 by Dwarf Music; "Clothesline Saga"—copyright © 1969, 1975 by Dwarf Music; "Get Your Rocks Off"—copyright © 1968, 1973 by Dwarf Music; "You Ain't Goin' Nowhere"—copyright © 1967, 1972 by Dwarf Music, renewed 1995 by Dwarf Music; "I'm Not There"—copyright © 1997 by Dwarf Music; "Tears of Rage"—copyright © 1968, 1970 by Dwarf Music; "All You Have To Do Is Dream"—copyright © 1997 by Dwarf Music; "I'm A Fool For You"—copyright © 1997 by Dwarf Music; "I Am A Teenage Prayer"—copyright © 1997 by Dwarf Music; "Baby, Won't You Be My Baby"—copyright © 1997 by Dwarf Music.

INDEX

Books and essays are noted parenthetically by author; films by director; sound recordings by performer. Sound recordings not noted parenthetically are generally credited to Bob Dylan or to Bob Dylan/Band.